THE
MANAGEMENT
GURUS

Chris Lauer is a senior editor at Soundview Executive
Book Summaries. He lives outside Philadelphia.

THE
MANAGEMENT
GURUS

LESSONS FROM THE
BEST MANAGEMENT BOOKS OF ALL TIME

CHRIS LAUER

AND THE EDITORS AT SOUNDVIEW
EXECUTIVE BOOK SUMMARIES

Atlantic Books
LONDON

First published in the United States of America in 2008 by Portfolio,
a member of Penguin Group (USA) Inc., 375 Hudson Street, New York,
New York 10014, USA.

First published in trade paperback in Great Britain in 2008
by Atlantic Books, an imprint of Grove Atlantic Ltd.

This paperback edition published in Great Britain
in 2009 by Atlantic Books.

The summaries of *The Leadership Challenge* by James M. Kouzes and Barry
Z. Posner and *Jack Welch and the 4E's of Leadership* by Jeffrey A. Krames
are published for the first time in this volume. The other summaries have
been previously published by Soundview Executive Book Summaries.

Permission acknowledgments appear on the last page of
the respective selection.

1 3 5 7 9 10 8 6 4 2

A CIP catalogue record for this book is available from the British Library.

ISBN 978 1 84354 934 5

Printed in Great Britain by CPI Bookmarque, Croydon

Atlantic Books
An imprint of Grove Atlantic Ltd
Ormond House
26–27 Boswell Street
London WC1N 3JZ

www.atlantic-books.co.uk

To Michelle, Toby, Camille, Renata, and the thousands
of Soundview subscribers

ACKNOWLEDGMENTS

Although my name appears on the cover of this remarkable management book, there are many other people behind the scenes who also deserve credit for making *The Management Gurus* possible.

First, special appreciation needs to be given to Soundview Executive Book Summaries chairman George Y. Clement, the man who interviewed and hired me as a writer and editor more than seven years ago. Guided by his vision and the leadership of Soundview's president Josh Clement and publisher Rebecca Clement, the company has evolved from a publisher of book summaries to a world-class multimedia resource for executives and businesspeople around the globe. Sincere thanks go to the Clements for creating the fertile foundation from which this book grew.

Soundview's Sabrina Hickman must also be given thanks for her outstanding work with the publishers of the books summarized in *The Management Gurus*. Without her ceaseless efforts, the book you are now reading would not exist. Thanks also go to Soundview's senior graphic designer, Christine Wright, for her valuable artistic input.

I would also like to give a personal thank-you to Jillian Gray at Penguin for her outstanding work throughout the writing and editing of this book. Working with the professionals at Penguin Portfolio, including Adrian Zackheim, Adrienne Schultz, and Courtney Nobile, has been both a pleasure and a rewarding learning experience.

And finally, a sincere thank-you goes to each of the publishers who allowed the words and works of their authors to be featured in *The Management Gurus*, including the helpful people at Wharton School Publishing, Jossey-Bass, AMACOM, Penguin Group, Portfolio, Hyperion, John Wiley & Sons, McGraw-Hill, Oxford University Press, and Thomas Nelson Publishers.

CONTENTS

INTRODUCTION

Soundview Executive Book Summaries has provided busy readers with summaries of exceptional business books for nearly thirty years. In 2006 we published our first full-length book, *The Marketing Gurus,* a collection of summaries from some of the most interesting and influential writings on marketing. Now, within the pages of *The Management Gurus,* we offer you fifteen summaries containing valuable lessons on people, management, and change.

The authors who appear in this book grasp management's fluid concepts and transform them into concrete actions that managers can take into the workplace. The discipline of management changes every day as organizations evolve in a marketplace that continues its eternal metamorphosis. Using the advice, strategies, tips, and techniques found in the following pages, managers and leaders can make better decisions while helping their organizations compete in that marketplace.

The juxtaposition of the management ideas in this volume creates a thought-provoking tool for managers and other students of management theory, starting with advice and insights from world-class leaders and managers. Best-selling author John C. Maxwell presents a compendium of twenty-five straightforward people principles for leadership and life in *Winning with People.* In *Topgrading,* management psychologist and consultant Dr. Bradford D. Smart shows executives and managers how the best organizations hire, coach, and promote their people to A-Player status.

In *Jack Welch and the 4E's of Leadership,* author Jeffrey A. Krames draws on the leadership model Welch used successfully at GE and describes how some of the best managers have created industry-changing profitability for their companies.

The leadership lessons executive educators James M. Kouzes and Barry Z. Posner offer within *The Leadership Challenge* help aspiring leaders become managers and executives while also helping those already in leadership positions use 360-degree feedback and a variety of other useful tools and techniques.

The next five summaries present vital insights into the more personal facets of leadership, including the self-discovery that is required to successfully accomplish the difficult work of a leader. Charles Handy begins his classic *Gods of Management* by explaining that he wrote the book to help more people understand the ways individuals and organizations work so they can better face the changing times.

Management researchers and trainers Kerry Patterson, Joseph Grenny, David Maxfield, Ron McMillan, and Al Switzler also aim to help individuals cope with change in *Influencer*, raising the art and science of management above factory floors, cubicles, and boardrooms to the places they live and play. In *True North*, legendary former Medtronic CEO Bill George and co-author Peter Sims describe the ways leaders develop their skills for personal introspection that increase self-awareness. Executive coach extraordinaire Marshall Goldsmith and co-author Mark Reiter offer leaders similar introspection techniques and guidance on the path to better leadership in *What Got You Here Won't Get You There*. The authors describe valuable practices that can help managers and executives solidify their beliefs and use this knowledge to improve their leadership behavior.

In *Judgment*, two top leadership experts combine their innovative ideas to show leaders how to develop the ability to make better decisions in their work. Noel M. Tichy and Warren G. Bennis offer the decision-making skills and wisdom they have gained over their remarkable careers as best-selling authors and respected advisers to some of the most powerful CEOs and leaders around the world.

The next four summaries reveal the secrets to developing world-class organizations on your own terms. Bo Burlingham delivers a unique and important message while focusing on a specific type of company: small giants. In *Small Giants*, Burlingham shows how several small companies rejected growth for growth's sake and, instead, dedicated themselves to the strategy of becoming the best at what they do.

To make decisions such as this, a leader must understand his or her company's role in its market ecosystem. Best-selling author Geoffrey A. Moore's *Dealing with Darwin* helps managers do this by turning a monumental management analysis of Cisco Systems into a groundbreaking unified theory on the evolution of markets that continues to help companies prevent extinction.

As the Internet revolution has matured, the market ecosystem has expanded to include new tools and techniques that help the practice of management move forward by leaps and bounds. In *Wikinomics*, management experts Don Tapscott and Anthony D. Williams outline the techniques used by the best companies to tap the power of new technology, global interconnectivity, and mass collaboration. Tapscott and Williams imagine a brighter future for management, filled with previously unimagined possibilities for better communication and teamwork.

Next comes *Managing Crises Before They Happen*, where crisis-management experts Ian I. Mitroff and Gus Anagnos offer strategic lessons about one specific aspect of managing an organization: dealing with crises. Since most managers can expect to face at least one calamity during their careers, the authors show them how to plan for and survive catastrophes.

The last part of this collection takes managers into the future with *The Leader of the Future* and *The Next Global Stage*. In *The Leader of the Future*, editors Frances Hesselbein, Marshall Goldsmith, and Richard Beckhard present the crucial ideas that make managers and their organizations more effective, and show how successful leaders put vision, development, and growth into action. In *The Next Global Stage*, Kenichi Ohmae presents a vital collection of managerial insights about the new, global economy and offers several radically new rules for business and personal success.

It is difficult for a summary to do justice to a book by Kenichi Ohmae, Charles Handy, John C. Maxwell, or any of the other authors represented here (Bradford Smart's *Topgrading* is 562 pages). An eight-page summary can only offer you a tiny taste of the lessons packed into the pages of any of these books. If any of these ideas motivates you, go to a library, bookstore, or other book outlet and search for more works by these authors. I hope this book will be a starting place in a much larger, more enlightening management adventure.

Chris Lauer
Senior Editor
Soundview Executive Book Summaries

WINNING WITH PEOPLE
by John C. Maxwell

J ohn C. Maxwell has a compelling way with words. In his books and during his leadership training seminars, he offers relationship-building insights with a storyteller's precision. The positive managerial ideas he shares are accented by his resonant voice and rural charm.

An expert on building great relationships, Maxwell connects naturally with others. The universal principles he described in his pivotal book *The 21 Irrefutable Laws of Leadership*—including "Trust is the foundation of leadership" and "Leadership develops daily, not in a day"—made it a *New York Times* bestseller that has sold more than a million copies since 1999. His other books include *Developing the Leader within You, The 360-Degree Leader, Relationships 101,* and *The Difference Maker.* Adding to his reputation as a leader of leaders, Maxwell's training seminars have been attended by more than a million corporate leaders worldwide.

With a talent for encapsulating valuable life lessons into succinct reflections on growing and thriving as a leader, Maxwell helps managers at all levels of the corporate hierarchy maximize and develop their leadership potential. He does this by handily enumerating and illustrating the people principles leaders can follow to managerial success.

In *Winning with People,* Maxwell describes twenty-five principles for getting along better with people and improving our abilities with the connections we make. He has studied the successful leaders in history and reveals the secrets of those with the best people skills, including Dale Carnegie, John Wooden, Ronald Reagan, and Norman Vincent Peale.

Maxwell started his mission to lead at a young age. As the son of an Ohio pastor, he says he knew as a child that he would follow in his father's footsteps. After earning a bachelor's degree from Circleville Bible College in Ohio, he and his wife, Margaret, moved to rural Hillham, Indiana, where he became a pastor at a small church. Today, he is a top expert on leadership with a devoted following around the world.

Maxwell makes friends and devotees wherever he speaks because he values relationships. He has spent his life helping others develop better and deeper relationships. By propagating the importance of relationships with the right people—those who are the "wrong" people are abusive, neglectful, or untrustworthy—Maxwell helps leaders become more effective.

Throughout *Winning with People* and Maxwell's other books, the human element remains at the core of his message. He recognizes that people and organizations perform better when the human element is embraced and nurtured. Many Fortune 500 companies invite Maxwell to share this message with their people. He has also worked with the U.S. military at West Point, the NCAA, the NBA, and the NFL to help leaders within these organizations improve their ability to lead others and succeed with others.

When Maxwell is not writing, he is involved in the organizations he has founded, including Maximum Impact and The INJOY Group, two companies that work to help people reach their personal and leadership potential.

In *The 21 Irrefutable Laws of Leadership,* Maxwell describes the laws of respect, intuition, magnetism, connection, priorities, sacrifice, and empowerment, among many others. In *Winning with People,* he reiterates the importance of these elements in the process of connecting with others and building strong relationships. Since we all rely on resilient relationships to make the most of our lives, Maxwell's advice for getting along better with others gives us tools we can use to create better organizations.

WINNING WITH PEOPLE

Discover the People Principles That Work for You Every Time

by John C. Maxwell

CONTENTS

THE SUMMARY IN BRIEF

What does it take to win with people? Good relationships are the foundation for achievement. Relationships are more than just the icing on the cake in life: They are the cake—the very substance we need to live successful and fulfilling lives.

Many people fall into the trap of taking relationships for granted. That's not good because our ability to build and maintain healthy relationships is the single most important factor in how we get along in every area of life. Our people skills determine our potential success.

In this summary, renowned leadership expert and author John C. Maxwell describes how anyone can improve his or her relationship skills. With twenty-five "People Principles" that anyone can learn and use anywhere he or she might be, Maxwell shows how relationships can be created and strengthened for success in work and life.

Fortunately, Maxwell explains, anyone can learn to become a people person and succeed in the things that matter the most. This summary provides the tools needed to immediately improve existing relationships as well as cultivate strong, exciting, and new ones. The skills used plus the relationships chosen equal success.

What You'll Learn in This Summary

- Better ways to prepare for relationships.
- How to examine ourselves.
- How to connect with others by focusing on them.
- How to put ourselves in other people's place.
- Ways to build mutual trust.
- How to make an investment in other people.
- Better ways to create synergistic, win-win relationships.
- How to increase your odds of winning with others.

THE COMPLETE SUMMARY

THE READINESS QUESTION: ARE WE PREPARED FOR RELATIONSHIPS?

Not everyone has the skills to initiate, build, and sustain good, healthy relationships. Many people grow up in dysfunctional households and never have positive relationships modeled for them. Some people are so focused on themselves and their needs that others might as well not even exist. Still others have been hurt so badly in the past that they see the whole world through the filter of their pain. Because of huge relational blind spots, they don't know themselves or how to relate to people in a healthy way. It takes relationally healthy people to build great relationships.

The Lens Principle

Who you are determines what you see and the way you see it. What is around us doesn't determine what we see: What is within us does. And who you are determines how you see others. If you are a trusting person, you will see others as trustworthy. If you are a critical person, you will see others as critical. If you are a caring person, you will see others as compassionate.

The way you view others is determined by who you are. If you don't like people, that really is a statement about you and the way you look at people. Your viewpoint is the problem. If that's the case, don't try to change others. Don't even focus on others; focus on yourself. If you change yourself and become the kind of person you desire to be, you will begin to view others in a whole new light. And that will change the way you interact in all of your relationships.

The Mirror Principle

People unaware of who they are and what they do often damage relationships with others. The way to change that is to look in the mirror. Consider these truths that we must learn about ourselves:

■ **Self-Awareness.** Human nature seems to endow people with the ability to size up everybody in the world but themselves.

■ **Self-Image.** Your image of yourself restricts your ability to build healthy relationships. A negative self-image will keep a person from being successful. If those with a poor self-image do somehow achieve success, it won't last because they will eventually bring themselves down to the level of their own expectations.

■ **Self-Honesty.** Comedian Jack Parr quipped, "Looking back, my life seems like one big obstacle race, with me being the chief obstacle." What can save us is a willingness to get honest about our shortcomings, faults, and problems.

■ **Self-Improvement.** Critic Samuel Johnson advised that "he who has so little knowledge of human nature as to seek happiness by changing anything but his own disposition will waste his life in fruitless efforts and multiply the grief which he purposes to remove."

■ **Self-Responsibility.** No significant accomplishments can be achieved by individual effort. However, every significant accomplishment begins with the vision of one individual. Once we possess the vision, we must take responsibility for carrying it to others.

The Pain Principle

German poet Hermann Hesse wrote, "If you hate a person, you hate something in him that is part of yourself. What isn't part of ourselves doesn't disturb us." When hurting people lash out, it is in response to what's happening inside them more than what's happening around them. They feel or believe something negative within themselves. The problem is that people who don't believe in themselves will never succeed, and they will also keep those around them from succeeding.

Not only do hurting people hurt others, but they are also easily hurt by others. As you interact with others, remember this: Any time a person's response is larger than the issue at hand, the response is almost always about something else.

If you find yourself dealing with a hurting person, don't take it personally. Look beyond the person and the situation for the problem. Try not to add to his or her hurt. Forgive those who lash out at you, try to help them, and move on.

The Hammer Principle

Psychologist Abraham Maslow observed, "If the only tool you have is a hammer, you tend to see every problem as a nail." People require more judicious treatment than that. When little things bother us, our primary objective must be putting our personal agendas aside and building relationships. When tempted to use overkill, the following four T's can help you temper your behavior:

■ **Total Picture.** If you come to conclusions long before the problem has been detailed, you should listen, ask questions, listen again, ask more questions, listen some more, and then respond.

■ **Timing.** Noted hostess and writer Lady Dorothy Nevill observed, "The real art of conversation is not only to say the right thing in the right place, but to leave unsaid the wrong thing at the tempting moment."

■ **Tone.** People often respond to our attitudes and actions more than to our words. Many petty conflicts occur because people use the wrong tone of voice.

■ **Temperature.** The size of a problem often changes based on how it is handled. If the reaction is worse than the action, the problem usually increases. If the reaction is less than the action, the problem usually decreases.

The Elevator Principle

People can be the wind beneath our wings or the anchor on our boat. People who add value to others almost always do so intentionally. Adding value to others requires a person to give of him- or herself. That rarely occurs by accident.

In relationships, receiving is easy. Giving is much more difficult. We all want to be a positive influence in the lives of others. If you want to lift people up and add value to their lives, keep the following in mind:

- Lifters commit themselves to daily encouragement.
- Lifters know the little difference that separates hurting and helping.
- Lifters initiate the positive in a negative environment.
- Lifters understand life is not a dress rehearsal.

HOW TO DEVELOP A SOFTER TOUCH

- Let the past stay in the past.
- Ask yourself, *Is my reaction part of the problem?*
- Remember that actions are remembered long after words are forgotten.
- Never let the situation mean more than the relationship.
- Treat loved ones with unconditional love.
- Admit wrongs and ask forgiveness.

THE CONNECTION QUESTION: ARE WE WILLING TO FOCUS ON OTHERS?

All human beings possess a desire to connect with other people. The need for connection is sometimes motivated by the desire for love, but it can just as easily be prompted by feelings of loneliness, the need for acceptance, the quest for fulfillment, or the desire to achieve in business.

To fulfill our desire for relationships, we must stop thinking about ourselves and begin focusing on the people with whom we desire to build relationships. When you stop worrying so much about yourself and start looking at others and what they desire, you build a bridge to other people and you become the kind of person others want to be around.

The Big Picture Principle

People who remain self-centered and self-serving will always have a hard time getting along with others. To help them break that pattern of living, they need to see the big picture, which requires perspective, maturity, and responsibility. Here are some steps to follow:

■ **Get Out of Your "Own Little World."** Go places you have never gone, meet the kinds of people you do not know, and do the things you have not done before.

■ **Check Your Ego at the Door.** If your focus is always on yourself, you'll never be able to build positive relationships.

■ **Understand What Brings Fulfillment.** Ultimately, the things that bring fulfillment involve others. A person who is entirely self-focused will always feel restless and hungry because he or she separates him- or herself from what's most important in life: people.

The Exchange Principle

Instead of putting others in their place, we must put ourselves in their place. When we fail to see things from the perspective of others, we fail in our relationships.

To become better at making the exchange, at seeing things from another person's perspective, do the following:

■ **Leave "Your Place" and Visit "Their Place."** Do whatever you can to change your perspective. Listen to people's concerns. Study their culture or profession. Read in their areas of interest. Or literally visit their place.

■ **Acknowledge That the Other Person Has a Valid Viewpoint.** People's belief systems and personal experiences are diverse and complex, and even if you do work to see things from another person's point of view, there will still be differences of opinion. Working to find the legitimacy of another person's point of view stretches your thinking.

■ **Check Your Attitude.** It is always easy to see both sides of an issue about which we are not particularly concerned. It is much harder when we have a vested interest in it. When that's the case, we are often more concerned with getting our way than connecting with others.

■ **Ask Others What They Would Do in Your Situation.** The key to the exchange principle is empathy. When you have empathy with others' points of view, it becomes much easier to connect with them because they know that you care.

The Learning Principle

Each person we meet has the potential to teach us something. All of us can learn things in unlikely places and from unlikely people. But that's only true if we have the right attitude. If you have a teachable attitude, you will be positioned well to learn from others. Then all you will need to do is to take the following five steps:

1. *Make learning your passion.* Management expert Philip Crosby notes, "There is a theory of human behavior that says people subconsciously retard their own intellectual growth. They come to rely on clichés and habits. Once they reach the age of their own personal comfort with the world, they stop learning and their minds run on idle for the rest of their days. They may progress organizationally, they may be ambitious and eager, and they may even work night and day. But they learn no more." If you desire to keep growing, you cannot sit back in a comfort zone.

2. *Value people.* People don't learn from people they don't value.

3. *Develop relationships with growth potential.* Find people who are especially likely to help you grow: experts in your field, creative thinkers who stretch you mentally, and achievers who inspire you to go to the next level.

4. *Identify people's uniqueness and strengths.* Philosopher and poet Ralph Waldo Emerson remarked, "I have never met a man who was not my superior in some particular." People grow best in their areas of strength—and can learn the most from another person's area of strength. For that reason, you can't be indiscriminate in choosing the people you seek out to teach you.

5. *Ask questions.* Learning begins with listening. The best way to learn is to watch others and ask questions.

The Charisma Principle

People are interested in the person who is interested in them. According to Dale Carnegie, "You can make more friends in two months by becoming interested in other people than you can in two years by trying to get other people interested in you." Carnegie's teachings in *How to Win Friends and Influence People* include:

- *Become genuinely interested in other people.* People don't care how much you know until they know how much you care.
- *Smile.* If you want to draw others to you, light up your face with a smile.
- *Remember names.* A person's name is the sweetest and most important sound to that person.
- *Be a good listener.* Encourage others to talk about themselves.
- *Talk in terms of the other person's interests.* Treat others the way they want to be treated.

- *Make the other person feel important.* Become sincerely interested in others.

The Number 10 Principle

All people have potential. Everyone you meet can be a 10. Believing in people usually brings out the best in them. If people believe in themselves, they can reach their potential and become the individuals they were created to be. If you've been hurt or disappointed in the past, don't let that negatively color your attitude in the future.

Philosopher and poet Johann Wolfgang von Goethe said, "Treat a man as he appears to be and you make him worse. But treat a man as if he already were what he potentially could be, and you make him what he should be."

The Confrontation Principle

Caring for people should precede confronting people. Conflict is like cancer: Early detection increases the possibility of a healthy outcome. While intellectually it's simple to resolve conflict, emotionally it can be difficult. It requires honesty, humility, and dedication to the relationship. Take these steps when confronting someone:

- *Confront a person only if you care about that person* It is more productive to go into a confrontation keeping the other person's interests in mind.
- *Meet together as soon as possible.* Putting off confrontation only causes the situation to fester.
- *First seek understanding, not necessarily agreement.* The person who gives an opinion before he or she understands is human, but the person who gives a judgment before he or she understands is a fool.
- *Outline the issue.* Be positive, describe your perceptions, state how this situation makes you feel, and explain why this is important to you.
- *Encourage a response.*
- *Agree to an action plan that clearly identifies the issue and spells out concrete steps that will be taken.* The action plan should include a commitment by both parties to put the issue to rest once resolved.

THE TRUST QUESTION: CAN WE BUILD MUTUAL TRUST?

Philosopher and poet Ralph Waldo Emerson said, "The glory of friendship is not the outstretched hand, not the kindly smile, nor the joy of companionship; it is the spiritual inspiration that comes to one when you discover that someone else believes in you and is willing to trust you with a friendship."

Why do many personal and business relationships fall apart? The reasons for such breakdowns are many, but the cause that outweighs all others is broken trust.

The Bedrock Principle

In his book, *On Becoming a Leader*, Warren Bennis says, "Integrity is the basis of trust, which is not so much an ingredient of leadership as it is a product. It is the one quality that cannot be acquired, but must be earned. It is given by coworkers and followers, and without it, the leader can't function."

That can be said not only of leaders and followers, but also of all relationships. Developing trust is like constructing a building. It takes time, and it must be done one piece at a time. As in construction, it's much quicker and easier to tear something down than it is to build it up. But if the foundation is strong, there is a good chance that what is built upon it will stand.

If you desire to build your trustworthiness—and as a result, your relationships—remember:

■ **Trust Begins with Yourself.** If you are not honest with yourself, you will not be capable of honesty with others. Self-deception is the enemy of relationships.

■ **Trust Cannot Be Compartmentalized.** Many people today try to compartmentalize their lives. They believe that they can cut corners or compromise their values in one area of life and it won't affect another area. But character doesn't work that way. And neither does trust.

■ **Trust Works Like a Bank Account.** Mike Abrashoff, author of *It's Your Ship*, states, "Trust is like a bank account—you have got to keep making deposits if you want it to grow. On occasion, things will go wrong, and you will have to make a withdrawal. Meanwhile, it is sitting in the bank earning interest."

The Situation Principle

Never let the situation mean more than the relationship. It is more rewarding to resolve a situation than to dissolve a relationship. Any time a person puts the situation ahead of the relationship, it happens for one reason: loss of perspective. People are always more important than mere things. Our property, our position, and our agenda are transitory.

Whenever we experience a rough time in a relationship, we need to remind ourselves of why that relationship is significant to us in the first place. Also, we must keep in mind that there is a big difference between a situation that occurs once and one that occurs again and again.

The Bob Principle

If Bob has problems with Bill, and Bob has problems with Fred, and Bob has problems with Sue, and Bob has problems with Jane, and Bob has problems with Sam, then Bob is usually the problem.

Every problem starter is like a fire lighter. And each of us is like a person carrying two buckets. One is filled with water and the other with gasoline. When we see a problem fire being lit, we can choose to douse it with water and put it out, or we can throw gasoline on it and make it worse.

If you have someone who creates and spreads problems, respond with a positive comment, show your concern for the person being criticized, and encourage steps toward resolution. Not everyone will respond positively to your suggestions. But if you have a strong connection with a Bob or you are in a position of authority with him, then ask him to THINK before he speaks using this acronym:

T   Is it true?
H   Is it helpful?
I   Is it inspiring?
N   Is it necessary?
K   Is it kind?

If he can answer yes to all of these questions, then it's appropriate for him to proceed.

The Approachability Principle

Being at ease with ourselves helps others be at ease with us. People miss many opportunities for connection and the chance to build deeper relationships because they do not make themselves approachable. Approachable people usually exhibit the following seven characteristics:

1. *Personal warmth.* Approachable people truly like people. To be approachable, you need to generate personal warmth toward the people you meet.
2. *Appreciation for the differences in people.* Approachable people appreciate people for who they are and what they have to offer.
3. *Consistency of mood.* Approachable people are even-keeled and predictable. You know what you'll get because they are basically the same every time you see them.
4. *Sensitivity toward people's feelings.* Although approachable people are emotionally

steady, they might not expect others to be that way. They tune in to the moods and feelings of others, and then adjust how they relate to them.

5. *Understanding of human weaknesses and exposure of their own.* Approachable people are honest about their abilities and shortcomings. They are willing to be told not what they want to hear but what they need to hear.

6. *Ability to forgive easily and quickly ask for forgiveness.* Approachable people quickly ask for forgiveness and easily grant it to others.

7. *Authenticity.* Approachable people are real. They engage with others on a genuine level, and don't pretend to be someone they're not. They don't go out of their way to hide what they think and feel. They have no hidden agenda.

The Foxhole Principle

We face many kinds of battles in life, and the "foxholes" we sometimes inhabit come in many shapes and sizes. These foxholes can include the home, a business, a sports team, a small group, a platoon, or something else. When preparing for battle, dig a hole big enough for a friend. The foxhole is for you and a friend, not a friend alone. You can ask a friend to fight with you, but you should never send someone else to fight your battles. And you should be willing to fight for any friend whose help you would request.

You might have many friends, but not all of them will be foxhole friends. For that matter, you will not be that kind of an ally to everyone in your life either. Foxhole friendships are special. Even before the battle, simply knowing that someone believes in you and will fight for you is uplifting. People who climb down into the foxhole with you see things from your point of view and they express empathy for your situation. That makes them not only a great help, but also a great comfort.

THE INVESTMENT QUESTION: ARE WE WILLING TO INVEST IN OTHERS?

Are you willing to invest in other people? You may build a beautiful house, but eventually it will crumble. You may develop a fine career, but one day it will be over. You may save a great sum of money, but you can't take it with you. You may be in superb health today, but in time it will decline. You may take pride in your accomplishments, but someone will surpass you.

Relationships are like anything else. The return you get depends on what you invest.

The Gardening Principle

All relationships need cultivation. You cannot neglect a relationship and expect it to grow. That's not to say that all relationships are the same and need the same amount of attention. The nature and purpose of the relationship will determine the energy and time needed to cultivate it.

You can start to cultivate a healthy, growing relationship by focusing on the following six things:

■ **Commitment.** Every long-lasting relationship suffers strains and setbacks. No two people agree on everything. Even the best friendships can expect to face conflict. The question is: What are you going to do when trouble comes?

■ **Communication.** A relationship begins with easy communication. It deepens with more difficult communication. And it is sustained with intentional communication.

■ **Friendship.** Critic Samuel Johnson remarked, "If a man does not make new acquaintances as he advances through life, he will soon find himself left alone; a man, sir, should keep his friendship in a constant repair." That goes for old friendships as well as new ones. We sometimes take for granted the people closest to us, and as a result, we neglect to try being good friends to them first.

■ **Memories.** Shared memories are a wonderful source of connection and bonding for people.

■ **Growth.** When you begin any friendship, it is filled with promise. But you have to find ways to keep it fresh and strong so that it continues to have potential and not just good memories.

■ **Spoiling Each Other.** Voltaire wrote, "If the first law of friendship is that it has to be cultivated, the second law is to be indulgent when the first law has been neglected." Let your friends and family members know how much you care as often as you can.

The 101 Percent Principle

Sometimes building relationships is an uphill battle, and connecting with another person can be particularly difficult. How do you connect with people when you seem to have nothing in common with them? Can you build relational bridges in such circumstances? And if so, can the relationships be healthy, long-lasting, and productive?

When the connection is difficult, you must find the one thing the two of you can agree upon. You can do that with just about anybody. The problem is that many people naturally take the opposite approach; they look for differences. Why? Sometimes it's due to natural competitiveness; people are often looking for an edge. Sometimes it's to make themselves stand out and to find their own distinctiveness. Other times, people focus on differences because they feel threatened by others.

When connection is difficult, you must find the one thing the two of you can agree upon. The greater the differences, the more important it is to focus on what you agree on. Once you do, give it 101 percent of your effort.

The Patience Principle

The journey with others is slower than the journey alone. Here are the steps you can take to become a more patient person in relationships:

■ **Prioritize Patience as a Virtue Worthy of Developing.** Oft-quoted Arnold Glasgow stated, "You get the chicken by hatching the egg, not smashing it." In the long run, you will find that patience with people is beneficial to you. But you may not see a return right away.

■ **Understand That It Takes Time to Build Good Relationships.** Relationships of any depth take time. The more people involved in the relational circle, the longer it takes.

■ **Practice the Exchange Principle.** Each of us thinks our circumstances warrant special consideration—people should be extra patient with us. Instead, put yourself in the other person's place and be extra patient with him or her.

■ **Realize That People Have and Create Problems.** When you decide to develop a relationship with another person, it's a package deal. You don't get to take only the good stuff and reject the bad. Try to give others the same kind of grace you'd like to receive for your shortcomings.

■ **Identify Areas Where People Need Patience with You.** It's a good idea for us to know what ours are.

The Celebration Principle

The true test of relationships is not only how loyal we are when friends fail, but how thrilled we are when they succeed. Everyone identifies with failure. The problem is that because people so readily identify with failure, they sometimes have a hard time connecting with success. And if they don't identify with success, they may resent it.

Frequently the very same qualities that prevent people from achieving success—emotional insecurity, a scarcity mind-set, petty jealousy, and the like—prevent them from celebrating others' successes. They constantly compare themselves to others and find themselves wanting.

How do you learn to celebrate with others instead of ignoring or undermining them? Realize it's not a competition. You must be willing to look at things from other people's points of view. When they achieve something that is important to them, celebrate with enthusiasm. Celebrate successes others don't yet see. Sometimes people make great strides and aren't even aware of it.

The High Road Principle

We go to a higher level when we treat others better than they treat us. If you're slinging mud, you're losing ground. There are really only three roads we can travel when it comes to dealing with others. We can take the low road where we treat others worse than they treat us. We can take the middle road where we treat others the same as they treat us. Or we can take the high road and treat others better than they treat us.

The low road damages relationships and alienates others from us. The middle road may not drive people away from us, but it won't attract them to us either; it is reactive rather than proactive and allows others to set the agenda for our lives. The high road helps to create positive relationships and attracts others to us; it sets a positive agenda with others that even negative people find difficult to undermine.

High roaders understand that it's not what happens to you but what happens in you that really matters. Newscaster David Brinkley observed, "A successful man is one who can lay a firm foundation with the bricks others have thrown at him." They commit to traveling the high road continually. Nearly anyone can be kind in the face of unkindness every once in a while: It's more difficult to sustain a high road attitude all the time. High roaders recognize their own need for grace, and extend it to others.

High roaders set higher standards for themselves than others would. They make excellence their goal. They care more than others think is wise. They risk more than others think is safe. They dream more than others think is practical. They expect more than others think is possible. And they work more than others think is necessary.

THE SYNERGY QUESTION: CAN WE CREATE A WIN-WIN RELATIONSHIP?

Some relationships add value to both parties, and that is rewarding. When both parties enter into a relationship with an investment mind-set—after having connected and built trust with each other—a win-win relationship can result.

The wonderful thing about win-win relationships is that they can be forged in every area of life and in all kinds of relationships: between husbands and wives, parents and children, friends and neighbors, and bosses and employees.

If both parties sustain a giving attitude and both are having their needs met, then the relationship can become something truly special.

In the long run, lopsided relationships don't last. If one person is doing all the giving and the other is doing all the receiving, the giver will eventually become worn out. And ironically the taker will become dissatisfied because that person will feel he or she is not receiving enough. The only way to build a positive, long-lasting, synergistic relationship is to make sure everybody wins!

The Boomerang Principle

When we help others, we help ourselves. Those who invest in others give and then receive. They believe that success comes from being helpful, caring, and constructive. They desire to make everything and everyone they touch better, and they understand the best way to accomplish that is to give of themselves. To enrich the world and become someone who invests in others, you must:

■ **Think "Others First."** Good, healthy, growing relationships begin with the ability to put other people first. Begin every relationship by giving the other person respect—even before he or she has had a chance to earn it.

■ **Focus on the Investment, Not the Return.** Investors in people are like investors in the stock market. In the long haul, they will benefit, but they have little control over what that return will look like or how it will occur. But they can control what and how they invest.

■ **Pick Out a Few People with Great Potential.** When people prepare to make financial investments, the wise ones don't put all their money into a single stock or fund. They diversify by investing in several areas. But good investors don't spread themselves too thin. They know they can give only so much time and attention to each particular investment. Wise investors in people follow a similar pattern. Pick only as many people as you can handle with intensity, choose only people with great potential for growth, and choose only people whose need for growth matches your gifts and talents.

■ **With Their Permission, Begin the Process.** You cannot help someone who does not want your help. The stronger the relationships and the greater the trust, the higher the likelihood that the investment process will work.

■ **Enjoy a Return in Due Season.** When people's motives are pure and they genuinely desire to add value to others, they cannot help others without receiving some benefit. The return may be immediate, or it may take a long time, but it will occur. And when it does, the relationship begins to resonate with synergy.

The Friendship Principle

Most people underestimate the power and importance of relationships in regard to business and career. They try to learn the most recent management fad, focus on product quality, or create programs and systems to improve productivity or increase repeat business. These things are helpful, but the real key is relationships. Never underestimate the power of friendship when it comes to doing business.

As soon as you understand the way that relationships affect business, you begin to realize that all business relationships are not created equal. Here are the four levels of business relationships:

■ **People Knowledge.** Your understanding of people helps build your business. All the product knowledge in the world won't help someone without people skills. Nor will technical expertise. Nor will the ability to build a brilliantly efficient organization. If individuals don't possess people skills, they very quickly hit a ceiling in their effectiveness.

■ **Service Skills.** Barry J. Gibbons, author of This Indecision Is Final, writes, "Between 70 percent and 90 percent of decisions not to repeat a purchase of anything are not about product or price. They are about some dimension of the service relationship." How you treat the people with whom you do business really matters, especially in a competitive market.

■ **Business Reputation.** Writer Howard Hodgson said, "Whatever business you are in, you are in a business of relationships. That's why your reputation is your greatest asset."

■ **Personal Friendship.** Your friendship with others builds your business. The highest level of business relationships is reached when people like your business, but more important, they like you!

The Partnership Principle

Working together increases the odds of winning together. Try to build relationships with everyone, but forge partnerships with only a few. Those closest to you determine your level of success. Move from simply working with good, capable people to partnering with difference makers. Find capable people with the same passion and mission as yours who also need others to make a difference. This will lead to many rewarding relational partnerships and together you will do things that make a positive impact by helping others.

Every person possesses one of two mind-sets: scarcity or abundance. People with a scarcity mind-set believe that there's only so much to go around so you have to scrape for everything you can and protect whatever you have at all costs. People with an abundance mind-set believe there's always enough to go around.

The Satisfaction Principle

In great relationships, the joy of being together is enough. A lasting relationship begins as a healthy relationship. The following four factors help to create the right climate for relationships where simply being together is enough:

- *Shared memories create a bonded environment.*
- *Growing together creates a committed environment.*
- *Mutual respect creates a healthy environment of trust and servanthood.*
- *Unconditional love creates a safe environment.*

TOPGRADING
by Bradford D. Smart, PhD

H undreds of thousands of managers and employees have felt the effects of Dr. Bradford D. Smart's techniques for hiring, training, and promoting people to top company positions, but his groundbreaking methods are often credited to other powerful people. Many managers associate the process of rewarding A-Players, improving B-Players, and getting rid of C-Players with General Electric's former CEO Jack Welch. Although Welch advocates this technique for hiring, training, and promoting whenever he speaks or writes about human resources issues, this method links back to the work of Brad Smart, the author of *Topgrading: How Leading Companies Win by Hiring, Coaching, and Keeping the Best People*.

Honeywell's retired CEO and Chairman Larry Bossidy also used Smart's ideas to help make his company a high-performance organization. With highly successful devotees such as Welch and Bossidy, among many others, Smart's "topgrading" techniques have had a vast impact on the entire field of corporate management.

Brad Smart says that when he received his PhD in management psychology from Purdue University, he was skeptical of the ways hiring interviews had been conducted in the past because studies showed that interviews failed to predict who would succeed in management positions. When he started out, Smart explains, he joined a group of fellow psychologists to do coaching, not hiring interviews. But in his first month on the job, he changed his mind. He says, "It gradually became clear that the terrible hiring success companies experienced was fixable."

His mission to change the ways hiring interviews were conducted began while he sat in with one of his firm's senior partners during an interview with a candidate for a vice president of marketing position at an insurance company. Smart says that he was disappointed to find the hiring company's job description so vague and general that it was practically worthless. In addition, he adds, top executives at the company each had their own ideas about the type of candidate they wanted in the position. The candidate's résumé and background information were also vague and incomplete.

Smart explains that the aptitude tests given to the candidate were the same tests he had seen at Purdue. He says these tests "had very low validity." He recalls that he also felt the behavioral interview questions from the senior partner were incomplete. After hearing glib answers to the same, old questions, and wondering about the competencies that went uncovered during the interview, Smart says he was left with the impression that the candidate had rehearsed all of the answers he provided, and was so selective when describing his competencies that weak points were left out.

Smart remembers that the entire interviewing process left him with only shallow insights about the candidate. Unsatisfied by the results of his firm's interview, he conducted his own interview with the candidate. Three hours later, he had discovered a much more complete description of the man's education, work history, and competencies. Smart had made an important discovery. He believed he had found a better hiring process that could identify high performers at a better rate than the usual 25 percent success rate.

Next, Bradford Smart started his own consultancy: Smart and Associates. With his new, in-depth hiring process, he explains, he soon had a 90 percent success rate of hiring top performers. After honing his methods over several years, he was hired as a consultant by Jack Welch, who was looking for a new way to identify top performers during GE's hiring process. Smart's work with GE led to the tandem interviewing process in which two interviewers work with a candidate to identify his or her competencies through a chronological interviewing process. By training managers how to perform these interviews, Smart says his consultancy has helped them to hire high performers between 75 percent and 90 percent of the time.

General Electric became so successful at the tandem Topgrading Interview process that many other companies sought out Smart's firm to help improve their hiring success rate. Soon, Smart's interview process for hiring was being used for promotions and manager assessments at many companies to determine who should stay and who should go.

To help companies reap the benefits of his new process for hiring, coaching, and promoting leaders, Smart published *Topgrading* in 1999. CEOs at companies such as Lincoln Financial, the American Heart Association, and MarineMax were inspired by the success of the hiring methods found in *Topgrading*. Leaders at these companies soon embraced Smart's top-performer standard, trained their managers in the tandem Topgrading Interview approach, and diligently used the "Topgrading Interview Guide" found in his book. New case studies in the 2005 edition of *Topgrading* describe the positive effects that Smart's interviewing methods have had on many companies since the book's first publication.

Smart says, "I think my reason for being on this planet is to help reduce the colossal pain and colossal costs of mis-hires and mispromotions." With *Topgrading,* he gives managers the tools they need to complete his mission.

TOPGRADING

How Leading Companies Win by Hiring, Coaching, and Keeping the Best People

by Bradford D. Smart, PhD

CONTENTS

THE SUMMARY IN BRIEF

Great companies are made by A-Players. The secret is to hire, promote, and retain only these individuals, but this is easier said than done. Research shows that typically only one-fourth of those hired or promoted turn out to be A-Players. The other three-fourths (the B- and C-Players) become mis-hires and mispromotions. And with the cost of a staffing mistake estimated at fifteen times base salary, the financial drain on the average company is huge.

Compare that with the 90 percent and higher success rate enjoyed by companies that use management psychologist and consultant Bradford D. Smart's topgrading practices for hiring, training, and promoting. Case studies of topgraded companies—including General Electric, Hillenbrand, and the American Heart Association—prove that it's possible to vastly improve how people are hired and promoted at companies large or small. By rewarding A-Players, improving B-Players, and weeding out C-Players, topgraded companies are much more successful. Great leaders like Jack Welch and Larry Bossidy know firsthand that topgrading can enable your company to gain a sizeable advantage over your competition.

This summary shows how premier companies topgrade and presents compelling statistics showing why they have embraced topgrading. The basics of how to use the most important technique in topgrading—the Topgrading Interview—and advice on legal considerations are given. This summary is for A-Players and all those aspiring to be A-Players.

What You'll Learn in This Summary

- How leading companies have embraced topgrading.
- A practical approach to the Topgrading Interview, the proven best practice for assessing talent.
- How to develop A-level talent.
- The most successful techniques for coaching A-Players to remain A-Players.
- How to turn some B- and C-Players into A-Players.
- How to gain a strong advantage over your competition.
- What management competencies to look for when hiring a potential A-Player.

THE COMPLETE SUMMARY

TOPGRADING: EVERY MANAGER'S FIRST PRIORITY

How dramatically can topgrading improve talent? The average company today hires only 25 percent A-Players, promotes only 25 percent A-Players, and has 25 to 40 percent A-Players in management. Topgraded companies hire 90 percent A-Players, promote 90 percent A-Players, and eventually have 90 percent A-Players in management.

What Is Topgrading?

Topgrading is filling every position in the organization with an A-Player, at the appropriate compensation level. Topgrading involves replacing underperformers until the entire team of ten consists of ten A-Players, or at least those who clearly exhibit A-potential. When you are topgrading, you are not accepting a mixture of A-, B-, and C-Players. You are proactively doing whatever it takes to pack your team with *all* A-Players. Topgraders are not cheap. Circumstances might justify paying above the *entire* accepted salary range. The topgrader is more rigorous than the "upgrader," more thorough in assessment, and more likely to get what he or she pays for.

Proactively seeking out and employing the most talented people can have a major effect on the creation of other competitive advantages. High performers contribute more, innovate more, work smarter, earn more trust, display more resourcefulness, take more initiative, develop better business strategies, articulate their vision more passionately, implement change more effectively, deliver higher-quality work, demonstrate greater teamwork, and find ways to get the job done in less time with less cost. It's no coincidence that A-Player managers attract and retain A-Players, who want to be part of organizations that succeed.

Who Is Topgrading?

McKinsey & Co., a premier global consultancy, is known for its commitment to seeking out and employing the best people available at every level. Intel, Dell, Goldman Sachs, and 3M attract and retain A-Players and quickly redeploy C-Players. Lincoln Financial, Hillenbrand Industries, General Electric, MarineMax, Hayes Lemmerz, the American Heart Association, and UBS increase their percentage of A-Players yearly and redeploy not just C-Players but B-Players too.

What Is an A-Player?

An A-Player is someone who qualifies among the top 10 percent of those available for a position. An A-Player is the best of class. Most fine companies use these definitions:

- *A-Player*: top 10 percent of talent available.
- *B-Player*: next 25 percent.
- *C-Player*: below the top 35 percent.

The Topgrading Calculator

The Topgrading Calculator helps to overcome talent self-delusion. If you are a perfect topgrader, you don't need a Topgrading Calculator to estimate the number of replacements necessary to achieve 100 percent A-Players. If your success rate is 100 percent, you need only hire one person (who will be an A) as a replacement. If your likely success rate is 25 percent, you need to hire four people to get an A—three mis-hires and your good hire. Topgrading promises to improve your success rate from 25 to 90 percent. In the meantime, to learn how many people you will have to hire to finally have 90 percent A-Players:

1. Estimate your current number of A-Players, including those with A-potential.
2. Estimate your hiring success rate (your percentage of A-Players and A-potentials after hiring and promoting people).
3. Use the Topgrading Calculator (see below). It will show the total number of people you must hire or promote in order to end up with *at least* 90 percent A-Players, after replacing all those who turn out not to be A-Players. For example, if you wish to replace 10 underperformers, you hire or promote 10 using topgrading, and end up with nine or more A-Players on your team.

Topgrading Calculator

**Total Number of Replacements to Achieve
90 Percent A-Players**

Number of Underperformers to Be Replaced	Your Current Success in Hiring/Promoting			
	25%	50%	75%	100%
10	31	17	11	10
20	67	35	24	20
40	141	72	48	40
100	357	179	120	100

THE FINANCIAL AND CAREER COSTS OF NOT TOPGRADING

Integrating topgrading into your interview process minimizes the firings and measurable costs of mis-hires, making your course of action relatively quick, seamless, and inexpensive.

Topgrading case studies for years have shown how to achieve a 90 percent success rate in hiring. The CEOs of the following organizations estimated the percentage of upper management hires who turned out to be A-Players as follows: Lincoln Financial, 90 percent; Hayes Lemmerz, 94 percent; ghSMART, 92 percent; MarineMax, 94 percent; and the American Heart Association, 95 percent.

Prior to topgrading, most of these organizations experienced a hiring success rate of about 35 percent; Topgrading Interviews took them to 90 percent and higher. Their typical topgrading discipline is for a group of managers to scrutinize each hire one year after the person was hired. B-Players without A-potential are deemed mis-hires.

In some companies that evaluation of the hiree is so tough that if the hiree turns out to be a B or C without A-potential, the bonuses of the hiring manager and HR professionals are reduced. So there is great confidence that those deemed A-Players truly are.

The Cost of Mistakes

It doesn't make any difference if a person is "hired" from outside or inside the company. Mispromoting internally is about as costly as mis-hiring an external candidate.

At the worker level there are plenty of published statistics on turnover and even a few studies of the costs associated with mis-hires. A computer search of more than two hundred studies and articles produced a hodgepodge of single-company results, with costs of mis-hiring factory workers to be $1,500 in one company and salespeople $6,000 in another. Government studies have placed the costs of mis-hiring programmers at two to three times their annual compensation. At the managerial and professional levels, the data are even more sparse.

The single biggest *estimated* cost of mis-hiring is the wasted or missed business opportunity. In recent years there have been many multimillion-dollar fiascos that clearly could have been avoided had an A-Player been hired instead of a B/C-Player.

One of the most insidious elements of wasted or missed business opportunity goes to the heart of topgrading. B/C-Players hire B/C-Players and drive away A-Players.

CEO mis-hires are the most serious. The media, if not behavioral scientists, cite at least some of the costs. Have you read enough about Ken Lay and Dennis Kozlowski? Their companies suffered because of their failures as CEOs. Michael Ovitz was hired and fired by his buddy Michael Eisner at Disney, and Ovitz walked away with $140 million in severance (challenged in later lawsuits). Not only are the stockholders hurt, but all business suffers a black eye when executives reap great financial rewards despite destroying companies and jobs.

The Career Setbacks

There is no clearer truth to a topgrading professional than this: *The most powerful lever for career success in management is topgrading.*

Its corollary is: *There is no more certain career derailer in management than failing to topgrade.*

More than six thousand senior managers have answered exhaustive topgrading questions about every job they held, an average of ten jobs. Successful careers all have a common pattern: Creating more talented teams accounts for better results, earning managers more promotions. Sometimes the managers admitted they were lucky—they inherited an A-Team because a boss assigned them the "best and brightest," or they went to work for a topgrading company that taught them how to do it. Most were motivated and resourceful, figuring out how to develop or replace non-A-Players.

The vast majority of managers interviewed in a recent study experienced a stutter step—a failure to topgrade and a resulting failure to perform—that led to career stagnation for a while or, in some cases, getting fired. The most successful leaders figure out the importance of topgrading, do it, get better results, and earn promotions.

HIRING AND PROMOTING TALENT: THE TOPGRADING PLATINUM STANDARD

The main responsibility for hiring good people rests on your—the manager's or CEO's—shoulders.

The CEO's job is to achieve results by getting the strategy, talent, and organizational culture right. Topgrading must be thought of as a function permeating the entire company, supported by HR but driven by the CEO. When delegated to HR, topgrading fails, even when HR is a fully topgraded function.

HR cannot drive topgrading, because it lacks the line authority and political clout and because many HR systems (compensation, performance management, hiring, succession planning) require CEO intervention to maintain the A-Player standard.

Anyone can topgrade—*any* department manager can topgrade a department; *any* division manager can topgrade a division. But from a corporate topgrading perspective, the CEO cannot assume that A-Player subordinates are doing it. That's why Jeffrey Immelt (CEO) and Bill Conaty (HR) literally spend months in the famous Session C talent meetings at GE.

The same principle holds for you if you are a function head or operating division head. As a division president you can topgrade, but it is foolish to assume that all your A-Player plant managers will topgrade (even though they would not be considered A-Players without being topgraders). In your talent meetings as well as daily discussions, you must be sure that no one is gaming the system or eroding your A-Player standard for political reasons.

Topgrading Assessments

In topgrading companies it is typical for everyone in management to be topgrading-assessed, to create an overall talent picture of A's, A-potentials, and non-A's. Managers are developed and become A's or are redeployed, and eventually there are 90 percent A-Players. Companies relying on a current performance review and a three-year-old topgrading assessment fail to achieve 90 percent success in promotions. To achieve a 90 percent success in promotions, you must supplement performance appraisals with a fresh, current, topgrading-based assessment.

INCENTIVES FOR BETTER HUMAN CAPITAL ALLOCATIONS

Armed with accurate ROI information on hires, teams can make better human capital allocations and all managers will embrace more rigorous selection. Why not raise the bonus of a manager who hires and retains A-Players and who becomes a provider of talent to other parts of the company? Why not lower the bonus of a manager who costs the company $2 million in mis-hires in a year and who drives away two A-Players? Topgrading companies use such incentives.

REDEPLOYING CHRONIC B- AND C-PLAYERS: A MORAL APPROACH

If topgrading means packing teams, even the entire company, with A-Players, then it usually involves removing chronic B- and C-Players. Chronic means they don't even try to become A-Players or else they have embraced their Individual Development Plan, or IDP (a performance plan to maximize strengths and minimize weak points), but simply aren't improving sufficiently to qualify as A-Players in a reasonable amount of time.

Some B/C-Players can be redeployed internally into jobs where they can be A-Players. If this isn't feasible, they are redeployed externally. They're let go or "changed out," though typically with an appropriate severance and outplacement counseling. Having worked on their IDPs, they also have good insights into themselves and a clear understanding of what sort of job would enable them to be happy and . . . A-Players! Unfortunately, topgrading requires some firing or asking people to resign. It's painful, but it's not immoral if companies:

- Use the best selection techniques, which lead to hiring 90 percent A-Players.
- Use the best assessment techniques, which identify as many people with A-potential as possible.
- Use the best coaching techniques, which give A-potentials the best chance of becoming A-Players.
- Look for other internal jobs where the person would be an A-Player.
- Fire people only if they fail to achieve agreed-upon standards for performance.

TOPGRADING CASE STUDY: LINCOLN FINANCIAL

In 1998 Jon Boscia was named chairman and CEO of Lincoln Financial, and he continued to execute the new business strategy, transforming Lincoln from a traditional life insurance company to a diversified financial services powerhouse. Topgrading was key to the success.

Today Lincoln, with $5.3 billion in revenues and $131 billion in assets, is a different company, one of the nation's leading providers of wealth accumulation and protection, financial planning, and investment advisory services for the fast-growing segments of affluent and retirement markets.

Topgrading required dramatic changes in management, not because the company had weak talent, but because some of the managers in the traditional insurance company lacked necessary competencies to drive the strategy.

Boscia said, "About half of the top 100 managers were A-Players in the old Lincoln and became A's in the new Lincoln, but others simply did not have the necessary skills for the new strategy."

Simple Topgrading Model

To qualify as a company that topgrades, the A-Player standard has to be embraced, but that alone is insufficient. The A-Player standard is not achieved without superb methods to assess and deploy internal talent and assess candidates for selection. The simplest model for topgrading includes these five essential components:

1. Topgrade from the top down.
2. Assess internal talent using Topgrading Interviews, a process that involves an in-depth review of an individual's education and work history, his or her core competencies, as well as a thorough background check.
3. Coach people using Topgrading-based Individual Development Plans.
4. Hire and promote people using Topgrading Interviews.
5. Redeploy (fire, demote, transfer) people who fail to achieve the A-Player standard.

OBSTACLES TO TOPGRADING AND HOW A-PLAYERS OVERCOME THEM

Ratcheting up an organization's talent involves many obstacles. Here are the top ten major obstacles to topgrading and the best practices to overcome them:

1. *"I can't get my B/C-Players to hire A-Players."* Topgrade from the top down, or require your A-Players to make the topgrading judgments for their B/C's.
2. *"We think we're hiring A-Players, but they turn out to be B/C-Players in disguise."* Perform more accurate assessments using the Topgrading Interview.
3. *"Our human resources people are overworked and understaffed, so we don't exactly have a pipeline of A Players going through the office."* Constantly recruit your "virtual bench," your network of A-Players in your Rolodex, who are ever available to join you. And require all your managers to constantly build their virtual bench.
4. *"Search firms just don't produce enough A-Player candidates."* Manage the search process, including search firms, much more thoroughly.
5. *"I want to raise the performance bar, but almost every talented person I bring in from the outside is rejected by the current organization culture and ends up quitting."* Provide new A-Players protection from undermining by existing personnel.
6. *"We can't afford to hire A-Players."* A-Players are available at all compensation levels.
7. *"I do not want to fire loyal B/C-Players."* Redeploy chronic B/C-Players because painful as it is to fire someone, failing to do so is almost always more painful—to the company, your career, and the underperformer.
8. *"Our problems will soon clear up because we engaged a management consulting firm and their report looks great, so topgrading isn't necessary."* Topgrade first. Organizations that topgrade are able to drive improvements in strategy, productivity, innovation, quality, customer service, and speed to market.

9. *"We could never attract A-Players because of our location, industry, current financial problems, and so on."* Pay more in compensation to attract the level of talent necessary to beat the competition.

10. *"My subordinates tend to give 'thumbs-down' on A-Players."* Don't let them have a vote. Make the hiring decision yourself.

THE TOPGRADING INTERVIEW GUIDE

The Topgrading Interview Guide provides you with the most accurate and valid insights when assessing internal talent and candidates for selection or promotion. Companies can achieve a record of 90 percent A-Players hired when a tandem interview (two interviewers) is conducted and the interviewers have been trained in Topgrading Interview techniques.

The Topgrading Interview Guide features comprehensive questions that cover college, work history, self-appraisal of strengths and weaknesses, leadership/management, topgrading, and competencies. It produces more valid results than so-called targeted, or competency-based, interviews that ignore dozens of important competencies as well as the chronology, the crucial patterns of how the interviewee developed throughout his or her career.

Interview Questions to Facilitate Topgrading

During the interview process, it's important to ask thorough questions about the interviewee's education and prior work history. Beginning with college, incorporate some of the following questions into your Topgrading Interview:

- What people or events during college might have had an influence on your career?
- What were the high points during your college years? (Look for leadership, resourcefulness, and particularly what competencies the interviewee exhibits *now* while discussing those years.)
- What were your career thoughts toward the end of college?

Following the questions about education, move into a discussion about the interviewee's work history. Based on his or her résumé, you will already have an overview, but the following questions will allow you to delve deeper:

- What were your expectations for the job? What did you find when you arrived to the position? What major challenges did you face?

- What results were achieved in terms of successes and accomplishments? How were they achieved?
- As a manager, what sort of talent did you inherit? What changes did you make, how did you make them, and how many A-, B-, and C-Players did you end up with?

It is also necessary to have the interviewee give a self-appraisal. This involves listing all of his or her strengths and assets, as well as any shortcomings and areas for improvement. After obtaining the list, go back through and have the interviewee elaborate upon each point. Finally, ask the interviewee to go over his or her competencies with you. These include intellectual, personal, interpersonal, management, leadership, and motivational competencies. A general question such as "Please describe _____ and what specific examples can you cite?" should be asked. This information will allow you to assess a number of the interviewee's competencies.

Interpreting All the Data

Here are some of the most important principles for valid interpretation of data:

1. *Observe patterns.* Patterns in many statements give multiple vantage points from which to find out what makes a person tick and what the person's strengths and weak points are.
2. *Assume that strengths can become shortcomings.* Under pressure, we all tend to overuse our strengths, and they can become shortcomings. During interviews, entertain this hypothesis frequently.
3. *Assume recent past behavior is the best predictor of near-future behavior.* As you review an individual's chronological history, weigh the most recent behaviors most heavily.
4. *Spot red flags and look for explanations.* Red flags are warning signals to the interviewer that something has gone wrong. Use follow-up questions to get additional information.
5. *Weigh negatives more heavily than positives.* Good-fit factors do not ensure success, but poor-fit factors can ensure failure.
6. *Watch out for strong feelings and beliefs.* Naturally, strong beliefs can be an asset for any candidate. It's when the beliefs are accompanied by rigidity, intolerance, and extreme emotionality that you begin to wonder if there might be accompanying shortcomings.

50 MANAGEMENT COMPETENCIES

A-Players need not be excellent in all competencies, but they must meet the minimum standard for a particular job on all of them. The following are fifty management competencies:

- *Intellectual competencies:* Intelligence, analysis skills, judgment/decision making, conceptual ability, creativity, strategic skills, pragmatism, risk taking, leading edge, education, experience, track record.
- *Personal competencies:* Integrity, resourcefulness, organization/planning, excellence, independence, stress management, self-awareness, adaptability.
- *Interpersonal competencies:* First impression, likability, listening, customer focus, team player, assertiveness, oral communication, written communication, political savvy, negotiation, persuasion.
- *Management competencies:* Selecting A-Players, coaching, goal setting, empowerment, accountability, redeploying B/C-Players, team building, diversity, running meetings.
- *Additional leadership competencies:* Vision, change leadership, inspiring "followership," conflict management.
- *Motivational competencies:* Energy, passion, ambition, compatibility of needs, balance in life, tenacity.

COACHING 101: THE TOPGRADING-BASED MODEL

Coaching is a one-to-one dialogue in which a coach helps a person understand his or her strengths and weak points and build commitment to improve performance. Coaching helps unlock someone's potential. This involves:

- Counseling—to help someone improve self-awareness and change points of view.
- Mentoring—sharing sage advice to help someone become more savvy in matters of organizational culture, networking, and career planning.
- Teaching—instructing someone in order to improve expertise.
- Confronting—addressing nonperformance to help someone either achieve performance goals or accept the necessity of redeployment.

Ordinary solid human qualities blended with topgrading best practices frequently result in leaders being rated "very high" on coaching scales. This becomes clear during assimilation coaching, a disciplined process to help your new hire adjust and to begin a comprehensive developmental process.

Assimilation Coaching

First-time topgrading interviewers have fun in assimilation coaching, a high-powered, positive coaching session. You feel empowered, so it is relatively easy to empower your new hire. There are fewer problems to fix with A-Players than with C-Players, so there is little inclination to push, cajole, or demand certain changes. With an initial coaching meeting a success, you become positively reinforced to polish your skills, to extend coaching to other subordinates. Hiring an A-Player using topgrading interviewing and thorough reference checking automatically endows you with supercoach characteristics.

A topgrading-based coaching meeting, whether for assimilation or another purpose, is not always warm and fuzzy. Even A-Players have weak points— plenty of them. Coaching need not be acrimonious, but to be effective, it must be hard-hitting.

The nicest thing you can do for high-potential managers is tell the truth and hold them accountable for growth. That means saying, "Improve, and only then will you get promoted." People change the most when they sense pain in not changing and benefits in changing, and fully embrace developmental activities to achieve their goals.

COACHING TO FIX WEAKNESSES

Having conducted a Topgrading Interview gives you instant coaching advantages. Having hired an A-Player, you automatically are 20 percent better as a coach.

The four essential steps in coaching a new hire to succeed are:

1. *Hire an A-Player* with a tandem Topgrading Interview, reference checks with all bosses in past ten years, a co-worker competency interview (one hour each), and conclusions stated in a Candidate Assessment Scorecard (CAS), a simple form used to assess the candidate on all competencies.
2. *Conduct oral interviews or e-mail 360 survey* two to four weeks after hire, with the purpose of measuring first impressions.
3. *Have a coaching interview* two to six weeks after hire; state conclusions, strengths, weak points; and create an Individual Development Plan together.
4. *Hold a mid-year career review* in which you discuss follow-up e-mail 360 survey results and include feedback to you.

This rather typical assimilation coaching session should progress through the seven psychological stages of change: awareness, rational acceptance, emotional commitment, program for development, reinforcement, monitoring progress, and conclusion.

Constructive Criticism

The business world is too fast-paced and too demanding for quiet, gentle little hints, except with a rare subordinate requiring your most flexible and sensitive care. This world requires hard-hitting constructive criticism. You want the straight scoop if your boss is dissatisfied. You want to be treated with respect, and you respond best when you are presented positively with an opportunity to improve. Your subordinates want and deserve the same thing.

AVOIDING LEGAL PROBLEMS

Topgrading can embrace the spirit and letter of employment law or it can be abused. An effort to remove chronic B- and C-Players can incur big risks if care is not taken to avoid a charge of discrimination—age discrimination, for example.

Developing future A-Players can trigger litigation if disabled people protected by the Americans with Disabilities Act are overlooked. The Equal Employment Opportunity Commission will be knocking on your door if your infusion of new A-Players systematically excludes minorities. Employees and managers have discovered not only their civil rights, but also their contract and tort rights. Unless your company protects itself, it could face serious employment-related claims, including claims of wrongful discharge, breach of contract, discrimination, negligent hiring, or harassment.

Topgrading will help you meet legal requirements during the hiring process. The leading-edge practices in recruitment and selection—job analyses, behaviorally anchored competencies, structured interviews, note taking, and so forth—must be coupled with working hand in hand with your partner in HR and your legal counsel to avoid legal problems. State laws vary and your company might be vulnerable. So check with your attorney before acting or failing to act.

Safe Hiring and Firing Practices

Despite the complexities of employment law, the answer is to focus on the fundamentals: (1) perform thorough job analysis; (2) write job descriptions with behavioral competencies; (3) use nondiscriminatory language in employment applications, topgrading forms and guides, job advertisements, and interviews; (4) use legally sound job offer letters; (5) avoid negligent hiring and retention claims; (6) use safe managing and firing practices; and (7) follow guidelines on how to topgrade outside the United States.

TOPGRADING IN THE FUTURE

It's hard to imagine an organization that cannot benefit from topgrading. From hot dog stands to the United Nations, A-Players get results, C-Players don't. What organization cannot benefit from a 90 percent success in hiring versus 25 percent?

Consider just a few future venues for topgrading:

1. *Community service.* Community-service organizations can attract more money in the future by topgrading them and advertising, "We have a team of A-Players who will spend your donations for maximum results."
2. *Government.* Why not screen political candidates for financial support by submitting them to Topgrading Interviews?
3. *Finance.* Half of all mergers and acquisitions fail, and the biggest reason is inadequate talent. The most successful venture capitalists are very rigorous in assessing management in organizations in which they invest; they qualify as topgraders. Topgrading offers the world of finance accurate insight into people.
4. *Governance.* To hire a CEO, boards have historically trusted the search firm's interviews and report, with directors performing perfunctory interviews. With directors taking more (deserved) heat and incurring more legal risk, it would seem prudent to select a CEO by topgrading.
5. *Legally mandated topgrading.* With race norming and quotas illegal, yet the pressure for affirmative action continuing, valid approaches for hiring truly talented protected groups is the solution.
6. *Education.* Are 90 percent of teachers in your school system A-Players? European high schools surpass U.S. schools on standardized tests, yet our per-pupil cost is sky-high (six times what French students are allocated, for example).
7. *Career planning.* Topgraded companies rarely promote people over their heads or leave a supertalent languishing and underutilized. Educational institutions could assess students' career talents much better if they would incorporate a Topgrading Interview.
8. *Future research on topgrading.* Talent as an issue, or opportunity, is as old as the human race. Many companies could contribute to the body of scientific

literature, and hundreds of master's theses and PhD dissertations could refine and connect individual corporate studies.

In the meantime, you can conduct your own research on talent maximization every day. Topgrading is not easy. There are lessons to be learned, by you and me, about what topgrading approaches work best. Your personal "case study" is an art form, a work in progress.

JACK WELCH AND THE
4E'S OF LEADERSHIP
by Jeffrey A. Krames

B usiness author Jeffrey A. Krames has spent many years researching and writing about the world's top business and political leaders. His award-winning management books are well-organized leadership training tools that present the latest in management thinking. His bestsellers include *The Welch Way, What the Best CEOs Know,* and *The Jack Welch Lexicon of Leadership.*

In *Jack Welch and the 4E's of Leadership,* Krames analyzes the enduring leadership principles of legendary General Electric CEO Jack Welch. He rounds out these rules by also examining a variety of case studies and ideas from other leaders inside and outside GE. Krames dissects Welch's organizational strengths and management wisdom while describing his talents and tactics for developing leaders at GE, a company that has cultivated more Fortune 500 CEOs than any other organization in history.

Welch and his winning ways have inspired countless books and articles that chronicle his decisive actions and controversial decisions while he was GE's CEO. Most avid business readers are aware of Welch's amazing legacy as the tough CEO who increased GE's market value by more than $400 billion over two decades. But the 4E's Krames describes in his collection of Welch-ian wisdom offer leaders ways they can tap into the strategies Welch used to make GE the most valuable corporation on the planet.

After his first ten years at the helm of GE—one of the world's most complex companies—Welch developed the 4E model of leadership. It reflects four specific traits: The exceptional leader has *energy, energizes* others, has a competitive *edge,* and *executes* for measurable results. Krames develops these concepts with quotes from Welch, Peter Drucker, Larry Bossidy, Peter Senge, and a plethora of other corporate, academic, and political leaders.

The principles found in Welch's 4E leadership formula contain valuable ideas every manager and executive needs in his or her repertoire of leadership knowledge. For example, Welch's first E is the *energy* to attack the job at hand. Welch says loving the thrill of the game is essential to the success of a leader. This energy is the key to building spirit and morale in any organization. Creating connections between people requires the physical and emotional energy to execute. Welch's principles proclaim the value of both the energy to fuel an organization's results *and* the ability to energize other people to work toward clear and simple goals.

Krames deciphers the Welch leadership formula into an outline of positive habits and topics that should remain on every leader's mind: performance, expertise, mentors, ownership, global perspective, and the other disciplines of excellence. But Krames is also a storyteller who provides important lessons about corporate renewal when he relates the tale of another GE CEO, Jeff Immelt. Krames describes how Welch trusted Immelt with the tasks of reinventing the company and carrying on his legacy of continual change. Through additional stories about Honeywell's Larry Bossidy, 3M's James McNerney, Wipro's Vivek Paul, and Home Depot's Bob Nardelli, Krames shows how Welch's ideas work and grow when cultivated by leaders at the top of other industries.

Jack Welch and the 4E's of Leadership offers leaders hands-on checklists, self-assessment quizzes, and training scenarios that can help them develop a deeper understanding of the specific ways Welch's management and training breakthroughs can be used in their own organizations.

JACK WELCH AND THE 4E'S OF LEADERSHIP

How to Put GE's Leadership Formula to Work in Your Organization

by Jeffrey A. Krames

CONTENTS

7. Make Leadership Development a Top Priority

8. Execution Is Everything

9. Enhance, Extend, Expand

10. Go on the Offense When Others Retrench

THE SUMMARY IN BRIEF

Jack Welch was one of history's most competitive corporate leaders, and he had a well-defined process for surrounding himself with individuals cut from the same cloth. This summary examines the model Welch used to identify and develop performance-based leaders and provides a template for incorporating Welch's tactics into your career and organization.

Best-selling author Jeffrey A. Krames details the inside secrets of Welch's success, including insights into the 4E's: Energy, the ability to Energize others, the Edge necessary to make the hard decisions, and the skill and confidence to Execute.

Under his watch, Welch and a handpicked team of 4E Leaders transformed General Electric from a lumbering manufacturing giant into one of the world's most agile enterprises that had "change in its blood."

During Welch's tenure as CEO, GE turned out more Fortune 500 CEOs than any other organization in history. This summary takes you step-by step through the reasons for that astonishing record, and provides you with specific actions for recognizing and rewarding authentic leaders and becoming a 4E Leader yourself.

In addition, this summary will show you:

- How to wage war on bureaucracy by eliminating walls between managers and employees.
- How to make your organization more customer-centric by basing each decision on customer needs and wants.
- How to make training a top priority, inside and outside the classroom.
- Why some senior managers fail, and what to do about it.
- How to achieve extraordinary results at every level of your organization.

THE COMPLETE SUMMARY

THE 4E LEADER: JACK WELCH'S WINNING
LEADERSHIP FORMULA

Jack Welch knows a great deal about what it takes to lead a large organization successfully, and the 4E Leadership model was central to that success. In his twenty-plus years at the helm of General Electric, Welch transformed a mature manufacturing company into an outstanding products-and-services juggernaut. He increased the value of his company more than thirty times over. He achieved all of this by defying some of GE's most venerated traditions (for example, by making hundreds of acquisitions), by making the "tough calls" (he laid off more than one hundred thousand workers), and by transforming GE's insular, hidebound culture (he fired the strategic planners and made sure that managers listened to workers).

But most of all, Welch selected and developed leaders. The discipline of the 4E's helped him find and develop leaders who would fit into GE's high-octane, performance-based culture. Those who scored high on all four "E" categories were the ones who ultimately helped him fulfill his goal of building the world's most competitive organization.

What are the four characteristics shared by these exceptional leaders?

- *Energy.* Welch says that individuals with energy love to "go, go, go." These are the people with boundless energy, who get up every morning just itching to attack the job at hand.
- *Energizers* know how to *spark others* to perform. They outline a vision and inspire people to act on that vision. They are selfless in giving others the credit when things go right and quick to accept responsibility when things go awry because they know sharing credit and owning blame energizes their colleagues.
- *Edge.* Those with edge are *competitive* types. They know how to make the really difficult decisions, never allowing the degree of difficulty to stand in their way. These are leaders who don't hesitate to make what management expert Peter Drucker called the "life and death" decisions: hiring, promoting, and firing.
- *Execute.* The first three E's are essential, but without *measurable results,* they are of little use to an organization. People who execute effectively understand that activity and productivity are not the same thing. The best leaders know how to convert energy and edge into action and results. They know how to execute.

THE 4E LEADER HAS ENERGY

Leaders must have other strengths, such as intelligence and decision-making ability, but it is energy that converts good ideas into measurable performance. Strictly defined, *energy* means a source of power, whether electrical, mechanical, or otherwise. There is more to energy than its physical properties. In addition to physical energy, there is also mental energy and what might be called "emotional energy"—the kind of energy that a leader projects to help build the spirit or morale of an organization.

It is an energy that reaches across people and binds together individual contributions into a purposeful whole. In that sense, emotional energy can be as important as or more important than physical energy. Emotional energy is the passion that gets the job done.

Simplify the Organization

Getting high-energy people into the company is only the first step—the organizational equivalent of setting the table. The next, and bigger, task is to create an organization that converts energy into results. Early in his tenure at GE, Welch set his sights on simplifying the organizational chart.

Why? Because when he surveyed GE's structure in the early 1980s, he saw a complex, lumbering, muddled organization with too many management layers, too many titles, too much of everything. To his eyes, the structure made no sense: 25,000 managers, more than 130 vice presidents, and more strategic planners than any one company would ever need.

With a speed and determination that shocked many of his colleagues, Welch de-layered the company. He fired the strategic planners and put the responsibility for plotting the direction of each of the business units into the hands of the people who led those units.

Later, he launched his now-legendary Work-Out™ initiative, aimed at getting good ideas out of the entire workforce (and compelling management to deal with those ideas). In all cases, Welch had three key goals in mind: making the organization more productive, weaving higher levels of self-confidence into the fabric of the firm, and throttling bureaucracy.

Energy and Change

Of all the words and ideas in the Welch lexicon, few are as important as *change*. Welch knew that everything was changing—the marketplace, GE's customers, the competitive landscape, and so on—and that he had to get ahead of that change.

How can a leader add energy to the organization during any large-scale change effort? The 4E Leader follows the Seven Steps of Dealing with Change:

1. *Explain the new rules of engagement.* In his first speeches as CEO, Welch explained that his goal was to create a company in which all the businesses were tops in their markets.
2. *Deal with change head-on.* Welch tackled change by owning it, spotlighting it, and incorporating it into the company's shared values.
3. *Paint a vivid picture of the finish line.* Get employees and managers to share a vision of the future.
4. *Candor first, foremost, and always.* Candor, openness, trust, boundarylessness: These were the watchwords that described Welch's ideal organization.
5. *Overcommunicate.* Welch served personally as the "champion" of all his strategies and initiatives.
6. *Exploit the opportunities that change brings.* Under Welch, GE made more than twelve hundred acquisitions. That change gave all GE's business leaders a chance to grow their businesses by means of acquisitions, and it fueled the majority of GE's growth during the Welch years.
7. *Reiterate that change never ends.* The trick is not to make change go away; the trick is to change the way you think about it.

CROTONVILLE

Even while he was making drastic budget cuts elsewhere, CEO Jack Welch invested heavily in Crotonville, GE's management training institute on the Hudson River, north of New York City.

Crotonville became the de facto headquarters of Welch's organizational transformation—a place where GE's best and brightest could go to both expand their intellectual horizons and recharge their batteries. *Fortune* called Crotonville "Harvard on the Hudson."

Welch considered Crotonville to be the glue that held the company together through all the change initiatives. Crotonville, he said, served as a "forum for the sharing of the experiences, the aspirations, and, often the frustrations of the tens of thousands of GE leaders who passed through its campus."

THE 4E LEADER ENERGIZES

The best energizers have an unvarnished, unqualified brand of enthusiasm. They can get their colleagues charged up about just about anything. People respond to them, and that response makes them particularly effective. They bring out the best in people, inject them with confidence, and give them the credit when things go right. They are the organization's confidence builders. That's why Welch decreed that "the ability to energize is the ingredient that counts."

Welch also said: "You have no right to be a leader if you don't have it in your soul to build others. Nothing is worse than a whirling dervish who bores everyone. You need fertilizer and water."

"Fertilizer and water," it turns out, is Welch's metaphor for effective leadership. The 4E Leader spreads confidence like gardeners spread fertilizer. That's why, according to Welch, the most important thing a leader does is to instill confidence into the soul of the organization.

New Ideas Energize Everyone

Few things got Welch more energized than new ideas. Extrapolating from his own experience, he was convinced that new ideas were the lifeblood of the organization. "The hero is the one with the idea," he once declared. Ideas, learning, training—all contribute to the collective intellect of the organization.

Energizers aren't necessarily the source of ideas; more likely, they encourage others to voice their ideas. They know that few things get people more excited than having one of their ideas lead to an important "win" for the organization.

HOW TO ENERGIZE EMPLOYEES AT REVIEW TIME

To energize employees, make a habit of asking these types of questions at review time:

- What do you want to achieve in the next twelve months? What do you want to achieve in the ensuing few years?
- What is it in the organization that will help you to make your goals? What roadblocks will interfere with your progress?
- What else do you need from the organization to help you accomplish your objectives?
- What things do I—your manager—do that hinder your efforts?
- What is your pattern of failure? What danger signals should I look for ahead of time so that I know to come talk to you and help you?

THE 4E LEADER HAS EDGE

To Welch, business is about winning: winning in the marketplace, winning customers, winning new business, winning for shareholders. But Welch's approach to winning was far from simplistic or one-dimensional. He knew that the path to winning is sometimes a winding one. Embracing complexity and paradox while still maintaining clarity of vision and edge is a difficult balancing act. Welch understood that, and he achieved it better than most.

Maintaining Edge in the Face of Paradox

Many of Welch's early moves confirmed what he had suspected from the beginning: that reinventing a company required many actions that tugged in contradictory directions. Most immediately, he had to tear down in order to build. He had to find a way of "managing long term while 'eating' short term." Welch did a great job of balancing the two, which is one of the reasons he was so successful.

One way he did so was to cut costs ruthlessly. In his first five years at the helm of GE, Welch cut one out of every four people on the GE payroll (118,000 people, including 37,000 people from businesses that were divested).

At the same time that Welch was cutting deeply into the payroll, he was spending millions on what he called "nonproductive" things. He upgraded the Crotonville facility, and he built a gym, a guesthouse, and a conference center for the Fairfield headquarters.

It took some time for many to see the logic of Welch's actions, but eventually they came around. The results were irrefutable. By the late 1980s, all the key metrics of productivity were up significantly: profit margins, inventory turns, and so on. By managing contradictory tugs within the organization while still defending his vision, Welch demonstrated that he was a manager with edge—someone who didn't shy away from the tough decisions. He and his team of consultants summed it up: "Paradox is a way of life. You must function collectively as one company and individually as many businesses at the same time. For us, leadership means leading while being led, producing more output with less input."

THE 4E LEADER EXECUTES

Creating a performance-based culture must begin at the top, with the chief executive officer. Of course, much depends on your starting point. As a rule, however, one of the keys to developing an execution culture is the recognition that altering the culture of a Fortune 500 company takes years—there is simply no quick fix or magic potion that can change a company overnight.

The following steps summarize twenty years of deep, difficult cultural change at GE:

1. *Establish performance as a key company priority.* From his first days on the job, Welch's edicts formed a powerful message: Execution was now the new order of things, and those businesses and individuals that could not help the company win would not be retained.
2. *Make sure that the company has a defining set of values.* Integrity, boundarylessness, seeing change as an opportunity, being open to ideas from anywhere, killing bureaucracy, being committed to Work-Out and Six Sigma, having global brains—these were the values and priorities that distinguished GE from other companies.
3. *Organize for execution.* Welch de-layered the company early on.
4. *Use differentiation to promote the A's, keep the B's, and fire the C's.* Welch said that differentiation was one of his most important tools in remaking GE's culture.
5. *Make execution a key part of the reward system.* Let managers know that bonuses and stock options will be based on consistent achievement of vital execution goals.
6. *Use Work-Out or a similar cultural initiative to instill candor and trust into the fabric of the organization.*
7. *Develop and train your best leaders.* Crotonville became the key to winning the hearts and minds of GE's managers.
8. *Make sure that there is an operating system in place that focuses on execution.* The GE operating system reinforced all of Welch's companywide initiatives, such as globalization and Six Sigma.
9. *Continue to winnow out weak businesses and weak performers.* There is no room for underperformers.

Why Some Senior Managers Fail

Welch sought reasons why people succeeded, but he also wanted to find out why some senior managers failed at GE. Here is the list that Welch and his team came up with, as well as some suggestions about what might be done to mitigate each of these failure-inducing factors:

1. *The wrong stuff.* These individuals did not behave or lead in a manner that was consistent with the company's belief and value system.

   The remedy: A senior manager who does not believe in the company's values should be eliminated as quickly as possible, lest he or she "infect" colleagues or direct reports.

2. *Poorly conceived organization.* Too many layers, the wrong structure, the wrong expectations or not giving a unit what it needs to succeed—all of these can derail a manager.

    The remedy: Work with your senior HR manager to reorganize the company, reducing layers.

3. *Wrong choices.* Organizations sometimes promote the wrong people. No one is perfect, so a manager is bound to make the wrong choice once or twice in his or her career.

    The remedy: Recognizing a bad selection is the first step to fixing this. Once you do, then you either fire that manager or (if appropriate) find him or her another position that he or she is truly suited for.

4. *Insufficiently heroic objectives.* This manager is not an effective energizer. He or she has difficulty inspiring others, articulating a vision, and so on.

    The remedy: Invite the manager to one or two of your meetings to show him or her how you get others to act.

5. *Poor start.* Some managers get off on the wrong foot and consistently lag behind.

    The remedy: Sit down with this manager to sort out the issues. If, after you talk with the manager, you determine that he or she will never do better than tread water, then you have no choice but to fire or reassign him or her.

6. *Cannot adapt.* Having the ability to live with paradox and change is an essential skill in a learning organization.

    The remedy: Sit down with the manager and provide very specific feedback on what is *not* getting done. Unless this manager is open to constructive criticism, however, it is unlikely that he or she will be able to turn this around.

7. *Can't get it done.* Managers must be able to do more than talk; they must be able to say yes or no (not maybe) when the situation demands it.

    The remedy: Let the manager know that you, the leader, will not punish him or her for honest mistakes. Tell the manager that it's not necessary to be right 100 percent of the time but to tilt the odds in his or her favor by making the right calculations.

8. *Not in focus.* Managers who are "out of focus" lack the ability to transform all the data and information into results that can be acted upon.

    The remedy: You need to show them what Welch calls the "leverage points": those things (e.g., decisions and actions) that will really move the needle. Ask them to carefully document leverage points and monitor their progress.

9. *Poor instincts.* This is a manager who cannot make the right calls with the limited information that he or she has.

   The remedy: The best chance you may have to turn around a manager with bad instincts is to do a postmortem on some of his or her recent misfires.

10. *Ego problems.* Some managers take themselves too seriously, and they don't often take responsibility for their actions.

    The remedy: Do not let a self-important manager destroy your unit or division. Deal with it head-on by removing the offending manager.

11. *Too slow.* Some managers, often those who lack the first E, energy, seem to move in slow motion.

    The remedy: Coaching is required to help turn these slowpokes around. In a constructive manner, point out what is not getting done quickly enough and why moving more quickly is so important to the success of the organization. Work closely with this manager until he or she develops quicker reflexes.

"BLOW IT UP"

Jeff Immelt was one of three candidates in contention for the most coveted job in corporate America: CEO and chairman of GE. Although Jack Welch was not scheduled to step down until 2001, he started working on the process of identifying his successor several years earlier. That is standard operating procedure at GE, a company that has led the way in succession planning for a century.

One of the key factors behind Immelt's selection was his devotion to Six Sigma, the quality program that consumed Welch in his last years on the job. But Immelt's relative youth also was important to Welch. Welch wanted to make sure that his successor had enough time to reinvent the company, much as he (and his six predecessors) had done. And there was another advantage to longevity in the CEO's post, as Welch saw it.

As he explained later, Welch's goal in selecting a successor was to choose someone who had enough time to stay in the post for about two decades. Welch had twenty years as CEO, and he wanted to make sure that the person who followed him had as much time as he did to reinvent the company. Of course, one of the other driving forces behind Welch's decision to promote Immelt was his ability to execute consistently.

Reinvent the Company—Again

As Welch's handpicked successor, no one had bigger shoes to fill than Jeff Immelt. Breaking with the past is a time-honored tradition of incoming CEOs at GE. Reg Jones, Welch's predecessor, gave Welch the same advice that Welch passed on to Immelt: "Blow it up." In other words, tear up the old game plan and create a new one tailored to whatever new realities the company was confronting.

Immelt has put his own stamp on the company's relationship with Wall Street. Welch held sway over analysts by setting lofty quarterly goals and beating them like clockwork. Immelt is taking the long view: outlining a long-term vision and de-emphasizing the short term. In fact, Immelt's entire approach is one that favors the next quarter century over the next fiscal quarter.

The real paradoxical twist is that by breaking with GE's past, Immelt is in fact being faithful to it. Most of GE's chairmen have carved their own paths, and this potentially risky penchant for reinventing the company every couple of decades or so has reaped great rewards for the company.

The Five-Initiative Growth Strategy

Like almost any truly effective CEO, Immelt is obsessed with growing the company. His stated goal is to make sure that the organic growth of GE comes in at 8 percent (excluding acquisitions) while simultaneously keeping the company's high margins. His mantra is: *Growth is the initiative, the core competency we are building at GE.*

He points to the company's five-initiative strategy as the key to creating "high-margin, capital-efficient growth":

■ **Technical Leadership.** Immelt puts technical expertise at the top of his list. He says that this kind of technical leadership, combined with GE's innovative spirit, infuses the company's key initiatives.

■ **Services.** Welch saw services as a critical growth engine, and Immelt certainly has picked up where Welch left off. Immelt also points out that GE has an incredible base of industrial products—including jet engines, power turbines, and medical devices—upon which future service lines may be built.

■ **Customer Focus.** Immelt has taken the concept of customer focus to the next level. He created a sales and marketing "council" designed to introduce Six Sigma to GE's customers, thereby improving the alignment of GE's sales force with its customers' needs.

■ **Globalization.** Welch's first initiative was globalization. Immelt understands that global success depends on the organization's ability to grow its businesses through relationships and on hiring and developing local managers who grasp the subtle cultural nuances that are so critical to success.

■ **Growth Platforms.** One of GE's key strengths, writes Immelt, is having the vision to see "unstoppable trends." For example, he predicts that in the near term, the organic growth rate of industrial platforms will be in double digits.

MAKE LEADERSHIP DEVELOPMENT A TOP PRIORITY

In 2000 James McNerney was one of the other two executives who did not get Welch's job. After McNerney found out that he had lost out to Immelt, he told Welch, flat out, that Welch had picked the wrong guy. But McNerney didn't waste time worrying about his lost opportunities at GE. He landed on his feet and then some, becoming chairman and CEO of corporate juggernaut 3M, the first outsider to head up that company in its one-hundred-plus-year history.

Don't Undervalue Leadership

In 2003 McNerney's 3M achieved record year-over-year earnings for the seventh quarter in a row—a lofty performance that has won the hearts of employees and shareholders alike.

McNerney's new agenda at 3M has included tighter fiscal management, more ambitious budget goals, and a greater emphasis on leadership development. Like Jack Welch, McNerney leads by example. He is intimately involved in the company's executive training program, declaring it "fundamental" for a CEO to take a leading role in the company's human-development efforts.

McNerney has established leadership development as one of the company's priorities. He turned 3M's R&D training center in St. Paul into the company's version of GE's Crotonville. Called the Leadership Development Institute, it trains some forty "high-potential people" at a time in a seventeen-day Accelerated Leadership Development Program.

The entire program is devoted to solving company problems personally identified and selected by CEO McNerney. On the final day of the course, McNerney listens to the class's solutions, some of which subsequently have been implemented companywide. Like GE's Crotonville, it is also a place that educates managers in key company initiatives, like Six Sigma. McNerney explains, "My experience is that if people are convinced they're growing as they pursue company goals, that's when you get ignition."

EXECUTION IS EVERYTHING

Larry Bossidy, former GE vice chairman and former Honeywell CEO, wrote the book on execution. *Execution: The Discipline of Getting Things Done* was co-authored with author and consultant Ram Charan, and it went on to become number one on *The New York Times* bestseller list in 2002.

Bossidy and Charan explained that execution was the new currency that would separate authentic leaders from the also-rans. Only through forging a genuine, execution-oriented culture, they argued, could leaders build real credibility. Bossidy and Charan also described the following three vital points on execution, and its importance to any organization's success:

- Execution is a discipline, and integral to strategy.
- Execution is the major job of the business leader.
- Execution must be a core element of an organization's culture.

Consistency

If you look more closely at the three points on execution, something interesting emerges: They're all about *consistency*. Execution can't be something that happens once in a while. It is a discipline, a core element, the major job of the leader—and, as it turns out, of *everybody*.

Bossidy also pointed out that execution, like other companywide initiatives such as Six Sigma, will only bear fruit if the company trains for execution and allows its people to "practice it constantly." He also notes that it will not take root unless a company trains the majority of its people in it.

To make sure that execution is ingrained in every corner of an organization, the leaders must keep it front and center at all times. Stated slightly differently, the responsibility for ensuring that execution remains a key company priority lies with senior management. It cannot be delegated, and it must be addressed on many different levels simultaneously.

DEVELOP AN "ARCHITECTURE FOR EXECUTION"

Execution must be integral to everything a company does, an overriding theme that permeates the organization's culture. Execution needs to be a reflex, something that becomes second nature. Make execution a prominent part of the incentive system, as well as a primary criterion for promotions. That will happen only if you incorporate it into goals, assignments, training, annual reviews, and everything else.

ENHANCE, EXTEND, EXPAND

Robert Nardelli spent nearly three decades at General Electric, holding more than a dozen different leadership positions, before making the move to run Home Depot.

Nardelli reinvented Home Depot the GE way. He recognized immediately that the company was behaving like a loosely knit confederation rather than like a Fortune 50 company. It had enormous clout on both the purchasing and the marketing ends that it was simply leaving on the table.

Nardelli wasted little time in implementing his makeover. He put in centralized vendor agreements. He transformed operations. He replaced most of the senior management team and he flattened the organizational structure. Nardelli's strategy was anything but complex, and could be articulated in nine words: *Enhance the core. Extend the business. Expand the market.*

Nardelli had some very specific ideas and initiatives associated with each component of his strategy:

■ **Enhance the Core.** Nardelli spent more than $10 billion on technology to spark productivity and bring the company's antiquated information systems into the new century. Some of that was used for inventory management systems and in-store Internet-based kiosks that offered customers thousands of special-order products. To better compete with Lowe's, he offered higher-margin products, thus increasing the average dollars per purchase.

■ **Extend the Business.** New stores, new formats, and new businesses would help fuel growth, argued Nardelli. In 2003, Home Depot added 175 new stores and added more net new jobs than any other established U.S. corporation. Training was also a top priority, and company associates received more than 21 million hours of training.

■ **Expand the Market.** Nardelli also reached beyond U.S. borders. By the end of 2003, the company had more than one hundred stores in Canada (with plans for more), stores in Mexico, and plans to expand in China and other high-growth markets. The company is also aggressively pursuing homebuilders and other professionals, including maintenance and repair professionals, as distinct growth markets.

A Customer-Based Strategy

Nardelli spoke with pride of his tri-tiered plan in 2005: "Under each of those three of enhance, extend and expand, the dynamics of the market and the customer will shape the initiatives of distinction and innovative merchandising, for example, store readiness digitization . . . all of those under the core which will result in same store sales improvement, sales per square foot productivity."

GO ON THE OFFENSE WHEN OTHERS RETRENCH

The true test of an organization's skill at creating effective leaders lies not in its ability to create what Peter Drucker called CEO "geniuses or supermen." Rather, it lies in the organization's ability to consistently and systematically develop strong managers at all levels of the hierarchy. An organization that has a strong senior management team but lacks bench strength will find itself in trouble sooner rather than later—particularly when it comes to execution.

Welch understood this. The GE operating system ensured a steady supply of capable leaders. Welch liked to say that GE's best products were not its aircraft engines or its medical devices, but its people. He thought more about the topic of leadership than almost any of his contemporaries, and this helped him create a leadership cadre with both strong skill sets and an affinity for change.

Vivek Paul's Story

Vivek Paul, an Indian national, was a senior executive in GE Medical in the 1990s. A generation "removed" from Welch; he reported instead to Jeff Immelt, who at the time headed GE's $8 billion medical systems division. Like his GE boss, Paul was a faithful follower of the company's predominant "religion," Six Sigma.

As the head of GE's global CT Division, Paul spearheaded a revolutionary application of Six Sigma design called "four-slice CT" that led to GE's ability to leapfrog the competition and stay at least one year ahead of its closest rival.

Paul also drove up profit margins and sparked the productivity of the entire CT product line in markets as far away as France, Japan, and China. Finally, Paul also was president and CEO of GE's medical equipment joint venture in India, which has been heralded as one of the best-run joint ventures in GE's vast portfolio.

Given those achievements, it is not hard to imagine why Immelt did everything he could to keep Vivek Paul within the GE fold. It proved an impossible task. Azim Premji, chairman of the Indian conglomerate called Wipro, offered Paul command of the company's $150 million software division, Wipro Technologies. "You can build another skyscraper in New York," Premji told Paul, "or you can build a completely new thing in India." For an ambitious executive like Paul, the challenge was irresistible.

Face Reality and Instill Confidence

Paul spent his first three months at the company meeting with customers and employees. At the conclusion of his first one hundred days on the job, he sent his employees a candid communiqué. He told them that despite the current IT boom, Wipro could not compete in the long term if it remained on its current path. The company had to change if it was to compete.

Even as the global recession at the turn of the century came on, hitting high-tech companies with special force, Paul increased spending selectively, trying to build new capacities in the company.

Spending while others were pulling back was a counterintuitive move that drew a lot of attention, but that was only a small piece of a much larger strategy. As he reinvented the business, Paul took a number of bold strategic steps that sealed Wipro's success and positioned it for strong growth for the future.

Think Long-Term

Paul's strategy was not a wave of the magic wand, with immediate and positive results. In fact, implementing that strategy took a heavy toll in the near term. Following a great year in 2000, growth slowed to the middle to upper 20 percent area in 2001 and 2002. Operating margins also fell by about a third. According to all these metrics, Wipro compared unfavorably with its competitors.

But ambitious strategies often take time to bear fruit. By 2004, Wipro was a $1.3 billion company and India's largest IT services corporation. Revenues once again grew by a stunning 60 percent over the previous year, and the stock price doubled in less than a year. Wipro also became the world's largest provider of outsourced technology R&D, which aided its efforts in attracting customers in new sectors, such as the electronics and car industries.

As a manager of managers, your job is very clear: It is to help others achieve and perform. That's how organizations, of any size and in any industry, produce winning results.

THE LEADERSHIP CHALLENGE
by James M. Kouzes and Barry Z. Posner

More than twenty-five years ago, James M. Kouzes and Barry Z. Posner conducted a research project to determine what people were doing when they were at their "personal best" while leading others. Hundreds, and then thousands of surveys and interviews were conducted. That research project resulted in the publication of the first edition of The Leadership Challenge in 1987. Today, it has sold more than 1.5 million copies and been translated into a dozen languages.

The Leadership Challenge introduces readers to the "Leadership Practices Inventory," which shows leaders how to use 360-degree leadership feedback to determine which leadership behaviors will serve them best. The input of tens of thousands of leaders from across the industry spectrum charges this leadership tool with the experiences that can help others make smart choices and avoid mistakes.

Offering a detailed map that describes how people at every level of an organization can make vital contributions as leaders, The Leadership Challenge shows readers how to use wisdom, courage, and compassion to make a positive difference. By marrying wisdom to the vision needed to lead others, and bringing courage into the challenge of choosing what is right, the authors connect with their readers at a very human level.

The summary offered here represents the latest evolution of the authors' work. By continuing to survey and interview thousands of leaders across almost every industry, Kouzes and Posner have updated their leadership handbook with a fourth edition for the latest crop of young employees and managers who strive to become effective leaders, as well as those already in leadership positions who want to improve how they lead their organizations. Their research offers lessons that managers can use to seize the opportunities of leadership that are available to them in whatever field they work or play.

The fourth edition of The Leadership Challenge continues to evoke praise from top leaders and experts who use its guidance every day. In it, the authors point out that the original practices and commitments that they advocated in the first edition of their book remain the same today. One thing that has changed in the latest version of *The Leadership Challenge* is its worldview. In recognition of the globalization that has taken place since its initial publication, more case studies about leaders working beyond the borders of the United States are used to illustrate the Five Practices of Exemplary Leadership. These practices are simple yet amazingly effective: Model the behavior you expect from other people, inspire others to share your vision and dreams, challenge the process by experimenting and taking risks, help others act by fostering collaboration and building trust, and encourage the hearts of your people to carry on.

While illuminating these five aspects of leadership with numerous examples and practices, *The Leadership Challenge* makes one point very clear: Anybody can practice leadership anywhere. By focusing on the unsung heroes of leadership rather than those with higher profiles, Kouzes and Posner reveal that leadership skills and abilities are available to all people.

Over the past twenty years, Kouzes and Posner have written many other books together, including *A Leader's Legacy, Credibility, Encouraging the Heart,* and *The Leadership Challenge Workbook.* Their leadership manuals and workbooks are legendary in the field of leadership education. By focusing on leaders at all levels, rather than the celebrity leaders whose stories fill thousands of other business books, *The Leadership Challenge* offers an easily accessible formula for leadership that can be applied to any type of work that demands disciplined practice.

Although they cite numerous examples of how smart leadership made a difference on the front lines of the marketplace, Kouzes and Posner are not afraid to step back from these practical applications and specific actions to discuss more elusive concepts, such as courage and spirit. Their evidence-based advice is built on following time-tested values, setting an example, articulating a vision, building teams, taking responsibility, developing self-confidence, and improving leadership abilities.

In his review of *The Leadership Challenge,* fellow management guru Marshall Goldsmith writes that he considers it to be "the best research-based book ever written in the field of leadership." He goes on to say he loves the book because it was written for regular readers who might not be CEOs of billion-dollar companies, even though it can help those men and women too.

At the heart of *The Leadership Challenge* is a very human message: Leadership is a relationship. By showing readers how to improve the quality of their relationships through mutual respect and confidence, Kouzes and Posner have created a guidebook to leadership that moves beyond leadership into the realm of helping people get along. The universal importance of this message will surely keep their book in print for many more years to come, extending the authors' impact on the world of management and leadership into future generations of leaders.

THE LEADERSHIP CHALLENGE, 4TH EDITION

by James M. Kouzes and Barry Z. Posner

CONTENTS

1. Getting Extraordinary Things Done in Organizations

2. What Leaders Do and What Constituents Expect

3. Ten Commitments of Leadership

4. Model the Way

5. Three Ways to Clarify Values

6. Inspire a Shared Vision

7. Challenge the Process

8. Enable Others to Act

9. Encourage the Heart

10. Leadership for Everyone

THE SUMMARY IN BRIEF

The fundamentals of leadership are not a fad. While the context of leadership has changed dramatically, the content of leadership has endured the test of time.

When leaders understand that leadership is a relationship and they begin to engage in the Five Practices of Exemplary Leadership®—Model the Way, Inspire a Shared Vision, Challenge the Process, Enable Others to Act, and Encourage the Heart—they are better able to embark on a lifetime of success and significance, according to authors James M. Kouzes and Barry Z. Posner.

This summary is about how leaders mobilize others to want to get extraordinary things done in organizations. It is about the practices leaders use to transform values into actions, visions into realities, obstacles into innovations, separateness into solidarity, and risks into rewards. It's about leadership that creates the climate in which people turn challenging opportunities into remarkable successes.

This *evidence-based* summary assists people—managers and individual contributors alike—in furthering their abilities to lead others to get extraordinary things done. It helps you develop your capacity to guide others to places they have never seen before.

What You'll Learn in This Summary

- How to utilize the five practices common to personal-best leadership experiences.
- How to improve your performance and the performance of your team with commitment and consistency.
- How to strengthen your abilities and uplift your spirits, as well as those of others.
- How the "magic" word we can help you enable people to act.
- How ordinary people exercise leadership at its best.

THE COMPLETE SUMMARY

GETTING EXTRAORDINARY THINGS DONE IN ORGANIZATIONS

When they are doing their best, leaders exhibit certain distinct practices, which vary little from industry to industry, profession to profession, community to community, and country to country. Good leadership is an understandable and universal process. Though each leader is a unique individual, there are shared patterns to the practice of leadership. And these practices can be learned.

The Future of Leadership

The domain of leaders is the future. The leader's unique legacy is the creation of valued institutions that survive over time. The most significant contribution leaders make is not simply to today's bottom line; it is to the long-term development of people and institutions so they can adapt, change, prosper, and grow.

Leadership is important, not just in your career and within your organization, but in every sector, in every community, and in every country. We need more exemplary leaders, and we need them more than ever. There is so much extraordinary work that needs to be done. We need leaders who can unite us and ignite us.

In the end leadership development is self-development. Meeting the leadership challenge is a personal—and a daily—challenge for all of us. If you have the will and the way to lead, you can.

WHAT LEADERS DO AND WHAT CONSTITUENTS EXPECT

Leadership can happen anywhere, at any time. It can happen in a huge business or a small one. It can happen in the public, private, or social sector. It can happen in any function. It can happen at home, at school, or in the community. The call to lead can come at 4:00 AM or it can come late at night. The energy and motivation to lead can come in ways you'd least expect.

Personal-Best Leadership

From an analysis of thousands of personal-best leadership experiences, leadership researchers Kouzes and Posner discovered that ordinary people who guide others along pioneering journeys follow rather similar paths. Though each experience was unique in expression, every case followed remarkably similar patterns of action. Kouzes and Posner have forged these common practices into a model of leadership that provides guidance for leaders as they attempt to keep their own bearings and steer others toward peak achievements.

Leadership is not about personality; it's about behavior. The Five Practices of Exemplary Leadership are available to anyone who accepts the leadership challenge. And they're also not the accident of a unique moment in history. The Five Practices have stood the test of time, and the most recent research confirms they're just as relevant today as they were more than twenty-five years ago.

The Five Practices of Exemplary Leadership

This research has uncovered five practices common to personal-best leadership experiences. When getting extraordinary things done in organizations, leaders engage in these Five Practices of Exemplary Leadership:

1. *Model the way.* Exemplary leaders know that if they want to gain commitment and achieve the highest standards, they must be models of the behavior they expect of others. To effectively model the behavior they expect of others, leaders must first be clear about guiding principles. They must *clarify* values.

Exemplary leaders go first. They go first by *setting the example* through daily actions that demonstrate they are deeply committed to their beliefs.

2. *Inspire a shared vision.* As Mark D'Arcangelo, system memory product manager at Hitachi Semiconductor, said about his personal-best leadership experience, "What made the difference was the vision of how things could be and clearly painting this picture for all to see and comprehend."

   Leaders gaze across the horizon of time, imagining the attractive opportunities that are in store when they and their constituents arrive at a distant destination. They *envision exciting and ennobling possibilities.*

   Leaders have to *enlist others in a common vision.* To enlist people in a vision, leaders must know their constituents and speak their language. Leadership is a dialogue, not a monologue.

3. *Challenge the process.* Jennifer Cun, in her role as a budget analyst with Intel, noted how critical it is for leaders "to always be looking for ways to improve their team, taking interests outside of their job or organization, finding ways to stay current of what the competition is doing, networking and taking initiative to try new things."

   Leaders are pioneers. They are willing to step out into the unknown. They *search for opportunities to innovate, grow, and improve.*

   Leaders know well that innovation and change involve *experimenting and taking risks.*

4. *Enable others to act.* Hewlett-Packard's Angie Yim was the technical team leader on a project involving core team members from the United States, Singapore, Australia, and Hong Kong. In the past, she said, she "had a bad habit of using the pronoun I instead of *we,*" but she learned that people responded more eagerly and her team became more cohesive when people felt part of the *we.* "This is a magic word," she realized. "I would recommend that others use it more often."

   Leaders *foster collaboration and build trust.* They engage all those who must make the project work—and in some way, all who must live with the results.

   Leaders make it possible for others to do good work. Exemplary leaders *strengthen everyone's capacity* to deliver on the promises they make.

5. *Encourage the heart.* Genuine acts of caring uplift the spirits and draw people forward. *Recognizing contributions* can be one-to-one or with many people. It's part of the leader's job to show appreciation for people's contributions and to create a culture of *celebrating values and victories.*

What People Look For and Admire in Leaders

Research documents consistent patterns across countries, cultures, ethnicities, organizational functions and hierarchies, gender, educational, and age groups. For people to follow someone willingly, the majority of constituents believe the leader must be:

- *Honest.* Honesty is the single most important factor in the leader-constituent relationship. If people anywhere are to willingly follow someone, they first want to assure themselves that the person is worthy of their trust. They want to know that the person is truthful, ethical, and principled.
- *Forward-looking.* People expect leaders to have a sense of direction and a concern for the future of the organization. Leaders must know where they're going if they expect others to willingly join them on the journey. They have to have a point of view about the future envisioned for their organizations and they need to be able to connect that point of view to the hopes and dreams of their constituents.
- *Inspiring.* People expect their leaders to be enthusiastic, energetic, and positive about the future. It's not enough for a leader to have a dream. A leader must be able to communicate the vision in ways that encourage people to sign on for the duration and excite them about the cause.
- *Competent.* To enlist in a common cause, people must believe that the leader is competent to guide them where they're headed. They must see the leader as having relevant experience and sound judgment. If they doubt the person's abilities, they're unlikely to join in the crusade.

Credibility Is the Foundation

Above all else, we as constituents must be able to believe in our leaders. We must believe that their word can be trusted, that they're personally passionate and enthusiastic about the work that they're doing, and that they have the knowledge and skill to lead.

If leaders practice what they preach, people are more willing to entrust them with their livelihood and even their lives. This realization leads to a straightforward prescription for leaders on how to establish credibility: *Do what you say you will do.*

To be credible in action, leaders must be clear about their beliefs; they must know what they stand for. They must put what they say into practice: They must act on their beliefs and "do."

This consistent living out of values is a behavioral way of demonstrating honesty and trustworthiness. People trust leaders when their deeds and words match.

TEN COMMITMENTS OF LEADERSHIP

Embedded in the Five Practices of Exemplary Leadership are behaviors that can serve as the basis for learning to lead. Here are the Ten Commitments of Leadership:

1. Clarify values by finding your voice and affirming shared ideals.
2. Set the example by aligning actions with shared values.
3. Envision the future by imagining exciting and ennobling possibilities.
4. Enlist others in a common vision by appealing to shared aspirations.
5. Search for opportunities by seizing the initiative and by looking outward for innovative ways to improve.
6. Experiment and take risks by constantly generating small wins and learning from experience.
7. Foster collaboration by building trust and facilitating relationships.
8. Strengthen others by increasing self-determination and developing competence.
9. Recognize contributions by showing appreciation for individual excellence.
10. Celebrate the values and victories by creating a spirit of community.

MODEL THE WAY

CMP Media Electronics Group's Tim Avila said, "Having faith in my principles and beliefs gave me the courage to navigate difficult situations and make tough decisions."

To stand up for your beliefs, you have to know what you stand for. To walk the talk, you have to have a talk to walk. To do what you say, you have to know what you want to say. To earn and sustain personal credibility, you must first be able to clearly articulate deeply held beliefs.

Clarify Values

Clarifying values is where it all begins. To clarify values as a leader you must engage in these two essentials:

• *Find your voice.* You must know what you care about. To act with integrity, you must first know who you are. You must know what you stand for, what you believe in, and what you care most about. Clarity of values will give you the confidence to make the tough decisions, to act with determination, and to take charge of your life. Once you have the words you want to say, you must also give voice to those words.

• *Affirm shared values.* Shared values are the foundations for building productive and genuine working relationships. Although credible leaders honor the diversity of their many constituencies, they also stress their common values. Important as it is that leaders forthrightly articulate the principles for which they stand, what leaders say must be consistent with the aspirations of their constituents.

High-performance values stress the commitment to excellence, *caring* values communicate how others are to be treated, and *uniqueness* values tell people inside and outside how the organization is different from all the others. These three common threads seem to be critical to weaving a values tapestry that leads to greatness.

Set the Example

Leaders take every opportunity to show others by their own example that they're deeply committed to the values and aspirations they espouse. No one will believe you're serious until they see you doing what you're asking of others. Leading by example is how leaders make visions and values tangible. It's how they provide the evidence that they're personally committed.

To set the example you need to:

• *Personify the shared values.* Leaders are their organizations' ambassadors of shared values. Their mission is to represent the values and standards to the rest of the world, and it is their solemn duty to serve the values to the best of their abilities. Spend your *time and attention* wisely, watch your *language,* ask purposeful *questions,* and seek *feedback.*
• *Teach others to model the values. Teach others* what's expected so they can hold themselves accountable for living the values of the organization, *confront critical incidents, tell stories* about what team members do to live the values, and *reinforce the behavior you want repeated.*

In practicing these essentials leaders become role models for what the whole team stands for, and they also create a culture in which everyone commits to aligning themselves with shared values.

THREE WAYS TO CLARIFY VALUES

Here are three actions that you can use to clarify values for yourself and others:

- *Write a tribute to yourself.* Begin the process of clarifying your values by reflecting on your ideal image of yourself—how you would most like to be seen by others.
- *Write your credo.* Get a single sheet of paper and write a "Credo Memo."
- *Engage in a credo dialogue.* Gather together the people you lead for a dialogue about shared values. Tell them what you've learned about personal values and about shared values. Tell them that you've written a Credo Memo that you'd like to share with them, but before doing it you'd like them to do the same thing. Ask each person to share with a few colleagues in small groups what he or she wrote. Model the process by reading your memo to them and telling them why you prize the values you chose.

INSPIRE A SHARED VISION

Organized efforts—whether those of a company, a project, or a movement—begin in the mind's eye. Call it what you will—*vision, purpose, mission, legacy, dream, aspiration, calling,* or *personal agenda*—the point is the same. If we are going to be catalytic leaders in life, we have to be able to imagine a positive future. When we envision the future we want for ourselves and others, and when we feel passionate about the legacy we want to leave, then we are much more likely to take that first step forward. If we don't have the slightest clue about our hopes, dreams, and aspirations, then the chance that we'll lead is nil.

Ideal and Unique Image of the Future for the Common Good

Exemplary leaders are forward-looking. They are able to *envision the future,* to gaze across the horizon of time and imagine the greater opportunities to come. They are able to develop an *ideal and unique image of the future for the common good.*

Leaders develop the capacity to envision the future for themselves and others by mastering two essentials:

- *Imagine the possibilities.* There are ways we can improve our capacity to imagine exciting possibilities and to discover the central theme for our lives. Improvement comes when you engage in conscious introspection. You need to do more to *reflect* on your past, *attend* to the present, *prospect* the future, and *feel* your passion.

• *Find a common purpose.* What people really want to hear is not simply the
leader's vision. They want to hear about *their own* aspirations. They want to
hear how their dreams will come true and their hopes will be fulfilled.
They want to see themselves in the picture of the future that the leader is
painting.

Listen deeply to others. Determine what's meaningful to others. Make it a
cause for commitment. People commit to causes, not to plans.

Enlist Others

Keith Sonberg, director of site operations for Roche in Palo Alto, California,
said, "What really drives performance is not metrics. It's passion plus pride
equals performance. I call it the three P's. The leader's job is to create an environment where people are passionate about what they're doing and take pride
in what they're doing. The end result will always be performance." For Keith
and his team, the three P's are all about sustainability, a vision of a company
that delivers a triple bottom line. "We want to be environmentally sound, eco-
nomically viable, and socially just," Keith explained.

Beyond the vision and mission statements, Keith and his team developed
a program with seven categories of projects—including energy conservation,
natural resources conservation, recycling, green engineering and construction, and employee and community growth and development. They wanted to
become a model for what an organization could do to create sustainability.

Mobilizing a Crowd

Whether they're trying to mobilize a crowd in a grandstand or one person
in the office, to enlist others leaders must improve their capacities to act on
these two essentials:

• *Appeal to common ideals.* Ideals reveal our higher-order value preferences.
Connect to what's meaningful to others, take pride in being unique, and
align your dream with the dreams of others.
• *Animate the vision.* Leaders have to arouse others to join in a cause and to
want to move decisively and boldly forward. Use symbolic language,
make images of the future, practice positive communication, express
your emotions, and speak from the heart.

Successfully engaging in these two essentials can produce very powerful
results. When leaders effectively communicate a vision, constituents report sig-

nificantly higher levels of job satisfaction, motivation, commitment, loyalty, team spirit, productivity, and profitability.

CHALLENGE THE PROCESS

Leaders venture out. When it comes to innovation, the leader's major contributions are in the creation of a climate for experimentation, the recognition of good ideas, the support of those ideas, and the willingness to challenge the system to get new products, processes, services, and systems adopted.

Search for Opportunities

The work of leaders is change. And all change requires that leaders actively seek ways to make things better, to grow, innovate, and improve. To search for opportunities to get extraordinary things done, leaders make use of two essentials:

- *Seize the initiative.*
- *Exercise outsight.*

Sometimes leaders have to shake things up. Other times they just have to grab hold of the adversity that surrounds them. Whether change comes from outside challenges or inside challenges, leaders make things happen. And to make new things happen they rely on outsight to actively seek innovative ideas from outside the boundaries of familiar experience.

Seize the Initiative

When people think about their personal bests they automatically think about some kind of challenge. Why? The fact is that when times are stable and secure, people are not severely tested. They may perform well, get promoted, even achieve fame and fortune. But certainty and routine breed complacency. In contrast, personal and business hardships have a way of making people come face-to-face with who they really are and what they're capable of becoming.

Leaders must be innovators to navigate their organizations into and through the global economy.

Exercise Outsight

If leaders are going to detect demands for change, they must stay sensitive to external realities, especially in this networked, global world. They must go out and talk to their constituents, be they citizens, customers, employees, stockholders, students, suppliers, vendors, business partners, managers, or just interested parties. They must listen—in person, on the phone, via e-mail, via Web sites—and stay in touch.

As CEO of Bay Area Credit Services, Michael Priest learned firsthand that leaders must look forward to fresh ideas. "Sometimes you just can't predict where the change will come from," he says, "but you have to have your eyes wide open if you have any hope of even catching a glimpse of it."

Leaders can expect demand for change to come from both inside and outside the organization. Unless external communication is actively encouraged, people interact with outsiders less and less frequently and new ideas are cut off.

Experiment and Take Risks

To create a climate in which the norm is to experiment and take risks, it's essential for leaders to:

- *Generate small wins.* Leaders should dream big, but start small. Dream big about crossing that enormous cosmos to find some new world, but start small with a few short journeys to test your theories and your abilities.
- *Learn from experience.* Studies of the innovation process make the point: "Success does not breed success. It breeds failure. It is failure which breeds success."

These essentials can help leaders transform challenge into an exploration, uncertainty into a sense of adventure, fear into resolve, and risk into reward. They are the keys to making progress that becomes unstoppable.

ENABLE OTHERS TO ACT

The first order of business for Jill Cleveland when she became finance manager at Apple Inc. was "to learn how to trust my employees. After being responsible only for myself for so long, it was very difficult to have to relinquish control. But I understood that in order for my employees, and thus myself, to be successful I needed to learn to develop a cohesive and collaborative team, beginning with trust as the framework." This is a key realization for all leaders.

Foster Collaboration

World-class performance isn't possible unless there's a strong sense of shared creation and shared responsibility. To foster collaboration, leaders have to be skilled in two essentials. They must:

- *Create a climate of trust.* To build and sustain social connections, you have to be able to trust others and others have to trust you. Psychologists have found that people who are trusting are more likely to be happy and psychologically adjusted than are those who view the world with suspicion and disrespect. Be the first to trust. Be open to influence. Share information and resources.
- *Facilitate relationships.* To create conditions in which people know they can count on each other a leader needs to develop cooperative goals and roles, support norms of reciprocity, structure projects to promote joint efforts, and support face-to-face interactions.

A Climate of Trust

Collaboration can be sustained only when you create a climate of trust and facilitate effective long-term relationships among your constituents. To get extraordinary things done, you have to promote a sense of mutual dependence—feeling part of a group in which everyone knows they need the others to be successful.

Here are three action steps that you can take to fulfill the leader's commitment to fostering collaboration:

- *Show trust to build trust.* Building trust is a process that begins when one party is willing to risk being the first to ante up, being the first to show vulnerability, and being the first to let go of control. Since you're the leader, the first to trust has to be you.
- *Say we, ask questions, listen, and take advice.* When talking about what is planned or what has been accomplished, it's essential that you talk in terms of *our* vision, *our* values, *our* goals, *our* actions, and *our* achievements.
- *Get people interacting.* Create opportunities for people to interact with one another and in the process form more trusting, more collaborative relationships.

People can't all be in this together unless you get them interacting on both a personal and professional basis. People need these opportunities to socialize, exchange information, and solve problems informally.

Strengthen Others

Exemplary leaders enable others to take ownership of and responsibility for their group's success by enhancing their competence and their confidence in their abilities, by listening to their ideas and acting upon them, by involving them in important decisions, and by acknowledging and giving credit for their contributions.

Creating a climate in which people are fully engaged and feel in control of their own lives is at the heart of strengthening others. People must have the latitude to make decisions based on what they believe should be done.

Here are two leadership essentials that strengthen others:

- *Enhance self-determination.* Leaders accept and act on the paradox of power: *You become more powerful when you give your own power away.* Self-determination can be enhanced in a number of ways. The most significant actions a leader can take to ensure that people can decide for themselves are to provide more choices, to design jobs that offer latitude, and to foster personal accountability.
- *Develop competence and confidence.* Developing competence and building confidence are essential to delivering on the organization's promises and maintaining the credibility of leaders and team members alike. To get extraordinary things done leaders must invest in strengthening the capacity and the resolve of everyone in the organization.

By using these essentials, leaders significantly increase people's belief in their own ability to make a difference. Leaders move from being in control to giving over control to others, becoming their coaches and teachers. Leaders help others learn new skills and develop existing talents, and they provide the institutional supports required for ongoing growth and change.

Turning Constituents into Leaders

Strengthening others is essentially the process of turning constituents into leaders—making people capable of acting on their own initiative. A virtuous cycle is created as power and responsibility are extended to others and as people respond successfully.

Here are three action steps you can start taking to strengthen others:

- *Increase individual accountability.* Enhancing self-determination means giving people control over their own lives. Therefore you, the leader, have to give them something of substance to control and for which they are accountable.
- *Offer visible support.* Make others more visible. By fostering outside contacts, and by developing and promoting people with promise, you help build a

greater sense of personal power, increase confidence, and open doors for people so they can exercise more of their own influence.
- *Conduct monthly coaching conversations.* Schedule a once-a-month one-on-one dialogue with each of your direct reports.

ENCOURAGE THE HEART

In high-performing organizations—and when people reported being at their personal best—people work quite intensely and often put in very long hours, but this doesn't mean they don't or can't enjoy themselves. To persist for months at a demanding pace, people need encouragement. They need emotional fuel to replenish their spirits. They need the will to continue and the courage to do something they have never done before and to continue with the journey. One important way that leaders accomplish this is by recognizing individual contributions.

Recognize Contributions

Recognition is about acknowledging good results and reinforcing positive performance. It's about shaping an environment in which everyone's contributions are noticed and appreciated.

Exemplary leaders understand this need to recognize contributions and are constantly engaged in these essentials:

- *Expect the best.* Successful leaders have high expectations of themselves and of their constituents.
- *Personalize recognition.* To make recognition personally meaningful, you first have to get to know your constituents.

By putting these essentials into practice to recognize constituents' contributions, leaders stimulate and motivate the internal drive within each individual— and fulfill their commitment to encouraging the heart.

Celebrate the Values and Victories

Performance improves when leaders bring people together to rejoice in their achievements and to reinforce their shared principles. If leaders are to effectively celebrate the values and victories, they must master these essentials:

- *Create a spirit of community.* Celebrations are among the most significant ways we have to proclaim our respect and gratitude, to renew our sense of community, and to remind ourselves of the values and history that bind us together. Celebrations serve as important a purpose in the long-term health of our organizations as does the daily performance of tasks.

- *Be personally involved.* One of the most significant ways in which leaders show others that they care and that they appreciate the efforts of their constituents is to be out there with them. This visibility makes them more real, more genuine, more approachable, and more human.

Perpetuate the Stories

Leaders are on the lookout for "catching people doing things right," and this can't be easily done sitting behind a desk. They want to see and know firsthand what's being done right not only so that they can let that person know to "keep up the good work" but so that they can tell others about this and other examples of what it means to put into practice and live out shared values and aspirations.

LEADERSHIP FOR EVERYONE

Leadership is not about position or title. Leadership is about relationships, about credibility, and about what you *do.*

You Are the Most Important Leader in Your Organization

If you're a manager in an organization, to *your* direct reports *you* are the *most important* leader in your organization. You are more likely than any other to influence their desire to stay or leave, the trajectory of their careers, their ethical behavior, their ability to perform at their best, their drive to wow customers, their satisfaction with their jobs, and their motivation to share the organization's vision and values.

The leaders who have the most influence on people are those who are the *closest* to them. You have to challenge the myth that leadership is about position and power.

The Secret to Success in Life

Constituents look for leaders who demonstrate an enthusiastic and genuine belief in the capacity of others, who strengthen people's will, who supply the means to achieve, and who express optimism for the future. Constituents want leaders who remain passionate despite obstacles and setbacks. In uncertain times, leaders with a positive, confident, can-do approach to life and business are desperately needed.

Leaders must keep hope alive, even in the most difficult of times. Without hope there can be no courage—and this is not the time or place for the timid. This is the time and place for optimism, imagination, and enthusiasm. Hope is essential to achieving the highest levels of performance. Hope enables people to find the will and the way to unleash greatness.

U.S. Army Major General John H. Stanford

U.S. Army Major General John H. Stanford grew up poor, failed sixth grade, but went on to graduate from Penn State University on an ROTC scholarship. He survived multiple military tours in both Korea and Vietnam, was highly decorated, and the loyalty of his troops was extraordinary. John headed up the Military Traffic Management Command for the U.S. Army during the Persian Gulf War. When he retired from the Army he became county manager of Fulton County, Georgia, when Atlanta was gearing up to host the 1996 Summer Olympics, and then he became superintendent of the Seattle Public Schools, where he sparked a revolution in public education.

When asked how he'd go about developing leaders, whether in colleges and universities, in the military, in government, in the nonprofit sector, or in private business, he replied:

> When anyone asks me that question, I tell them I have the secret to success in life. The secret to success is to stay in love. Staying in love gives you the fire to ignite other people, to see inside other people, to have greater desire to get things done than other people. A person who is not in love doesn't really feel the kind of excitement that helps them to get ahead and to lead others and to achieve. I don't know any other fire, any other thing in life that is more exhilarating and is more positive a feeling than love is.

Many leaders use the word *love* freely when talking about their own motivations to lead.

Of all the things that sustain a leader over time, love is the most lasting. It's hard to imagine leaders getting up day after day, putting in the long hours and hard work it takes to get extraordinary things done, without having their hearts in it. The best-kept secret of successful leaders is love: staying in love with leading, with the people who do the work, with what their organizations produce, and with those who honor the organization by using its products and services.

Leadership is not an affair of the head. Leadership is an affair of the heart.

GODS OF MANAGEMENT

by Charles Handy

When management theorist, marketing executive, economist, and management educator Charles B. Handy writes or broadcasts his ideas about business, he enters the topic from the perspective of a social philosopher. His brilliance and eclectic history as a management thinker make him more than a famed professor at the London Business School. As the creator of many groundbreaking business books, articles, and radio programs, he has become a global management celebrity.

Born in Kildare, Ireland, in 1932, Handy was educated in England and the United States, studying the classics, history, and philosophy in Oriel College at the University of Oxford. His attention soon shifted to combining these elements when he went to work in marketing at Shell International in London and Southeast Asia. Next, he entered the Sloan School of Management at the Massachusetts Institute of Technology where he met investment guru Warren Bennis, organizational psychology maverick Edgar H. Schein, organizational theorist Mason Haire, and other luminaries who defined how organizations work.

In 1967, Handy returned to England where he managed the Sloan Program at Britain's first Graduate Business School in London. Five years later, he was a full professor at the school, specializing in managerial psychology. His work there led him to a five-year job at a conference and study center in Windsor Castle where he studied ethics and values in society. His achievements include three years as the chairman of the Royal Society of Arts in London and honorary doctorates from seven British universities. In July 2006, he received an honorary Doctor of Laws from Trinity College in Dublin. British radio listeners know him for his profound "Thoughts for Today" on *BBC Radio Today*.

Handy has written some of the most influential articles and books about management, including *Understanding Organizations, The Future of Work, Gods of Management, Twenty-One Ideas for Managers, The Age of Unreason, The Age of Paradox, The Elephant and the Flea,* and *The New Philanthropists.* Ciaran Parker, the author of *The Thinkers 50,* calls Handy the most influential living management thinker. He is also credited as one of the first to predict the massive downsizing of organizations and the emergence of self-employed professionals.

Gods of Management stands out among Handy's business classics as a valuable description of how the work of organizations can be improved to face the changes and challenges of the future by looking into lessons from the past. A lover of classical history, Handy presents four archetypal gods from Greek mythology to describe the distinct differences among four approaches to management and the cultures for which they are best suited. To show leaders how to tap into the universal power of these gods, he creates a framework from which executives and organizations can develop the most effective form of leadership for their companies. Following these gods through their personal habits and styles, Handy shows leaders how they can improve efficiency and productivity by examining and changing the ways they motivate their people.

By urging managers and executives to reflect on their own "gods" and the cultural choices they make, he shows them how to create more satisfaction in their workplaces. Gifted with the ability to connect ancient history with the knowledge necessary to improve the future, Handy shows leaders the path toward positive change and away from the inevitable decay of those unable to "contemplate a future different from all that they have been used to." By describing the possibilities open to managers, he provides a map to a well-equipped laboratory in which leaders can experiment with the future. As an advocate of more experimentation with the assumptions and fashions of the day, Handy explains that even if some of these experiments fail, society and its organizations need to dabble in them to survive and thrive.

GODS OF MANAGEMENT

Managing the Battle of Organizational Cultures

by Charles Handy

CONTENTS

4. Dionysus, God of Individualism

5. Balancing the Gods: How the Four Gods Mix in Organizations

6. Managing the Mix: How to Make the Gods Work Together

7. The Price of Imbalance: Slack

8. The Apollonian Crisis: To Be, or Not to Be, Apollonian

9. Resolving the Crisis: The Professional/Contractual Organization

THE SUMMARY IN BRIEF

If the authorities are correct, one young man in an overseas subsidiary office was able to bring down one of the oldest, most venerable investment banks in the world. Nicholas Leeson, a futures trader in Barings Bank's Singapore office, ran up $1.3 billion in losses on Asian markets, forcing the 233-year-old bank into bankruptcy. How could it happen?

Ask Zeus.

Zeus is one of Charles Handy's four gods of management. Drawn from ancient Greek mythology, the four gods symbolize and describe the four basic types of organizational cultures:

Zeus, the patriarch of all gods, represents the culture of charismatic leadership and professionals free to follow their instincts.

Apollo, the god of rules and order, represents the culture of traditional bureaucracy and management control.

Athena, the patroness of Odysseus, problem solver of craftsmen and pioneering sea captains, represents the culture of project-based teamwork.

Dionysus, the god of wine and song, represents the culture of individualism and independence.

In this summary, you will learn the detailed characteristics of the four gods of management, which gods are appropriate in which work situations, and how the different gods work together. You will learn the management implications of each god. And, most important, you will learn how to choose the balance or mix of gods for your organization.

Maintaining the right balance of the different gods and cultures is the key to organizational management—as Barings found out too late.

In its Singapore office, the Zeus culture of trust and instinct ruled uncontested. Apollonian management controls were totally absent.

The result was disastrous—a spectacular example of why no manager can afford to ignore the gods of management.

THE COMPLETE SUMMARY

ZEUS, GOD OF LEADERSHIP BY TRUST

Zeus was the king of the Greek gods. He ruled from Mount Olympus using thunderbolts (for those who crossed him) and showers of gold (for those he was trying to seduce).

He was feared, respected, and occasionally loved. He was the patriarchal ruler, impulsive, powerful, charismatic, and benevolent, all at the same time.

Zeus Leaders

In business, Zeus leaders look for power over people and events.

It's not a question of ego. It's the desire to be responsible for making things happen. Zeus leaders are excited by the challenge of uncertainty. And they want the freedom to act on their instincts.

Zeus individuals will seek money, information, and an extensive network of contacts and friends—not so much as rewards in themselves, but as the means to power.

Zeus figures are often, for example, the entrepreneurs who lead startup companies with their charismatic personalities, yet at the same time give trusted associates the freedom to take initiatives.

It is this combination of charismatic leadership with widespread independence that makes a Zeus organization feel more like a club than a corporation.

The Organizational Culture

In club cultures, individuals are independent but responsible. They're trusted to make the right decisions, understanding that they will bear the consequences of major mistakes.

For example, in brokerage firms, brokers have enormous decision-making power on how to spend investors' money. It is assumed they know what they are doing, so they are not directed from above. But if there is a problem, it is the brokers who will take the fall.

The club culture thus runs on trust and not controls. This means decisions are made faster, since employees don't have to get approval and input from hierarchical superiors. It also means that it is cheaper to run, since trust is less expensive than control procedures.

But trust is subjective, not objective. It is based on gut feelings and not cold, rational analysis.

For that reason, the club culture can favor old-boy networks. Managers will be more likely to trust long-time friends and exclude new employees or contacts, no matter how qualified—as author Charles Handy discovered (see story in box).

TRUSTED FRIEND OVERRULES FANCY REPORT

Charles Handy was once asked by the chairman of his company to investigate the economics of a possible investment in Africa.

For one week, Handy carefully researched and analyzed all variables related to the investment. He then spent two nights producing a detailed report with charts, estimates, and calculations.

Handy's conclusion: The investment would lead to a very respectable 15.7 percent rate of return after tax. It would be, without a doubt, a good investment.

The chairman was impressed with the report, but told Handy he wanted to check with his friend John, a merchant banker.

After a brief conversation with his friend, the chairman put the phone down and turned to Handy.

"No, it's not on," he said. "John says 'wrong place, wrong time, wrong company.' Thanks all the same, old boy."

At the time, Handy was offended by the victory of old-boy network over rational analysis. But the decision was reasonable: The chairman rightly trusted overseas investment experience over untested technical reasoning.

APOLLO, THE GOD OF TRADITIONAL BUREAUCRACIES

Apollo was the god of order and rules.

Today's traditional organization, with its detailed organizational chart and lengthy employee manuals, reflects Apollo more than any other god of management.

The Organizational Culture

Apollonian management brings order and control to organizations by breaking down the work into separate, specific job descriptions.

Job descriptions control what people do. Employees must fulfill the tasks in the job description—nothing more, nothing less.

Supervisors are in place to make sure people don't stray from their job descriptions.

Making decisions is in the job description of top management only. Top managers are the thinkers in the organization, as opposed to the doers at the lower levels.

Thus, everyone from the lowest-level operational employee to the highest-level manager has a role to fulfill. While Zeus inspires a club culture based on trust and freedom, Apollo inspires a role culture based on assigned tasks and supervision.

The Inhuman Organization

Because rules, not personalities, decide actions, people are interchangeable. The person in job position X will do task X, no matter who that person is.

People are simply cogs in a machine. Machines, however, have a fatal flaw: They are not flexible. They can't respond to extraordinary or unexpected circumstances.

Machines work well in predictable situations. But what if there are drastic changes in the environment—changing consumer preferences or new, market-changing technologies, for example?

Apollo and Change

Apollo cultures hate change. They usually respond to it first by ignoring it, then simply by doing more of what they're already doing.

For example, if costs go up, Apollo cultures are going to raise their prices. They aren't going to explore alternatives to reduce costs.

If change is absolutely required, it is the systems and procedures that must be changed. Because it is the systems and procedures, not employees, that decide what happens.

Apollonian Leaders

Apollonians are logical, sequential, and analytical. They believe in a scientific world in which everything moves for a reason. If you have all the facts, and the required knowledge, skills, and experience to analyze those facts, you will make the right decisions.

Apollo cultures, unlike Zeus cultures, are not looking for seat-of-the-pants intuitive people to make decisions. They want people who have been taught the right skills and knowledge.

Training and experience eventually lead to positions of authority. In Apollonian organizations, only people officially given titles and positions—the role—of authority are allowed to lead.

THE GODS IN PICTURES: ZEUS AND APOLLO

Charles Handy selected a picture to represent each of the four gods of management.

The symbol for Zeus is a spider's web.

At the center is the spider, the leader, the person who inspires the whole organization.

Radiating in straight lines out from the center are the traditional functional departments.

But in Zeus organizations, the lines connecting the departments—the encircling lines—are as important as the connections between departments and the leader.

The reason: In Zeus organizations, decision making is not concentrated in the leader, but rather spread around to trusted colleagues. Thus department employees are taking initiatives and interacting directly with other departments along the circular strands of the web.

The image for the Apollo organization is a Greek temple.

Greek temples draw strength from their unbending pillars. The pillars represent the functions and divisions of the organization.

At the top, the pillars are linked by management. For example, the heads of each department join together to form a board or management committee.

Also linking the department pillars at the top are sets of organizational rules and procedures.

The Apollo organization is the picture of the traditional top-down bureaucracy—solid but inflexible.

In contrast, Zeus leaders in club cultures gain their authority through their charisma, based on proven track records and the force of their personalities.

The function of leadership is also different between Apollo and Zeus cultures. In Apollonian management, there is less decision making.

The Apollo organization is a machine, which, at its purest, is something you turn on and let run. The responsibility of Apollonian managers, therefore, is to make sure the machine is running.

Apollonian managers are administrators. Zeus managers are more leaders.

ATHENA, GODDESS OF PROBLEM-SOLVING TEAMS

Athena is the warrior goddess, the patroness of Odysseus, arch problem solver of craftsmen and pioneering sea captains.

For Athenians, management is continuously finding solutions to problems. Management first defines the problem. It then assigns the necessary personnel and equipment resources to problem-solving "commando" units in the organization.

The Organizational Culture

In Athenian cultures, the only thing that counts is how well people can find solutions. Talent, creativity, initiative, and intuition are all prized characteristics in Athenian organizations.

Since different problems call for different combinations of talents and intuition, the commando units are constantly changing. People come together in groups to solve a problem, then split apart and separately move on to whatever other groups require their talents.

Thus, Athenian organizations have task cultures. It is the task, the problem to solve, that drives the organization—not the job descriptions as in Apollonian organizations, nor the personalities as in Zeus organizations.

The Athenian culture works for an organization whose product is a solution to a problem. Consultancy companies, research and development departments, and advertising agencies are some examples.

Athenian Leadership

Athenian leaders are dealing with creative problem solvers who use talent and ingenuity to find solutions. These kinds of people are more impressed by expertise and experience than by titles and positions.

Instead of giving orders, Athenian leaders must be able to convince those they want to lead that they have the right solutions. They must be able to build a case for credibility.

Unlike in Zeus organizations, where leaders have to build up trust through direct experience and personal charisma, expertise credentials in Athenian companies will be taken at face value. New leaders can therefore enter the organization endowed with the credibility of an expert.

But they must back up that credibility with a track record in the company.

New leaders get the benefit of the doubt, but if they can't solve problems, the credibility "credit" will evaporate.

Getting the Job Done

Athenians, like Zeus figures, enjoy variety.

The difference is that Athenians are problem solvers, while Zeus managers are visionary leaders.

Athenians are more narrowly focused than Zeus managers. They like boundaries around their problems, not the wide-open challenges that Zeus leaders in Zeus organizations relish.

But although less adventurous than Zeus personalities, Athenians would find the treadmill of an Apollonian job dull and repetitive.

Getting the job done for Athenians means finding solutions. Then they want to move on to new problems.

Apollonians don't move on. For them, "getting the job done" is more "getting on with the job."

Thus, the Athenian attitude toward work falls between the visionary, long-term approach of Zeus leaders and the day-to-day grind of Apollonians. In the Apollo world, Athenians would become restless. But in the Zeus world, they would be too indecisive.

WHEN ATHENA RULED AEROSPACE

In the 1960s, Athena ruled at the aerospace companies of Southern California.

The U.S. Defense Department, then the world's largest consumer, kept them supplied with a long succession of high-technology problems to resolve.

As many as 30 percent of their managers had PhDs. The formal organization structure was the matrix type. They worked in groups that came together and disbanded with each project.

An engineer from a traditional British company was impressed. "In those companies," he told Handy, "not only did the sun shine all day outside, but the managers were young, intelligent, earning high salaries, and having fun, and the organization was making money.

"In my company," he added a bit sadly, "we believe that these things are incompatible."

When Apollo Replaces Athena

As Athenian companies become more successful, they become bigger—and bigger means less ad hoc activity and more standard procedures and routines. Eventually, the task culture is replaced by the Apollonian role cultures.

Many organizations start off Athenian and end up Apollonian.

THE GODS IN PICTURES: ATHENA

The image for Athena is a net.

Power in Athena companies lies at the interconnections of the net, not at the top, as in Apollo organizations, or center, as in Zeus organizations.

The Athena company is a network of loosely linked problem-solving groups, each largely self-contained but part of the overall strategy for the organization.

DIONYSUS, GOD OF INDIVIDUALISM

Dionysus, the god of wine and song, represents individualism. In the Dionysian organization, the organization is the servant of the individual. In the other three organizational cultures, it is the opposite: The individual is the servant of the organization.

An example of how an organization serves individuals is a doctor's office. Four doctors, each with their own specialty, agree to share an office, a telephone, and a secretary.

Each doctor conducts his business as he wishes, keeping his individualism. The organization is only there as support.

The Organizational Culture

The Dionysian culture is essentially an existential one. Existentialists believe that the world is not some part of a higher purpose. Humans exist and must take responsibility for their existence. They are in charge of their own destinies.

At the same time, what they wish for themselves has to apply to everyone.

This is not a moral imperative, but a logical one: If we want a safe and lawful society, we have to be lawful ourselves.

Each individual in a partnership is responsible for his or her individual business. But, if the partnership is to work, that is, if the organization really helps the individuals to achieve their purposes, conditions have to be the same for everyone.

One doctor cannot monopolize the secretary's time, for example. The other doctors will be shortchanged, and the partnership will fall apart.

The partners in a Dionysian culture thus help themselves, but they are not mutually dependent. A leaving partner can be replaced with a new one without any change in the organization.

Dionysians at Work

The management challenge of the existentialist, Dionysian organization is that there cannot be a boss. Since all partners are equal, no partner has decision-making authority over the other ones. Thus any decisions affecting the organization—such as whether to move to a new office—must be done by consent.

DIONYSIAN MASOCHISM

Dionysians think, whether or not it's true, that they have nothing to learn from anyone—except life.

For those at the top of their professions, this may be an accurate reflection of their achievements. For others, it's just plain arrogance.

Dionysians enjoy learning from their experiences. If the job they're in, or the project they're working on, is teaching them nothing new, they will often just get up and leave—to the consternation of employers and clients alike.

Here are two examples of how Dionysians flee the comfort of familiarity:

- Conductor André Previn was asked why he left Hollywood, where he had built up a reputation as a composer of musical scores. "Because," Previn said, "I began to wake up in the morning without any pain in my stomach. I was no longer unsure of my capabilities."
- A publisher noted that "academic authors are always bored by the books we want them to write, which build on their established reputation, whereas publishers are always worried by the books academics want to write, which are about fields and topics new to them."

Since individual partners in Dionysian organizations are alone in their part of the business, these individuals must have the individual talent to succeed by themselves. Thus, professionals such as doctors and lawyers are the prototypical Dionysian jobs.

The New Dionysians

Today, Dionysians also include professional contractors such as computer consultants, public relations advisers, systems analysts, and any other number of independent, talent-based professions.

The Dionysian tendency is even starting to break away from the professions and invade traditionally Apollonian occupations.

Dionysians on the factory shop floor, for example, are beginning to demand a greater freedom of decision-making and greater control over their work.

How Apollo is losing his hold in even the most traditional of occupations is the subject of pages ninety-three and ninety-four.

THE GODS IN PICTURES: DIONYSUS

The Dionysian organization is depicted by a cluster of stars gathered in a circle.

The stars represent individuals with separate goals and talents. The Dionysians gather in the circle only because they know that joining with a group helps them achieve their individual goals.

There are no direct connections between the individuals in the picture—unlike in the web of Zeus, the temple of Apollo, or the net of Athena.

Therefore, the stars can come and go without changing or destroying the organization.

BALANCING THE GODS: HOW THE FOUR GODS MIX IN ORGANIZATIONS

Different organizations emphasize different gods or cultures. Bureaucratic companies can be labeled Apollonian, for example.

But no organization is exclusively dedicated to one god. Instead, organizations balance the right mix of all four gods.

Maintaining that balance is what Handy calls the *theory of cultural propriety*. According to this theory, the task of management is getting the right culture in the right place for the right purpose.

Now we'll look at the forces that influence the balance of the gods.

Why All Gods Are Present

All four gods are present in all organizations because different activities within organizations call on the characteristics of different gods.

Steady-state activities, for example, are the predictable, routine Apollonian jobs that you program in advance. Processing invoices is a steady-state activity.

The goal of *development* activities is to create things, not run them. Product development, for example, creates new products, and the procedures to make them.

Development activities call for the creative Athenians.

Asterisk activities deal with exceptions, emergencies in which the rules can't be applied. A hostile takeover attempt is an asterisk job.

Asterisk activities demand the intuition and risk-taking skills of a Zeus or a Dionysus. (Both gods can lead in emergencies. The difference is that Zeus draws his authority from charisma while Dionysus draws his from competence.)

Management activities, coordinating the other three types of activities, call on the skills of all four gods.

Finding the Balance

Four different factors influence the mix of the four gods or cultures present in organizations:

■ **Size.** Size has a major influence. Athenian systems, for example, depend on small groups working together to solve problems. The larger the group, or number of groups, the less effective the system.

Once you have more than ten people in a group, for example, or ten groups in a division, or ten divisions in a company, you must rely on formal methods of control and coordination. It's time for Apollo.

■ **Life Cycle.** The length of a life cycle in an organization also influences which god dominates.

For example, in a factory making the same product year after year (a steady-state activity) Apollo rules.

In an industry in which the product's life cycle is short, such as computer chip manufacturing, developing new products is as important as manufacturing them.

Apollo keeps the steady-state factory going, but Athena's creative skills are needed to develop new products.

■ **Work Patterns.** Work comes in different patterns.

In the flow pattern, one section's work is input for the next section—for example, the assembly line. In a copy pattern, the work in different sections is identical. For example, the different stores in fast-food chains do the same work.

Flow and copy patterns call for Apollo because the work is routine and repetitive. In a unit pattern, the work is always changing. The job of an artist or a consultant, for example, depends on the current project. Unit patterns call for the variety-loving Zeus and Dionysus, or Athena if the work is done in groups.

■ **People.** People are different, and although there may be a bit of every god in all of us, usually one god dominates. Which god depends on all kinds of influences, such as culture, age, and education.

The Japanese culture, for example, emphasizes Apollonian conformism over Dionysian free flights. Young people don't like Apollo's routine. And higher education often grants people, such as doctors and architects, the skills to be independent Dionysians.

Like size, life cycle, and work pattern, the types of people working in an organization will help influence the balance of the gods.

Two Examples

In summary, four forces influence the proportion of activities, and thus cultures, in organizations.

For example, a canning factory, which features long life cycles, operates in a flow work pattern, and staffed by uneducated workers, is likely to feature a large number of steady-state activities. The Apollo role culture will dominate.

On the other hand, an advertising agency, which is smaller, has short life cycles, and requires talented groups of people working on development-type jobs, will likely be an Athenian task culture.

MANAGING THE MIX: HOW TO MAKE THE GODS WORK TOGETHER

The previous section showed the different forces that create the mix of gods and cultures in an organization.

Even given the right mix, the organization still needs to be held together. In this section, we will explore how to link the different, and often conflicting, cultures so that they are working together in harmony.

Cultural Tolerance

One of the prerequisites to a harmonious organization is cultural tolerance. The different cultures must not try to impose their preferences on others.

An Apollonian, for example, shouldn't try to set up rigid procedures for a small company made up of independent Dionysians. The Dionysians will consider the procedural rules as a bureaucratic waste of time that distracts them from their activities.

Bridges

Another key to helping the cultures work together is to build as many bridges—coordination mechanisms—between them as possible. Without bridges, cultures go their separate ways.

Many organizations are content with one bridge at the top; for example, an executive board coordinating the different functions and cultures. The drawback is that this solitary bridge can become crowded with problems, leading to delays and inefficiency.

Most organizations locate bridges at the points of major interaction between the cultures—for example, where research meets production, or where purchasing, production, and sales meet over production schedules.

Types of Bridges

There are different ways to coordinate activities between cultures.

A human bridge is one example. Managers who are skilled in interpersonal relationships and have the credibility to command attention, can act as a liaison between different functions and cultures.

The centralized information bank is another organizational bridge. All information needed for coordination is routed to a computer, where it can be accessed by the different cultures.

Computerized stock control systems is one example.

Another option is to group activities by project rather than by function, thus tearing down the walls that traditionally separate functions. A manufacturing company, for example, would create a product-development team that consists not only of product designers, but also of production and sales managers.

A Common Language

A common language is also important in linking different parts of the organization. Shared organizational buzzwords and jargon, and a shared understanding of what words mean (for example, how productivity is measured) ensure that different cultures can communicate.

CHANGING THE BALANCE: A CASE STUDY

Pharmaceutical distributor Bosco Chemicals U.K. Ltd. decided to expand into production.

It hired a top-notch team of nine highly qualified, highly paid production experts to build and run its first factory.

The team spent two years meeting around a table and planning, one by one, every facet of the factory: a prototypical Athenian effort.

In the first two years of operation, equipment, staffing, quality, and other problems appeared in an endless string of disasters. The team, still collaborating around the table, couldn't solve the problems and disbanded.

A production manager took over. Systems replaced projects. Participative problem solving was eliminated: The production managers solved problems and told the others what to do.

The results are good.

In this case, Athena was the right god for creating, but it is Apollo who was needed to run the factory.

THE PRICE OF IMBALANCE: SLACK

If the mix of the gods is wrong, or is not changed when it needs to be, the result is organizational *slack*.

For example, Apollonians believe in coordination and control systems. Athenians, working in small groups, don't need those systems.

Creating an expensive system of coordination and control for a small staff is a waste of time (for both employees and management) and money. This is an example of *systems* slack, which can be loosely defined as "oversystemizing."

Other types of slack include error slack (leaving room to make mistakes), staffing slack (overstaffing), and investment slack (overinvestment).

All slack is not bad. Athenians, for example, like investment slack. Their job is to solve problems and they want the resources possible to reach a solution, even if they don't end up using all of these resources.

Zeus club cultures, such as investment banks, give their employees error slack (room to make errors).

But the key, once again, is to find the right balance. Too much Zeus-like trust and not enough Apollonian controls is what bankrupted Barings—Leeson had been given too much error slack.

THE APOLLONIAN CRISIS: TO BE, OR NOT TO BE, APOLLONIAN

Organizations are traditionally Apollonian, featuring top-down management control. And in one sense, they are under pressure to be even more Apollonian.

The Drift to Apollo

Organizations are becoming bigger, because bigger means less dependency and more flexibility. In a big company, for example, a loss in one area can be offset by profits in another.

Given the rapid and constant change in the current business environment, flexibility is a must for survival.

Organizations are also becoming more internally consistent. Information technology, for example, requires that all departments use the same forms and language. Government regulations and union bargaining also result in consistency across the organization.

Size necessitates more control rules and procedures. Consistency implies standardized methods, fixed reporting periods, and so forth.

Thus, greater size and consistency are pushing organizations toward Apollonian bureaucracies.

Resistance to Apollo

But what about the people?

Today, employees demand more from their jobs than just a paycheck. They want to be recognized as thinking assets, not just machines.

Employers today know the value of fulfilling the desires of employees to increase motivation and productivity.

As a result, employee empowerment and participation is replacing command-and-control management. The independence of Dionysus and the problem-solving teamwork of Athena are replacing the management vs. employee hierarchies of Apollo.

In summary, organizations are being pulled in two opposite directions: to be at once more and less Apollonian.

Which way should managers go? The answer is in the professional/contractual organization described below.

RESOLVING THE CRISIS: THE PROFESSIONAL/ CONTRACTUAL ORGANIZATION

The Apollonian crisis can be resolved if organizations adapt their managerial philosophies to the needs, aspirations, and attitudes of individuals.

Instead of cogs in a machine, employees should be considered individual craftsmen contributing qualifications, experience, and intelligence to the organization.

These individuals have personalities, desires, and rights that the organization must respect—including the right to be consulted on major decisions and changes.

When Dionysian individualism meets Apollonian structures, the result is an organization of consent—individuals belong to the organization but input in decision making.

Management Implications

As respected, individual craftsmen, employees in the new organization don't like to be "managed"—that is controlled, manipulated, or directed.

Management impinges on the freedom that, as qualified and competent professionals, they have earned.

These professionals can think for themselves, so why should there be a higher level of "thinkers" managing them?

In the new organization, groups of employees take over many of the management functions—such as planning or quality control—previously reserved for higher rungs of the hierarchy—a Dionysian approach to Apollonian tasks.

The leadership function, however, remains in the hands of the top rank.

Dionysians and Athenians are professionals and craftsmen, not visionaries or motivators. Therefore, they need a charismatic, energizing figure to lead them. In sum, the new organization needs to be led, not managed.

The Contractual Organization

Having professionals on staff is not the only option.

Many professional jobs can be contracted out. Thus organizations can grow without adding staff. And contracting covers the freedom requirements of individuals.

Contracting, or outsourcing, also reconciles Dionysus and Apollo.

Dionysus Satisfied

In sum, the new organization is an organization of consent (for the professionals employed) and contract (for the professionals outsourced). The individualistic Dionysian urges are satisfied without sacrificing Apollonian growth or structure.

A KINDER, GENTLER APOLLO

Not every task in the new organization is professional. There are still mundane, repetitive tasks that need to be covered.

The new organization realizes, however, that even employees who do repetitive tasks are human. Although under more management control than their professional colleagues, they are still treated as individuals.

In the new organization, even the most Apollonian task has a Dionysian tinge.

The image for this new Apollo is not the Greek temple, but the village: a small and personal place where everyone has a name, character, and personality.

INFLUENCER

by Kerry Patterson, Joseph Grenny, David Maxfield, Ron McMillan, and Al Switzler

The authors of *Influencer* have become masters of their latest book's topic—the power of influence—by positively influencing a wide range of readers and leaders for many years. Thirty years ago, they founded Vital-Smarts to help individuals, teams, and organizations get better results from their work. So far, more than three hundred of the Fortune 500 companies have put VitalSmarts's training products and services into action. To share some of their organization's discoveries with readers from around the world, four of Vital-Smarts's top leaders put their brains, stories, and research together to write *Crucial Conversations: Tools for Talking When Stakes Are High*. Their first book, filled with highly useful tips and techniques for creating more effective communication patterns and dialogue habits between people, became a *New York Times* bestseller. Combining innovative methods for helping people work together and reap the benefits of constructive dialogue, the leaders from VitalSmarts created a valuable guidebook to the skills needed to master crucial conversations at work, at home, and at play.

To follow up their incredibly successful book, the four authors of *Crucial Conversations*, Kerry Patterson, Joseph Grenny, Ron McMillan, and Al Switzler, wrote their next *New York Times* bestseller, *Crucial Confrontations: Tools for Resolving Broken Promises, Violated Expectations, and Bad Behavior*. This book raised the rules of dialogue to the next level by showing readers how to apply the skills of crucial confrontations to the hard work of resolving conflicts while creating positive outcomes for teams, organizations, families, and individuals.

In their third book together, *Influencer,* the VitalSmarts leaders brought in master researcher David Maxfield to help them describe what they have learned while studying the ways people can resolve conflicts better and become more effective in their personal and professional lives. *Influencer* carries on the authors' tradition of framing a complex and baffling human concept, such as how we can better influence those around us, and creating a process by which we can improve our abilities by following the habits of those who have mastered the difficult skills required for success.

The team of authors who have helped to make VitalSmarts one of the fastest-growing companies in America include some of the world's top experts on training leaders to manage change. Kerry Patterson's education includes doctoral work in organizational behavior at Stanford University. He is also the author and leader of many award-winning training programs. In 2004, he received the coveted Brigham Young University Marriott School of Management Dyer Award for his outstanding contributions to organizational learning.

Similarly, Patterson's co-author Joseph Grenny has spent twenty years designing and implementing major corporate change initiatives. Grenny has also been pivotal in helping the world's poor achieve economic self-reliance through the nonprofit micro-financing organization Unitus, which he co-founded in 2000.

Like Grenny, co-author Ron McMillan is also an acclaimed speaker and consultant who works with leaders ranging from first-level managers to corporate executives. In addition, he is a co-founder of the renowned Covey Leadership Center, where he was vice president of research and development.

Co-author Al Switzler is another renowned speaker and consultant who has directed training and management initiatives with dozens of global companies. He also serves as a faculty member of the Executive Development Center at the University of Michigan.

Influencer is the first book by the VitalSmarts experts to include the research experience and work of co-author David Maxfield. As a leading researcher and expert on dialogue skills and performance improvement—among a range of other vital business topics—he is an expert on the personality theory and interpersonal-skills development that help make *Influencer* such a vital collection of research-based principles, skills, and techniques. His doctoral work in psychology at Stanford University shines through the human stories and research in *Influencer* that turn it into a valuable inroad to important management tools and techniques.

Together, these five VitalSmarts experts have written a modern management classic in solving problems, managing people, and creating the achievable and sustainable changes required by organizations and individuals to survive in today's marketplace.

INFLUENCER

The Power to Change Anything

by Kerry Patterson, Joseph Grenny, David Maxfield, Ron McMillan, and Al Switzler

CONTENTS

THE SUMMARY IN BRIEF

If you're like most people, you face several influence challenges that have you stumped. For instance, at work your best efforts to make quality part of the everyday culture have yielded no improvements. Or maybe at the personal level you're fighting a problem that has gone on for years.

Whether you're a CEO, a parent, or merely a person who wants to make a difference, you probably wish you had more influence with the people in your life. Most of us stop trying to make change happen because we believe it is too difficult, if not impossible. Instead we develop complicated coping strategies when we should be learning the tools and techniques of the world's most influential people. Almost all the profound, pervasive, and persistent problems we face in our lives, our companies, and our world can be solved.

Over the past half century, a handful of behavioral-science theorists and practitioners have discovered the power to change just about anything. From high-powered influencers from all walks of life, we can learn every step of the influence process—including robust strategies for making change inevitable. Through years of careful research and studied practice, the authors have developed powerful influence principles and strategies that can be replicated and that others can learn.

Not everyone will become influencers with a capital "I," but everyone can learn and apply the methods and strategies the world's best influencers use every day.

What You'll Learn in This Summary

- How to identify a handful of high-leverage behaviors that lead to rapid and profound change.
- How to apply strategies for changing both thoughts and actions.
- How to marshal six sources of influence—such as finding strength in numbers, changing the environment, and harnessing peer pressure—to make change inevitable.
- What steps you need to take in order to become an opinion leader.
- How to reward vital behaviors and not just good results.
- Why studying positive deviance can help you identify vital behaviors and how to do it.

THE COMPLETE SUMMARY

YOU'RE AN INFLUENCER

There are a handful of brilliant social scientists routinely studied by influence masters, but the one cited as the scholar of scholars is the legendary father of social learning theory, Dr. Albert Bandura. Dr. Bandura generated a remarkable body of knowledge that led to rapid changes in behaviors that other theorists had dawdled over for years.

He demonstrated, for example, how powerfully our behavior is shaped by observing others. This came at a time when most psychologists believed that behavior was solely influenced by the direct rewards and punishments people experienced. He also taught us where not to waste our time. For instance, if you want others to change, you don't have to put a person on a couch for ten years to learn about his or her critical childhood moments.

Study with the Best Scholars

There is a growing body of knowledge as well as an impressive supply of real-life success stories that teach exactly how to change almost any human behavior. The influencers noted below demonstrate that, if you know what you're doing, you can indeed change remarkably resistant behaviors.

Dr. Mimi Silbert in San Francisco, California, is the founder of the Delancey Street Foundation. It consists of several dozen businesses, all headed by Silbert, and is part corporate conglomerate, part residential therapy. What's unique about the institution is the employee population, which consists of thieves, prostitutes, robbers, and murderers. Dr. Silbert's typical new hires have had four felony convictions, they've been homeless for years, and most are lifetime drug addicts. Within hours of joining Delancey, they are working in either a restaurant, moving company, car repair shop, or one of the many Delancey companies. Other than Silbert herself, these felons and addicts make up the entire population at Delancey. No therapists. No professional staff. Her remarkable influence strategy has profoundly changed the lives of fourteen thousand employees over the past thirty years. Of those who join Delancey, over 90 percent never go back to drugs or crime.

Since 1986, Dr. Donald Hopkins and his team at The Carter Center in Atlanta, Georgia, have focused on the eradication of the Guinea worm disease. The Guinea worm is one of the largest human parasites, and it has caused incalculable pain and suffering in millions of people. Hopkins knew that if 120 million people in twenty-three thousand villages would change just a few vital behaviors for just one year, there would never be another case of the infection. But imagine the audacity of intending to influence such a scattered population in so many countries. And yet, this is exactly what Hopkins's team has done. They are overcoming enormous disadvantages and will have beaten the disease with nothing more than the ability to influence human thought and action.

What This Means to You

There's good news in all of this. Since our ineffectiveness at influencing others stems from a simple inability rather than a character flaw or lack of motivation, the solution lies in continued learning. We can become powerful influencers. It also means that the changes we need to make won't be too intrusive. Instead, we need to expand our self-image by seeing ourselves as influencers; it's the one job that cuts across every domain of our life.

All this is important to know because if you want to change how people behave, you have to first change how they think. There is no one strategy for resolving profound, persistent, and resistant problems. It takes an entire set of influence methods.

FIND VITAL BEHAVIORS

Before you can influence change, you have to decide what you're trying to change. Influence geniuses focus on behaviors. They're universally firm on this point. Enormous influence comes from focusing on just a few vital behaviors. Take care to ensure that you do not confuse outcomes with behaviors. In most failed influence strategies, you're likely to find at least one example of means/ends confusion, in which the focus is on achieving a specific end result instead of a focus on what actually needs to be done. Without a behavioral focus, often people will not choose to enact the right behaviors.

Study the Best

How do legitimate researchers actually discover the handful of behaviors that typically lead to success? The science of identifying which actions lead to key outcomes—no matter the domain—has already been carefully developed by those who study "best practices." Researchers compared the best to the rest and then discovered the unique and powerful behaviors that led to success. They watched top performers at work, compared them with others who were decent but not quite as good, and identified the sets of behaviors that set apart the best from the rest.

The real test of best-practice research comes when scholars take newly discovered vital behaviors and teach them to experimental groups. If they have indeed found the right behaviors, experimental subjects show far greater improvement in both the vital behaviors and the *desired outcome* than do control subjects. From this best-practice research we learn two important concepts:

- First, there is a process for discovering what successful people actually do. We know what to look for when examining others' claims that they've found vital behaviors. If the individuals who are offering up best practices haven't scientifically compared the best to the rest, found the differentiating behaviors, taught these behaviors to new subjects and then demonstrated changes in the outcomes they care about, they're not the people we want to learn from.
- Second, in many of the areas where you'd like to exert influence, the vital-behaviors research has already been done. If you search carefully, you'll find that good scholars have found the vital behaviors that solve most challenges affecting a large number of people.

Study Positive Deviance

"Positive deviance" can be extremely helpful in discovering the handful of vital behaviors that will help solve the problem you're attacking. Look for people, times, or places where you or others don't experience the same problems and try to determine the unique behaviors that make the difference.

- First, dive into the center of the actual community, family, or organization you want to change.
- Second, discover and study settings where the targeted problem should exist but doesn't.
- Third, identify the unique behaviors of the group that succeeds.

In the case of the Guinea worm disease, researchers focused on the third methodology of identifying unique behaviors and flew into sub-Saharan Africa. Once there, researchers decided to study villages that should have the disease but didn't. They were particularly interested in villages that were immediate neighbors to locations that were rife with the Guinea worm disease.

It didn't take long to discover the vital behaviors. Researchers knew that behaviors related to the fetching and handling of water would be crucial, so they zeroed in on those successful behaviors, which could then later be taught to the worm-struck villages.

Test Your Results

Finally, if you've conducted your own research and found what you think are high-leverage vital behaviors, test your ideas. Implement the proposed actions and see if they yield the results you want. Don't merely measure the presence or absence of the vital behaviors; also check to see whether the results you want are happening. To make it easy to both surface and test vital behaviors, conduct short-cycle-time experiments. Don't hypothesize forever or put massive studies into place. Instead, develop the habit of conducting rapid, low-risk miniexperiments.

CHANGE THE WAY YOU CHANGE MINDS

Once you've identified the behaviors you want to change, you're ready to convince others to change their minds. But as you might suspect, convincing others to see the world differently isn't easy.

People will attempt to change their behavior if they believe it will be worth it, and they believe they can do what is required. Instill these two views, and individuals will at least try to enact a new behavior or perhaps stop an old one.

To change one or both of these views, most people rely on verbal persuasion. Talk is easy, and it works a great deal of the time. However, with persistent and resistant problems, talk has very likely failed in the past, and it's time to help individuals experience for themselves the benefits of the proposed behavior.

Dr. Bandura and his team found that if you want people to change their persistent and resistant view of the world, come up with innovative ways to create personal experiences. Second, when you can't take everyone on a field trip, create vicarious experiences.

The good news is that vicarious modeling is one of the most accessible influence tools that can be employed. For most of us, that means we'll make use of a well-told story.

Create Profound Vicarious Experiences

Stories provide every person, no matter how limited his or her resources, with an influence tool that is both immediately accessible and enormously powerful. Poignant narratives help listeners transport themselves away from the content of what is being said and into the experience itself. Because stories create vivid images and provide concrete detail, they are:

- More understandable than terse lectures.
- More focused on the simple reality of an actual event.
- More often credible than simple statements of fact.

Finally, as listeners dive into the narrative and suspend disbelief, stories create an empathic reaction that feels just as real as enacting the behavior themselves.

Tell the Whole Story

Don't make the mistake of shortcutting the story—stripping it of its compelling narrative and leaving out much of the meaning and all of the emotion. And make sure that the narrative you're employing contains a clear link between the current behaviors and existing (or possibly future) negative results. Also make sure that the story includes positive replacement behaviors that yield new and better results. Remember, stories need to deal with both "Will it be worth it?" and "Can I do it?" When it comes to changing behavior, nothing else matters.

MAKE CHANGE INEVITABLE

We now know enough about the forces that affect human behavior to place them into a coherent and workable model that can be used to organize our thinking, select a full set of influence strategies, combine them into a powerful plan, and eventually make change inevitable.

Master the Six Sources of Influence

With this model, influence geniuses know exactly what forces to bring into play in order to overdetermine their chances of success.

Source 1: Personal Motivation—work on connecting vital behaviors to intrinsic motives.

Source 2: Personal Ability—coach the specifics of each behavior through deliberate practice.

Source 3: Social Motivation—draw on the enormous power of social influence to both motivate and enable the target behaviors.

Source 4: Social Ability—people in a community will have to assist each other if they hope to succeed.

Source 5: Structural Motivation—attach appropriate reward structures to motivate people to pick up the vital behaviors.

Source 6: Structural Ability—ensure that systems, processes, reporting structures, visual cues, and so forth support the vital behaviors.

Model of the Six Sources of Influence

	Motivation	**Ability**
Personal	Make the Undesirable Desirable	Surpass Your Limits
Social	Harness Peer Pressure	Find Strength in Numbers
Structural	Design Rewards and Demand Accountability	Change the Environment

MAKE THE UNDESIRABLE DESIRABLE

If you can't find a way to change a person's intrinsic response to a behavior—if you can't make the right behaviors pleasurable and the wrong behaviors painful—you'll have to make up for the motivational shortfall by relying on external incentives or possibly even punishments.

Can you actually change how humans experience a behavior? Is it possible to change the meaning of a behavior itself from loathsome to gratifying, from pleasurable to disgusting, or from insulting to inspiring? If you ask gifted influencers, their unequivocal answer will be, *of course you can*. And you must. Specifically, there are two very powerful and ethical ways of helping humans change their reaction to a previously neutral or noxious behavior: creating new experiences and creating new motives.

Create New Experiences

Sometimes people loathe the very thought of a new behavior because they lack adequate information to judge it correctly. Get people to try it. The "try it, you'll like it" strategy can be further aided by the use of models. Many influence masters have found that vicarious experience can work in situations where they can't get people to try a vital behavior based on faith alone.

When dealing with activities that are rarely satisfying or unhealthy activities that are very satisfying, take the focus off the activity itself, and reconnect vital behavior to the person's sense of values. Don't be afraid to talk openly about the long-term values individuals are currently either supporting or violating.

Create New Motives

Help individuals see their choices as moral quests or as personally defining moments, and that they must keep this perspective despite distractions and emotional stress. Help them to take their eyes off the demands of the moment and view the larger moral issues at hand by reframing reality in moral terms. Spotlight human consequences and rehumanize targets that people readily and easily abuse. Don't let people minimize or justify their behavior by transforming humans into statistics. If people can make their behavior part of a broader and more important moral mission, they can do almost anything.

When facing highly resistant people, don't try to gain control over them by wowing them with logic and argument. Instead, talk with them about what they want. Through a skillful use of open and nondirective questions, called motivational interviewing, examine what is most important to the person and what changes in their life might be required in order for them to live according to their values. When you listen and they talk, they discover on their own what they must do.

SURPASS YOUR LIMITS

Many of the profound and persistent problems we face stem more from a lack of skill (which in turn stems from a lack of deliberate practice) than from a genetic curse, a lack of courage, or a character flaw. But we often underestimate the need to learn and actually *practice* the desired skill. For example, self-discipline, long viewed as a character trait, and elite performance, similarly linked to genetic gifts, stem from the ability to engage in guided practice of clearly defined skills. There is little evidence that people who achieve exceptional performance ever get there through any means other than carefully guided practice. Learn how to practice the right actions, and you can master everything from withstanding the temptations of unhealthy food to holding an awkward discussion with your boss.

Perfect Complex Skills

Not all practice is good practice. For example, most professionals progress until they reach an "acceptable" level, and then they plateau. Beyond this level of mediocrity, further improvements are not correlated to years of work in the field.

So what creates improvement? According to psychologist Dr. Anders Ericsson, improvement is related not just to practice, but to a particular kind of practice—called *deliberate practice*. The techniques of deliberate practice are:

- *Demand full attention for brief intervals.* The ability to concentrate at a heightened level is usually the limiting factor to deliberate practice. Most people can maintain a heightened level of concentration for only an hour straight.
- *Provide immediate feedback against a clear standard.* The number of hours one spends practicing a skill is far less important than receiving clear and frequent feedback against a known standard.
- *Break mastery into minigoals.* Concentrate on specific goals where the process is controllable.
- *Prepare for setbacks; build in resilience.* The practice regime should gradually introduce tasks that require increased effort and persistence. As learners overcome more difficult tasks and recover from intermittent defeats, they see that setbacks aren't permanent roadblocks, but signals that they need to keep learning.
- *Build emotional skills.* To regain emotional control over your genetically wired responses, take the focus off your instinctive objective by carefully

attending to distraction activities. For example, as a strategy to help obsessive-compulsives cope with their tendencies, therapists teach them to wait fifteen minutes before giving in to a maddening mental demand.

HARNESS PEER PRESSURE

When seeking influence tools that have an impact on profound and persistent problems, no resource is more powerful and accessible than the persuasion of the people who make up our social networks. The ridicule and praise, acceptance and rejection, approval and disapproval of our fellow beings can do more to assist or destroy our change efforts than almost any other source.

The Power of One

To harness the immense power of social support, sometimes you need to find only one respected individual who will fly in the face of history and model the new vital behaviors. When a respected individual attempts a vital behavior and succeeds, this one act alone can go further in motivating others to change than almost any other source of influence. But take note, the living examples of other humans exert power only to the extent that the person who is modeling the vital behaviors is truly respected.

Enlist Social Support

When it comes to creating change, you no longer have to worry about influencing everyone at once. Your job is to find the opinion leaders who are the key to everyone else. Spend disproportionate time with them. Listen to their concerns. Build trust with them. Be open to their ideas. Rely on them to share your ideas, and you'll gain a source of influence unlike any other.

On a more personal note, if you're trying to change something within your own life, co-opt the power of those who have an influence on you. If you make a commitment and then share it with friends, you're far more likely to follow through than if you simply make your commitment to yourself. Better still, team up with someone who is attempting to make the same changes you are.

Make Undiscussables Discussable

Sometimes change efforts call for changes in widely shared norms. In that case, almost everyone in a community has to talk openly about a proposed change in behavior before it can be safely embraced by anyone. This calls for public discourse. Detractors will often suggest that it's inappropriate to hold such an open discourse, and they may even go so far as to suggest that the topic is undiscussable. Ignore those who seek silence instead of healthy dialogue. Make it safe to talk about high-stakes and controversial topics.

Create a Village

Some challenges are so profound that they won't vanish, even if everyone talks openly and new norms are formed. For instance, some personal changes are so significant that asking people to embrace many new behaviors requires that you shape them into entirely new people; this level of transformation calls for the work of an entire village.

When breaking away from habits that are continually reinforced by a person's existing social network, people must be plucked from their support structure and placed in a new network, one where virtually everyone in their new social circle supports and rewards the right behaviors while punishing the wrong ones.

BECOME AN OPINION LEADER

If you aspire to become an effective influencer, you should also aspire to become an opinion leader within your own work and family circle. Here's what it takes to become and remain an opinion leader. People, including children, pay attention to individuals who possess two important qualities:

- First, these people are viewed as knowledgeable about the issue at hand. They tend to stay connected to their area of expertise, often through a variety of sources.
- Second, opinion leaders are viewed as trustworthy. They have other people's best interest in mind. This means that they aren't seen as using their knowledge to manipulate or harm, but rather to help.

FIND STRENGTH IN NUMBERS

As the Beatles suggested, we're most likely to succeed when we have "a little help from our friends." These friends provide us with access to their brains, give us the strength of their hands, and even allow us to make use of their many other personal resources. In effect they provide us with social capital. In fact, with a little help from our friends, we can produce a force greater than the sum of our individual efforts. But we can do this only when we know how to make use of social capital—the profound enabling power of an essential network of relationships.

So, when exactly should you build social capital to bring about challenging changes?

- When others are part of the problem.
- When you can't succeed on your own.
- When facing changing, turbulent, or novel times—calling for novel solutions.

Blind Spots

Perhaps the most obvious condition that demands social support as a means of influencing vital behaviors comes with the need for feedback that can be offered only by a pair of outside eyes. When it comes to business and other settings, leaders rarely think of using real-time coaches. Some of today's companies provide their leaders with call-in advisers who discuss what happened yesterday when the leader faced a challenge and didn't do all that well. But few provide real-time coaching. This should change.

DESIGN REWARDS AND DEMAND ACCOUNTABILITY

Stories of well-intended rewards that inadvertently backfire are legion. The primary cause of most of these debacles is that individuals attempt to influence behaviors by using rewards as their first motivational strategy. In a well-balanced change effort, rewards come third. Influence masters first ensure that vital behaviors connect to intrinsic satisfaction. Next, they line up social support. They double-check both of these areas before they finally choose extrinsic rewards to motivate behavior.

Making use of extrinsic rewards can be complicated. Not every reward has its desired effect. Sometimes extrinsic programs can completely backfire and serve as punishment. For example, reward ceremonies honor a select few top performers but leave others who are not recognized feeling discouraged.

Use Incentives Wisely

Influence masters eventually use rewards and punishments, so the question is how to use incentives wisely.

Take care to ensure that the rewards come soon, are gratifying, and are clearly tied to vital behaviors. When you do so, even small rewards can be used to help people overcome some of the most profound and persistent problems.

If you're doing it right, less is more. When it comes to offering extrinsic rewards, the rewards typically don't need to be very large—at least if you've laid the groundwork with the previous sources of motivation. The thought behind an incentive often carries symbolic significance and taps into a variety of social forces that carry a lot of weight.

Reward Vital Behaviors, Not Just Results

Don't wait until people achieve phenomenal results, but instead reward small improvements in behavior. As simple as this sounds we're bad at it, especially at work. When polled, employees reveal that their number-one complaint is that they aren't recognized for their notable performances.

Each year a new survey publishes the fact that employees would appreciate more praise, and each year we apparently do nothing different. There seems to be a permanent divide between researchers and scholars who heartily argue that performance is best improved by rewarding incremental improvements, and the rest of the world where people wait for a profound achievement before working up any enthusiasm.

Influence by rewarding right results and right behaviors. If employees' current performance level is unacceptable, and you can't wait for them to come up to standard, then either terminate them or move them to tasks that they can complete. On the other hand, if an individual is excelling in some areas while lagging in others—but overall is up to snuff—then set performance goals in the lagging areas and don't be afraid to reward small improvements. This means that you shouldn't wait for big results but should reward improvement in vital behaviors along the way.

Watch for Divisive Incentives

People are so often out of touch with the message they're sending that they inadvertently reward exactly the wrong behavior. Just watch coaches as they speak about the importance of teamwork and then celebrate individual accomplishment. Kids quickly learn that it's the score that counts, not the assist, and it turns many of them into selfish prima donnas. So when behaviors are out of whack, look closely at your rewards. Who knows? Your own incentive system may be causing the problem.

Punishment Sends a Message, and So Does Its Absence

Sometimes you don't have the luxury of rewarding positive performance because the person never actually does the right thing. In fact, he or she does only the wrong thing—and often. In these cases, if you want to make use of extrinsic reinforcers, you're left with the prospect of punishing this person.

Punishment can create all sorts of serious and harmful emotional effects, particularly if it is only loosely administered. When it comes to punishment, you must be very careful.

Before punishing, place a shot across the bow—provide a clear warning to let people know exactly what negative things will happen to them should they continue down their current path, but don't actually administer discipline yet.

When all else fails, punish. The lack of punishment for routine infractions sends a loud message across an organization. If you aren't willing to punish people when they violate a core value (such as giving their best effort), that value will lose its moral force in the organization. On the other hand, punishing sends a powerful message about your values when you do hold employees accountable.

CHANGE THE ENVIRONMENT

For the final source for increasing our ability ("Can I do it?"), we examine how nonhuman forces—the world of buildings, space, sound, sight, and so forth—can be brought to bear in an influence strategy.

Consider the profound and yet mostly unnoticed effect of things on entire communities. Realizing the physicality of a neighborhood can send out unspoken messages that encourage socially inappropriate behavior, George Kelling started a community movement that is largely credited for reducing felonies in New York City by as much as 75 percent.

Committed to lessening the effect things were having on the community, Kelling advised the New York Transit Authority to start paying attention to environmental cues that provided a fertile environment for criminal behavior. Kelling's crew began a systematic attack against graffiti, litter, and vandalism. Over time, a combination of cleanup and prosecution for minor offenses began to make a difference. Surroundings improved, community pride increased, and petty crimes declined. So did violent crime.

Environmental factors affect much of what we do, and yet we often fail to make good use of things as much as we should. There are two reasons for this:

- We often fail to notice their profound impact. More often than not, powerful elements in our environment, such as work procedures, job layouts, reporting structures, etc., remain invisible to us.
- Even when we do think about the impact the environment is having on us, we rarely know what to do about it.

Make the Invisible Visible

Once you've identified environmental elements that are subtly driving your or others' behavior, take steps to make them more obvious. That is, you make the invisible visible.

Provide actual cues in the environment to remind people of the behaviors you're trying to influence.

For example, Dr. Leon Bender tried several methods to encourage doctors to wash their hands more thoroughly. He finally realized that he needed to make the invisible visible. At a routine meeting, he handed each doctor a petri dish with a layer of agar, collected a culture of their hands, and sent the dishes to the lab for culturing and photographing. When the photos came back from the lab, the images were frightfully effective. When it came to changing physicians' behavior, photos created poignant vicarious experiences and visual cues that reminded them of the need to properly wash their hands.

Mind the Data Stream

As in the hand-washing example, small cues in the environment can draw attention to critical data points and change how people think and eventually how they behave. Influence geniuses understand the importance of an accurate data stream and do their best to ensure that their strategies focus on vital behaviors by serving up visible, timely, and accurate information that supports their goals.

One warning about data: There is such a thing as "too much of a good thing." Corporate leaders often undermine the influence of the data they so carefully gather by overdoing it. The incessant flow of reports, printouts, and e-mails transforms into numbing and incoherent background noise. Influence masters never make this mistake. They understand that the only reason for gathering or publishing any data is to reinforce vital behaviors.

Make It Easy

Rather than constantly finding ways to motivate people to continue with their boring, painful, dangerous, or otherwise loathsome activities, find a way to change things in order to make the right behaviors easier to enact.

Making use of things to enable behavior works best when you can alter the physical world in a way that eliminates human choice entirely. You don't merely make good behavior desirable, you make it inevitable. This is where structure, process, and procedures come into play. An example of this is the fast-food industry where employees can simply push picture buttons when taking an order. The process has all been routinized, and it's almost impossible to do the wrong thing.

BECOME AN INFLUENCER

There is a growing body of knowledge as well as an impressive supply of real-life success stories that teach exactly how to change almost any human behavior. Scholarly works by Dr. Albert Bandura and others demonstrate that, if you know what you're doing, you can indeed change remarkably resistant behaviors.

To become an effective influencer, it is important to address all six sources of influence when designing an influence strategy. Stop thinking of influence tools as a buffet and recognize them as a comprehensive approach to creating systematic, widespread, and lasting change. Diagnose both motivational and ability sources of influence and then lock in the results by applying individual, social, and structural forces to the solution. You now have a powerful six-source diagnostic tool at your fingertips. Use it liberally.

TRUE NORTH
by Bill George with Peter E. Sims

W hile Harvard Business School Professor of Management Bill George was CEO at Medtronic, his leadership skills helped him increase the growth of the company to more than $60 billion in ten years, making it one of the world's leading medical technology companies. His success at that company has exemplified for many leaders and managers how smart management leadership is executed. In 2004, he published *Authentic Leadership* to relate his pivotal experiences at Medtronic and describe how honest leadership works.

In his second leadership book, *True North,* George turns lessons learned by 125 other top leaders, such as Howard Schultz of Starbucks, Andrea Jung of Avon, and Chuck Schwab, into effective management practices while describing what it takes to develop and follow one's own internal compass toward authentic leadership. He writes that authentic leadership begins in a leader's life story and inner wisdom, and then manifests itself as a force that draws people toward the leader and helps him or her lead others toward success.

George explains that while he was searching for the traits and characteristics that determine great leaders, he found that leaders were more likely to talk about the personal stories that shaped them early in their lives than discuss clear lists of management do's and don'ts. Sometimes those personal experiences were shaped by early childhood memories of poor homes or difficult family lives, he explains, and other times they were dramatic moments early in a career. George found that, from those experiences, the passion for leadership was developed and charged with the principles and values that helped the leaders he researched make critical choices. Those decisions built the teams that grew their companies into successful businesses. By integrating all aspects of their lives into their work, George explains, the leaders stayed grounded in who they were born to be and became authentic leaders. That's how a leader's personal biography plays a vital role in the overall management picture.

Shortly after the publication of *True North,* George discussed his own experiences with journalist Charlie Rose. George explained that his father saw himself as a failure, although he was a successful business consultant, because he never became a leader himself. By instilling his son Bill with the desire to lead a large company at an early age, he helped George realize his dreams. George said early setbacks and many lost student government elections in high school and college helped to teach him valuable lessons about leadership that have stayed with him for years.

Although George is a management professor at Harvard, he told Rose that he doesn't believe leadership can be taught. "I think you can learn about it. I think you've got to learn about yourself. It comes from within, from who are you inside and what makes you tick, and what are those tapes playing in your head that tell you about what you want to be and what your limitations are."

In *True North,* George explains that leadership is best practiced when leaders stay true to their own principles, values, and beliefs. These elements lead to each leader's own "True North." When leaders are drawn away from this direction by distractions such as salaries, celebrity, and power, their ability to deal with the challenges and demands of leadership is diminished. By showing how 125 of today's top leaders stay on course toward their own True North, in spite of outside pressures, he shows others how to stay true to what they believe.

According to George, the discovery of a leader's True North is only a part of the journey to personal fulfillment. He explains that the real satisfaction that comes from following this path is a result of working past mistakes and making a difference in the world through teamwork and effort. By seeking honest feedback, listening, and "knowing who you are at a deep level," he adds, leaders with character, substance, and integrity, rather than style, image, and charisma, can make the best decisions for their organizations and make a difference in the world.

He explains that today's great leaders are able to align their people around a consistent sense of purpose and values. They are also able to empower others to "step up and lead," George explains. This comes from the crucial ability to see their people's potential and bring it out of them.

TRUE NORTH

Discover Your Authentic Leadership

by Bill George with Peter E. Sims

CONTENTS

THE SUMMARY IN BRIEF

According to Warren Bennis, as the world becomes more dangerous and our problems become more complex and dire, we long for truly distinguished leaders, men and women who deserve our respect and loyalty. True North is about this kind of leader.

True North is the internal compass that guides you successfully through life. It represents who you are as a human being at your deepest level and is based on what is most important to you.

Author Bill George shows how anyone who follows his or her internal compass can become an authentic leader. This leadership examination is based on research and first-person interviews with 125 of today's top leaders—with some surprising results.

The leaders interviewed for *True North* ranged in age from twenty-three to ninety-three and were chosen based on their reputations for being authentic and successful. They make up a diverse group of women and men from an array of racial, religious, and socioeconomic backgrounds and nationalities. Among them are Howard Schultz of Starbucks, Andrea Jung of Avon, and Chuck Schwab, founder of Charles Schwab & Co. Half of the group are CEOs, and the other half includes a broad range of nonprofit leaders just starting on their journey.

Discovering your True North takes a lifetime of commitment and learning. But as long as you are true to who you are, you can cope with the most difficult circumstances that life presents. When you are aligned with who you are, you find coherence between your life story and your leadership. Can you recall the time when you felt most intensely alive and could say with confidence, "This is the real me"? When you can, you are aligned with your True North and are prepared to lead others authentically.

What You'll Learn in This Summary

- The five dimensions that make up an authentic leader.
- How to identify the five types of leaders who have derailed.
- How to build your support team.
- How to empower people to lead.
- How to optimize your leadership effectiveness.
- How to link your leadership style with your sense of power.

THE COMPLETE SUMMARY

LEARNING FROM AUTHENTIC LEADERS

It is understandable why academic studies have not produced a profile of an ideal leader. Leaders are highly complex human beings, people who have distinctive qualities that cannot be sufficiently described by lists of traits or characteristics.

Authentic leaders not only inspire those around them, they empower people to step up and lead. Thus, there is a new definition of leadership: *The authentic leader brings people together around a shared purpose and empowers them to step up and lead authentically in order to create value for all stakeholders.*

There are five dimensions that make up an authentic leader:

- *Pursuing purpose with passion.* Without a real sense of purpose, leaders are at the mercy of their egos and narcissistic vulnerabilities.
- *Practicing solid values.* Leaders are defined by their values, and values are personal—they cannot be determined by anyone else.
- *Leading with heart.* Authentic leaders lead with their hearts as well as their heads.
- *Establishing enduring relationships.* The ability to develop enduring relationships is an essential mark of authentic leaders.
- *Demonstrating self-discipline.* Authentic leaders know competing successfully takes a consistently high level of self-discipline in order to produce results.

There are two key steps to becoming an authentic leader. First, you have to understand yourself, because the person you will always find hardest to lead is yourself. Second, you must take responsibility for your own development. You must devote yourself to a lifetime of development in order to become a great leader.

THE JOURNEY TO AUTHENTIC LEADERSHIP

Authentic leaders consistently say they find their motivation through understanding their own stories. What makes leaders' stories different from everyone else's? Many people with painful stories see themselves as victims, feeling the world has dealt them a bad hand. Or they lack the introspection to see the connection between their life experiences and the goals they are pursuing. The difference with authentic leaders lies in the way they frame their stories. Their life stories provide the context for their lives.

Many learn the hard way that leadership is not a simple destination of becoming CEO. Rather, it is a marathon journey that progresses through many stages until you reach your peak leadership. Of all the leaders over forty who were interviewed, none wound up where they thought they would.

■ **Phase I: Preparing for Leadership.** The first thirty years is the time to prepare for leadership, when character is formed and people become individual contributors or lead teams for the first time.

■ **Phase II: Leading.** The second phase of your leadership journey begins with a rapid accumulation of leadership experiences and culminates in the fifties, when leaders typically reach their peak leadership.

■ **Phase III: Giving Back.** Many leaders are bypassing retirement to share their experience with multiple organizations. They serve on for-profit or nonprofit boards, mentor young leaders, take up teaching, or coach newly appointed CEOs.

Lord John Browne, who led BP to new heights in his eleven years at the helm, supports the idea of giving back. In announcing he would step down as CEO, Browne said, "I don't believe in retirement. The idea seems a touch out of date." He suggested he would be looking for an interesting new position with a purpose.

THE AUTHENTIC LEADERSHIP COMPASS

WHY LEADERS LOSE THEIR WAY

Why do people with excellent potential get derailed just as they appear to be hitting the peak of their leadership? People who lose their way are not necessarily bad leaders. They have the potential to become good leaders, but somewhere along the way they get pulled off course.

Before people take on leadership roles, they should first ask themselves two fundamental questions: "What motivates me to lead?" and "What is the purpose of my leadership?" If honest answers to the first question are simply power, prestige, and money, leaders risk being trapped by external gratification as the source of their fulfillment. There is nothing wrong with desiring these outward symbols as long as they are combined with a deeper desire to serve something greater than oneself.

While many leaders have a deep-seated fear of failure, the irony is that they learn the most from their failures. Some rising leaders have such a fear of failing that they avoid risks. When they reach the top, they are not prepared to cope with the greater challenges they face.

Derailment: Losing Sight of Your True North

In observing leaders who have derailed, five types who lose sight of their True North have been identified.

Impostors rise through the organizational ranks with a combination of cunning and aggression. They understand the politics of getting ahead and let no one stand in their way. They have little appetite for self-reflection or for developing self-awareness.

To people outside their organizations, **Rationalizers** always appear on top of the issues. When things don't go their way, they blame external forces or subordinates or offer facile answers to their problems. They rarely step up and take responsibility themselves.

Glory Seekers define themselves by acclaim of the external world. Money, fame, glory, and power are their goals as they pursue visible signs of success. Often it seems more important to them to appear on lists of the most powerful business leaders than it does to build organizations of lasting value.

Loners avoid forming close relationships, seeking out mentors, or creating support networks. They believe they can and must make it on their own. Not to be confused with introverts, loners often have a myriad of superficial relationships and acolytes, but they do not listen to them.

The lives of **Shooting Stars** center entirely on their careers. To observers, they are perpetual motion machines, always on the go, traveling incessantly to get ahead. They rarely make time for family, friends, communities, or even themselves. As they run ever faster, their stress mounts. They move up so rapidly in their careers that they never have time to learn from their mistakes.

TRANSFORMATION FROM "I" TO "WE"

To become authentic leaders, we must discard the myth that leadership means having legions of supporters following our direction as we ascend to the pinnacles of power. Only then can we realize that authentic leadership is about empowering others on their journeys.

This shift is the transformation from "I" to "We." It is the most important process leaders go through in becoming authentic. How else can they unleash the power of their organizations except by motivating people to reach their full potential? Only when leaders stop focusing on their personal ego needs are they able to develop other leaders.

Jaime Irick on Transforming

Jaime Irick, a West Point graduate and rising star at General Electric, offered insight into the process of transforming from "I" to "We." "You have to realize that it's not about you," he explained.

"We spend our early years trying to be the best. To get into West Point or General Electric, you have to be the best. That is defined by what you can do on your own—your ability to be a phenomenal analyst or do well on a standardized test. When you become a leader, your challenge is to inspire others, develop them and create change through them. If you want to be a leader, you've got to flip that switch and understand that it's about serving folks on your team. This is a very simple concept, but one many people overlook. The sooner they realize it, the faster they will become leaders."

KNOWING YOUR AUTHENTIC SELF

In their interviews, leaders said that gaining self-awareness was central to becoming authentic leaders. For this reason it is at the center of your compass. When you know yourself, you can find the passion that motivates you and the purpose of your leadership.

Your Emotional Intelligence

Self-awareness is the first element of emotional intelligence, or EQ. While intellectual intelligence, or IQ, has long been thought of as an essential characteristic for managers, EQ may be more important for authentic leaders. Leaders with an exceptionally high IQ get too intellectually involved and have trouble being tolerant of others. You have to have a certain level of intelligence at the top. Above that level, you need leadership skills, interpersonal skills, and teamwork.

Dirk Jager, the former CEO of Procter & Gamble, is an example of a failed leader because he imposed his intellect on others. Jager was a brilliant strategist who had excellent ideas about the strategic and cultural changes needed at P&G, but his style was so abrasive that he threatened the essence of P&G's culture. As a result, his management team rebelled, and the board asked him to step down in less than two years as A.G. Lafley, a longtime P&G executive, took his place. Using a combination of wisdom, humility, and personal engagement with employees, Lafley is transforming P&G into one of the great success stories of the twenty-first century.

Why Knowing Yourself Is So Important

The better you know yourself, the more likely you are to choose the right role. When leaders know themselves well, they become comfortable in their own skins, act consistently in different situations, and gain the trust of others. Most leaders see the process of gaining self-awareness as crucial to their ability to build strong relationships. Those who are comfortable with themselves tend to be more open and transparent. Leaders who know their strengths and weaknesses can fill their skill gaps with colleagues who complement them.

Becoming Self-Aware

Without self-awareness, it is easy to get caught up in chasing external symbols of success rather than becoming the person you want to be. It is difficult to regulate your emotions, control your fears, and avoid impulsive outbursts when you feel threatened or rejected. Without being aware of your vulnerabilities, fears, and longings, it is hard to empathize with others who are experiencing similar feelings.

One of the most difficult things in becoming self-aware is seeing ourselves as others see us. Although it can be difficult to hear, leaders need accurate feedback to identify their blind spots. When you can do that and be open to new ways of doing things, the change you can accomplish is almost unlimited.

Accepting Yourself

Self-awareness is only half the challenge. You still have to accept yourself. But with self-awareness, accepting your authentic self becomes much easier. You see yourself clearly and accurately, and you know what you truly believe. The key to self-acceptance is to love yourself unconditionally. This level of self-compassion enables you to get to the source of your True North and to accept yourself as you are.

PRACTICING YOUR VALUES AND PRINCIPLES

In gaining a clear awareness of who you are, you must understand your values and the principles that guide your leadership. Staying centered on your values is not easy. You can easily drift off course as the temptations and pressures of the outside world pull you away. But if you are centered by a high level of self-awareness, your compass can help you get back on track.

Values, Leadership Principles, and Ethical Boundaries

The values that form the basis for your True North are derived from your beliefs and convictions. In defining your values, you must decide what is most important in your life. When you have a clear understanding of your values and their relative importance, you can establish the principles by which you intend to lead. *Leadership principles are values translated into action.*

Your ethical boundaries set clear limits on what you will do when you are tempted or are under pressure or when you start rationalizing a series of marginal decisions. One way leaders understand their ethical boundaries is to use the *New York Times* test. Before proceeding with any action, ask yourself, "How would I feel if this entire situation, including transcripts of discussions, were printed on the first page of the *New York Times?*" If your answers are negative, then it is time to rethink your actions; if they are positive, you should feel comfortable proceeding.

WHAT MOTIVATES YOU TO BE A LEADER?

Chuck Schwab's strengths, talents, and motivations all came together when he founded Charles Schwab & Co. He combined his investment research skills with the persistence and resilience learned from years of suffering with dyslexia and an upbringing that instilled an enormous respect for individuals who want to achieve financial independence.

Building a company with a cause in which he passionately believes, he has helped millions become more confident while achieving financial independence himself. Schwab's company is an American icon, with fourteen thousand employees and market capitalization of $20 billion.

Like Chuck Schwab, you need to know what motivates you and have a realistic understanding of your strengths and weaknesses so you can put your best capabilities to work.

Intrinsic and Extrinsic Motivations

There are two types of motivation—extrinsic and intrinsic. Extrinsic motivations, such as getting good grades, winning athletic competitions, or making money, are measured by the external world.

Intrinsic motivations, on the other hand, are derived from your sense of the meaning of your life—your True North. They are closely linked to your life story and the way you frame it. Examples include personal growth, helping other people develop, and making a difference in the world. Schwab's passion for helping Americans achieve financial independence is an intrinsic motivation, even if the end result made him wealthy.

Avoiding Traps

Moving away from external validation of personal achievement is not easy. Achievement-oriented leaders grow so accustomed to successive accomplishments throughout their early years that it takes courage to pursue their intrinsic motivations.

But at some point, most leaders recognize that they need to address more difficult questions in order to pursue their true motivations. As a star consultant for global management firm McKinsey & Co., Alice Woodwark had achieved success at every stage of her life by age twenty-nine. She noted: "My version of achievement was pretty naive, born of things I learned early in life about praise and being valued. But if you're just chasing the rabbit around the course, you're not running toward anything meaningful." Many leaders turned down higher-paying jobs in early career decisions in order to pursue roles they would enjoy. They came out ahead in the end—in both satisfaction and compensation—because they were successful in doing what they loved.

However, many young leaders are tempted to take high-salaried jobs to pay off loans or build their savings, even if they have no interest in the work and do not intend to stay. Some become so dependent on maintaining a certain lifestyle that they get trapped in jobs where they are unmotivated and unhappy. Locked into the high-income/high-expense life, they cannot afford to do work they are passionate about. Ironically, not one of the leaders interviewed wound up taking a position predicated upon establishing wealth early. This course enabled them to later pursue roles they would enjoy.

BUILDING YOUR SUPPORT TEAM

Your support team is a key element of your personal development plan. Members of your team help you stay focused on your True North, keep you grounded in reality, and provide the support you need as you venture on your leadership journey. Leaders do not succeed on their own; they must give as much to their relationships as they get from them.

The Most Important Person to Your Leadership

Your support team starts with having at least one person in your life with whom you can be completely vulnerable and open. Often that person is the only one who can tell you the honest truth. Most leaders have their closest relationships with their spouses, although some develop these bonds with other family members, a close friend, or a trusted mentor.

Mentors

Many authentic leaders have had a mentor who has changed their lives by helping them develop the skills to become better leaders and the confidence to lead authentically. But what some people, especially aspiring leaders, fail to recognize is the importance of the two-way relationship with their mentors. *Lasting relationships must flow both ways.* The best mentoring interactions spark mutual learning, exploration of similar values, and shared enjoyment.

Current chairman and former CEO of Intuit Bill Campbell is the dean of mentoring in Silicon Valley. Many venture capitalists and board members in northern California will not hire a new CEO without first checking with Campbell. Although he keeps a low public profile, "Coach Campbell" is one of Silicon Valley's most respected executives.

Campbell has mentored dozens of entrepreneurs and business leaders. People are drawn to him because they consider him a great mentor and leader who has helped them unleash their own leadership potential. His selfless spirit, cultivated on the football fields of his youth, has enabled him to develop a loyal network of mentees, supporters, and friends.

The best mentors put the interests of those they are mentoring above their own. These relationships can grow into strong personal friendships, especially when the participants are no longer in the same professional context. The cycle then continues when those who benefited from strong mentoring mentor others.

Creating a Professional Support Network

Many leaders develop professional peer networks both within and outside their organizations to consult with about important issues and to provide counsel and guidance. Having a peer support structure within your organization can be invaluable, because colleagues may be facing comparable experiences, have insights about things you do not see, or be in a position to offer you real-time feedback on your leadership.

STAYING GROUNDED: INTEGRATING YOUR LIFE

Integrating their lives is one of the greatest challenges leaders face. To lead an integrated life, you need to bring together the major elements of your personal life and professional life, including work, family, community, and friends, so that you can be the same person in each environment.

Authentic leaders are constantly aware of the importance of staying grounded. In doing so, they avoid getting too arrogant during the high points and forgetting who they are during the low points. Spending time with their families and close friends, getting physical exercise, practicing spirituality, doing community service, and returning to places where they grew up are all ways they stay grounded. This grounding is essential to their effectiveness as leaders because it enables them to preserve their authenticity.

Measuring Success

Have you defined what success means for you and for your life? Unless you have thought through the answer to that question, you are at risk of letting others define success for you. Only when you can define what is most important in your life can you set the right priorities and become an integrated leader.

LEADERSHIP WITH PURPOSE AND PASSION

In 1998, Andrea Jung was facing the most difficult decision of her long and successful career. Four years after joining Avon Products, she had been passed over for promotion to CEO in favor of one of the company's outside board members. "I had an offer to become CEO at another company, but Ann Moore, CEO of Time Inc. and an Avon board member, advised me to stay," she recalled. "She told me, 'Follow your compass and not your clock.'"

Jung decided to stay, becoming president of Avon and a board member. The decision changed her life. Just twenty months later, the new CEO retired, and Jung was named his successor in November 1999, becoming Avon's first female CEO.

What is the purpose of your leadership? Are you following the True North of your compass or the timetable of your clock? If you examine your True North again, you will find that it points the way to the purpose of your leadership. When you understand your purpose, you are ready to find an organization—or create one—where you can fulfill that purpose.

Discerning Your Passions

How do you discern your passions? For most leaders passion comes from their life stories. By understanding the meaning of key events in your life story and reframing them, you can discern your passions. Following your passions will enable you to discover the purpose of your leadership. Leaders can sustain their effectiveness only if they empower employees around a shared purpose. As a leader, you must convey passion for the business every day while maintaining clarity about the mission of your organization.

EMPOWERING PEOPLE TO LEAD

If mutual respect provides the foundation for bringing out the best in people, what are the steps needed to empower them? Effective leaders use the following approaches at different times, depending on the capabilities of the people involved and the situation they are facing:

- Showing up.
- Engaging people.
- Helping teammates.
- Challenging leaders.
- Stretching people.
- Aligning everyone around a mission.

Woody Allen once remarked, "Eighty percent of success is showing up." Surprisingly, many leaders get so busy they don't take the time to be there for people. Showing up at important events or at unexpected times means a great deal to people and enables them to take their leaders off their proverbial pedestal and see them as real people.

The most empowering leaders are those who engage a wide range of people. That means being with them face-to-face; inquiring about their work, their families, their personal lives, and their careers; and being open and vulnerable with them. Authentic leaders help their teammates, whether it is with a personal problem or a career problem, by counseling them, offering suggestions, or assisting them in making vital contacts.

Most people want to be stretched in assignments that enable them to develop. The leader's key is to sense when people are ready for such challenging experiences. Yet it is important for your team to know that you will be there to support them if necessary.

The most empowering condition of all is when the entire organization is aligned with its mission and people's passions and purpose are in sync with each other. Individuals usually have their own passions. If the organization's leaders can demonstrate how they can fulfill their purpose while achieving the organization's mission, then alignment can occur.

HONING YOUR LEADERSHIP EFFECTIVENESS

Once you empower people to lead around a shared purpose, you are well positioned to achieve superior results through your organization. The final step in maximizing your effectiveness as an authentic leader is to hone your leadership style and make authentic use of your power. The process produces a virtuous circle that will encourage others to join you and sustain your effectiveness on an ongoing basis.

Optimizing Your Leadership Effectiveness

The style of an effective leader must come from an authentic place. That will only happen when you have a high level of self-awareness, are clear about your values, and understand your leadership purpose. Without this clarity, your style will be shaped by the expectations of your organization or the outside world, and will not be seen as authentic.

Yet your use of style and power must fit the situation you are facing, and you have to be versatile to maximize your effectiveness in that situation. In the aftermath of the attack of 9/11, New York Mayor Rudy Giuliani acted decisively to get urgently needed resources in place. He had no time to build consensus. In situations like these, people need decisive leaders to guide them efficiently and calmly to solutions. In other instances, such as when trying to create a future vision for their organizations, leaders need to use a more participative style that involves a wide range of people and gets them engaged and committed to that vision.

As you think about your leadership style and power, ask yourself these questions:

- Is your leadership style consistent with your leadership principles and values? Is it ever inconsistent?
- How do you adapt your style to the circumstances facing you and to the capabilities of your teammates?
- How do you optimize the use of your power in leading others?
- In situations in which you used your power over others inappropriately, how did they respond?
- How do you respond to powerful people who use their power over you?

Your Leadership Style

How do you know what leadership style fits you best? Many organizations work hard to get young leaders to embrace the company's normative leadership style, sending them to training programs to bring their styles into line. If you simply adopt an organization's normative style or try to emulate someone else's style, your lack of authenticity will show through. That's why you should find a leadership style that is authentic to you and continue to refine it.

Using Power Wisely

The effective use of power in relationships is essential to achieving one's goals. Many leaders in high-level organizational roles use their positional power to dominate others. They do not realize that their intimidating style and excessive use of power shuts down the contributions of others.

The irony is that the more power one accumulates, the less it should be used. By exerting your power, you are taking away the power of others. Authentic leaders understand they need power to get things done, but they learn to use it in subtle ways. They prefer to persuade others to adopt their point of view or to build a consensus rather than force subordinates to go along with them.

Adapting to the Situation and to Your Teammates

As leaders mature through multiple experiences, they develop an authentic primary leadership style that works well for them. That style is effective as long as their situation or context stays the same. But what happens when the context changes?

In leading, you must always understand the situation in which you are operating, as well as the performance imperative. Once you understand the context, you can adjust your leadership style to get results.

In determining the style and power you want to use in a given situation, you should consider the readiness of your teammates to accept greater power and authority. For example, teammates who are used to taking clear direction may not be ready to adapt to a leader with a consensus style; conversely, followers who are highly creative and independent will not respond positively to a directive style. You should also think carefully about the kind of relationship you want to have with your teammates and what type of relationship will enable your team or organization to achieve its business imperatives. These relationships generally fit one of three types: dependent, independent, or interdependent.

In creating *dependent relationships*, leaders must recognize that their teammates will rely entirely on their direction and their decisions. *Independent relationships* give teammates the autonomy and freedom to act on their own, but there is little bonding or group support. In creating *interdependent relationships*, expert, coaching, consensus, and affiliative leaders share power with teammates and bring out their best qualities. They believe interdependence creates better decisions and greater commitment to ensuring success.

The bottom line for all leaders is to optimize their effectiveness to achieve superior long-term results. Authentic leaders are more effective at doing this because they have a clear sense of their moral compass and are explicitly committed to building their organizations over time. By developing an authentic leadership style, they get the best from their teammates and their organizations.

LINKING LEADERSHIP STYLE AND POWER

Your style conveys your sense of power, just as your use of power reflects your leadership style.

- *Directive leaders* create dependent relationships with their subordinates, who obediently carry out their orders and respond to their demands.
- *Coaching leaders* create interdependent relationships.
- *Consensus leaders* use power in subtle ways to reach agreement without hurting others' feelings or isolating people with different points of view.
- *Affiliative leaders* are embraced by others for their highly empathic relationships.
- *Expert leaders* believe knowledge is power and being right and efficient is more important than relationships.

WHAT GOT YOU HERE
WON'T GET YOU THERE
by Marshall Goldsmith with Mark Reiter

Many misconceptions about being the boss continue to pervade the upper tiers of the world's organizations. It is executive coach Marshall Goldsmith's job to pinpoint the weaknesses that hold corporate leaders back and turn them into strengths before their repercussions harm the organizations they head. He has made a career of carefully teaching leaders how to overcome the management myopia that keeps them from seeing how effective they really are, and helping them improve in their weakest areas. Goldsmith's career has been extremely successful thanks to his ability to shed light into the dark corners of a leader's behaviors to reveal the great leader lurking behind bad habits.

Marshall Goldsmith knows more about how to be the boss than most bosses know about themselves. That's why he is one of the most influential executive coaches in the world. When he works with the top executives in the global corporate marketplace, he helps them discover the aspects of their leadership skills that are holding them back from achieving their true potential. In his *New York Times* bestseller and *Wall Street Journal* number-one book *What Got You Here Won't Get You There: How Successful People Become Even More Successful,* he shows leaders how to find flaws in their behavior and overcome them with techniques that have helped the best leaders stay on top.

By revealing the most common ways that managers and executives sabotage their own success, Goldsmith shows others how to improve their behavior. His explorations into the dysfunctions of leadership open up possibilities for leaders that can lead them to stronger organizations.

Early in his long career as an executive educator and coach, Goldsmith was pivotal in pioneering the use of the customized, 360-degree feedback leadership development tool, which involves confidential feedback from direct reports, peers, and managers. His focus on feedback and follow-up to measure changes in behavior provided the foundation for what would eventually become the field of executive coaching. Lately, he has reworked the idea of feedback into a concept he calls "feedforward," which focuses on providing suggestions for the future rather than the past. This role of coach differs dramatically from that of the judge, critic, or cynic.

Goldsmith's consultancy has worked with more than eighty of the top corporate CEOs in the world. These experiences have provided him with the vast insight needed to help others develop as leaders who have a greater impact on the people they lead. His successes have made him one of the most sought-after executive coaches in the world.

His impressive credentials speak volumes about his ability to help leaders lead. Not only does he hold a PhD in organizational behavior from UCLA, he is also on the faculty of the executive education programs at Dartmouth College's Tuck School of Business. Forbes named him as one of the five most-respected executive coaches. BusinessWeek has listed him as one of the most influential practitioners in the history of leadership development. Goldsmith also writes a regular column in Fast Company. Most big business publications recognize him as one of America's leading executive educators and coaches. His work has also brought him the honor of being named by the American Management Association as one of the fifty great thinkers and business leaders who have had a valuable impact on the field of management. And in 2006, he was honored by Alliant International University when they renamed their schools of business and organizational psychology the Marshall Goldsmith School of Management. Through twenty-two books on leadership that he has either written, co-authored, or edited, including The Leader of the Future, Best Practices in Organization Development and Change, Global Leadership: The Next Generation, Coaching for Leadership, The Art and Practice of Leadership Coaching, Leading for Innovation, and The Many Facets of Leadership, Goldsmith has been impacting the leaders of today and tomorrow for decades.

Today, Goldsmith is famous worldwide as the founder of Marshall Goldsmith Partners LLC, a leadership development firm focused on delivering superior executive coaching and other leadership development services to global clients. This is where he propagates his renowned Goldsmith Coaching Process, a coaching method that helps human resources professionals and other coaches consistently enable their clients to get their desired results.

Goldsmith's role as a management guru emerges from his ability to create and share leadership insights that result from decades immersed in the field of leadership behavior change. By examining how leaders develop and grow themselves, and develop and grow other leaders, he has left an indelible mark on leadership and management that continues to have a positive impact on people and organizations around the world.

WHAT GOT YOU HERE WON'T GET YOU THERE

How Successful People Become Even More Successful

by Marshall Goldsmith with Mark Reiter

CONTENTS

THE SUMMARY IN BRIEF

In this book, Marshall Goldsmith begins by examining the trouble with success, explaining how previous accomplishments often prevent leaders from gaining more success. He analyzes why high achievers are so resistant to change due to their delusion of success, pointing out that they can't see that what got them here won't get them there.

These are people who do one annoying thing repeatedly on the job and don't realize that this small flaw may sabotage their otherwise golden careers. Worse yet, they do not realize that it's happening and that they can fix it. Goldsmith details the twenty habits that hold you back from the top rung of the corporate ladder. In his experience, these are the most irritating interpersonal issues in the workplace. For each habit, he gives examples and practical solutions you can implement. He then describes the twenty-first habit, which stands separate from the other twenty habits—not because it is a flaw, but because it is often the root of an annoying behavior.

Finally, Goldsmith addresses the problem of how you can change your interpersonal relationships for the better, and ensure that you make your behavioral changes permanent.

This summary reveals how you can identify which of these twenty habits apply to you, and how to choose the one or two you should focus on.

In addition, you will learn:

• The four key beliefs that make you successful but also resistant to change.
• Why the higher you go, the more your problems are behavioral.
• Why the twenty-first habit, goal obsession, may be the most destructive of all.
• How to get good 360-degree feedback from your colleagues on your own.
• How to overcome special challenges if you're the one in charge at the workplace.

THE COMPLETE SUMMARY

Part I: The Trouble With Success

YOU ARE HERE

You know those maps in shopping malls that say, "You Are Here"? They exist to orient you in unfamiliar territory, to tell you where you are, where you want to go, and how to get there. A few people never need these maps. They're blessed with an internal compass that orients them automatically.

Some people go through life with this unerring sense of direction—it guides them through their school years, careers, marriages, and friendships.

When we meet people like this, we say they're grounded. They know who they are and where they're going.

In the arc of what can be a long and successful career, you will always be in transit from "here" to "there." Here can be a great place. If you're successful, here is exactly the kind of place you want to be. But here is also a place where you can be a success in spite of some gaps in your behavior or personal makeup.

That's why you want to go "there." There can be a better place, where you can be a CEO who is viewed as a great leader because he doesn't get in the way of his people. You are here. You can get there. But you have to understand that what got you here won't get you there.

THE SUCCESS DELUSION, OR WHY WE RESIST CHANGE

In the workplace, many of us overestimate our contribution to a project, have an elevated opinion of our professional skills and standing among our peers, and take credit—partial or complete—for successes that truly belong to others.

We also conveniently ignore the costly failures and time-consuming dead ends we have created, while exaggerating our projects' impact on net profits because we discount the real and hidden costs built into them (costs are someone else's problems; success is ours).

All of these delusions are the result of success, not failure. That's because we get positive reinforcement from our past successes and think that type of validation is predictive of great things in our future. But our delusions become a serious liability when we need to change and someone tries to make us change.

First, we tend to think the other party is confused. Second, we go into denial. The criticism does not apply to us, or we wouldn't be so successful. When all else fails, we discredit the messenger: "Why is a smart guy like me listening to a loser like you?"

Couple these with the positive interpretations successful people assign to their past performance—their ability to influence their success, their belief that their success will continue in the future, and their sense of control over their own destiny—and you have a volatile cocktail of resistance to change.

The Four Key Beliefs of Successful People

There are four key beliefs that help you become successful. However, each can make it rough for you to change.

1. *I have succeeded.* To successful people, the past is always the prologue—and always rose-colored. This belief only becomes an obstacle when behavioral change is needed.

2. *I can succeed.* Successful people believe they have the capability within themselves to make desirable things happen—through sheer force of personality, talent, or brainpower, they can steer a situation in their direction.

3. *I will succeed.* Successful people have unflappable optimism. But it can easily mutate into excessive optimism. It explains why successful people tend to be extremely busy and face the danger of overcommitment. When the "do-nothings" are asked, "Why didn't you implement the behavioral change you said you would?" the most common response is, "I meant to, but I just didn't have time."

4. *I choose to succeed.* Successful people believe they are doing what they choose to do, because they choose to do it. Unfortunately, the more you believe your behavior is a result of your own choices and commitments, the less likely you are to want to change your behavior.

We All Obey Natural Law

The main natural law that has been witnessed while observing successful people's efforts to become more successful is: *People will do something—including changing their behavior—only if it can be demonstrated that doing so is in their own best interests as defined by their own values.* This is natural law. Every choice, big or small, is a risk-reward decision where your bottom-line thinking is, "What's in it for me?"

Most people's resistance to change can be overcome by invoking natural law. Everyone, even the biggest ego in the room, has a hot button that can be pushed—and that button is self-interest. It usually boils down to four items that are the standard payoff for success: money, power, status, and popularity.

Part II: The Twenty Habits That Hold You Back from the Top

THE TWENTY HABITS

When was the last retreat or training session at your organization titled, "Stupid Things Our Top People Do That We Need to Stop Doing Now"? Can you imagine your CEO (or immediate supervisor) admitting a personal failing in public and outlining his or her efforts to stop doing it? Probably not. Instead of your usual "To Do" list, start your "To Stop" list.

What's Wrong with Us?

The most common faults are a very specific breed of flaws. What we're dealing with are challenges in interpersonal behavior, often leadership behavior. They are the everyday annoyances that make your workplace more noxious than it needs to be. They are transactional flaws performed by one person against another.

These faults are simple to correct. For example, the cure for not thanking others enough is remembering to say "Thank you." For punishing the messenger, it's imagining how we'd like to be treated under similar circumstances. Check yourself against the list, then whittle it down to one or two vital issues, and you'll know where to start.

Habit No. 1: Winning Too Much

This is the most common behavioral problem in successful people. There's a fine line between being competitive and overcompetitive, between winning when it counts and when no one's counting—and successful people cross that line with alarming frequency.

Winning too much is the number-one challenge because it underlies nearly every other behavioral problem. If we argue too much, it's because we want our view to prevail. If we put down other people, it's our stealthy way of positioning them beneath us. If we ignore people, again it's about winning—by making them fade away. If you've achieved any modicum of success, you're guilty of this every day.

Habit No. 2: Adding Too Much Value

It is extremely difficult for successful people to listen to other people tell them something they already know without communicating somehow that "We already knew that" and "We know a better way."

The higher up you go, the more you need to make other people winners and not make it about winning yourself. This means closely monitoring how you hand out encouragement. If you find yourself saying, "Great idea," then dropping the other shoe with a "but" or "however," try cutting your response off at "idea." Even better, take a breath before you speak and ask yourself if what you're about to say is worth it.

Habit No. 3: Passing Judgment

There's nothing wrong with offering an opinion in the normal give-and-take of business discussions. But it's not appropriate to pass judgment when we specifically ask people to voice their opinions about us.

Try this: For one week treat every idea that comes your way from another person with complete neutrality. Don't take sides. Don't express an opinion. If you find yourself incapable of just saying "Thank you," make it an innocuous "Thanks, I hadn't considered that" or "Thanks, you've given me something to think about." You will significantly reduce the number of pointless arguments at work or home. If you continue this for several weeks, at least three good things will happen:

1. This sort of neutral response will become automatic.
2. You will dramatically reduce the hours you devote to contentious interfacing. When you don't judge an idea, no one can argue with you.
3. People will gradually begin to see you as a much more agreeable person, even when you are not agreeing with them. Do this consistently and people will eventually brand you as a welcoming person, someone whose door they can knock on when they have an idea.

Habit No. 4: Making Destructive Comments

These are the cutting sarcastic remarks that run the gamut from a thoughtless jab in a meeting to comments about how someone looks—"Nice tie" (with a smirk)—to elaborately planned critiques of people's past performances that everyone but you has forgotten ("Do you remember the time you . . .").

Before speaking, ask yourself:

1. Will this comment help our customers?
2. Will this comment help our company?
3. Will this comment help the person I'm talking to?
4. Will this comment help the person I'm talking about?

Habit No. 5: Starting with "No," "But," or "However"

When you start a sentence with any of these words or a variation thereof, no matter how friendly your tone or how many mollifying phrases you throw in to acknowledge the other person's feelings, the message to the other person is: *You are wrong.*

Stop trying to defend your position and start monitoring how many times you begin remarks with those three words. Pay special attention to moments when you use these words in a sentence whose ostensible purpose is to agree with what the other person is saying, for example, "That's true, however, . . ."

(meaning: You don't think it's true) or the very common opener, "Yes, but . . ." (meaning: Prepare to be contradicted).

Habit No. 6: Telling the World How Smart We Are

This is another variation on our need to win. We need to be the smartest person in the room, but it usually backfires. We do it when we agree with someone offering us practical advice, whenever we nod our heads impatiently while people are talking, when we drum our fingers on the table. We do it more overtly when we tell someone, "I already knew that" or alternative phrasings such as, "I didn't need to hear that," or "I'm five steps ahead of you." We're insulting the other person.

Stopping this behavior is not hard. Try this three-step drill:

1. Pause before you open your mouth to ask yourself, "Is anything I say worth it?"
2. Conclude that it isn't.
3. Say "Thank you."

Habit No. 7: Speaking When Angry

When you get angry, you are usually out of control. It's hard to lead people this way. The worst thing about anger is how it stifles our ability to change. Once you get a reputation for emotional volatility, you are branded for life. Pretty soon that is all people know about you. To lose your reputation as a person who gets angry, just follow one simple piece of advice: *If you keep your mouth shut, no one can ever know how you really feel.*

Habit No. 8: Negativity, or "Let Me Explain Why That Won't Work"

We all know negative people in the workplace. They're incapable of saying something positive or complimentary to any of your suggestions. You could walk into the office with a cure for cancer and the first words out of their mouths would be, "Let me explain why that won't work."

That is the telltale phrase of negativity. It's a major annoyance because it's emblematic of our need to share our negative thoughts even when they haven't been solicited. It is pure, unadulterated negativity under the guise of being helpful.

If you catch yourself saying this frequently, you know what needs fixing. Seeing how people relate to you provides proof that your flaw is serious, it matters to people, and it's a problem.

Habit No. 9: Withholding Information

In the age of knowledge workers, information is power. Intentionally withholding information is the opposite of adding value. Yet it has the same purpose—to gain power. Reflect how you feel about these events:

- A meeting you weren't told about.
- A memo or e-mail you weren't copied on.
- A moment when you were the last person to learn something.

Not sharing information rarely achieves the desired effect. In order to have power, you need to inspire loyalty rather than fear and suspicion. Here are the unintentional or accidental ways you can withhold information:

- Being too busy to get back to someone with valuable information.
- Forgetting to include someone in your discussions or meetings.
- Delegating a task to a subordinate, but not taking the time to show them how to get it done.

So how do you stop withholding information? Start sharing it.

Habit No. 10: Failing to Give Proper Recognition

This is a sibling of withholding information. In withholding recognition of another person's contribution to a team's success, you are not only sowing injustice and treating people unfairly, but also depriving people of the emotional payoff that comes with success. They feel forgotten, ignored, and pushed to the side.

Habit No. 11: Claiming Credit That We Don't Deserve

When someone steals the credit for a success you created, they're committing the most rage-inducing interpersonal "crime" in the workplace. It creates a bitterness that's hard to forget. You can forgive someone for not recognizing your stellar performance. You can't forgive that person for recognizing it and brazenly claiming it as his or her own.

The best way to stop being a credit hog is to do the opposite—share the wealth. Here's a simple drill:

For one day (or longer) make a mental note of every time you privately congratulate yourself on an achievement, large or small. Then write it down. You'll find you pat yourself on the back more often than you think.

Once you've assembled the list, ask yourself if it's in any way possible that someone else might deserve the credit. For example, if you showed up on time for a meeting, is it because you are punctual and thoughtful? Or because your assistant hounded you about the meeting, chased you off a phone call, and made sure you were out the door to get there in time?

As you go through your list, consider this make-or-break question: If any of the other people involved in your episodes were looking at the situation, would they give you as much credit as you are claiming for yourself? Or would they hand it to someone else, perhaps even themselves?

Habit No. 12: Making Excuses

You can divide excuses into two categories: blunt and subtle. Blunt excuses sound like: "I'm sorry I missed our lunch date. My assistant marked it down for the wrong day on my calendar." However, the message is: "See, it's not that I forgot the lunch date. It's not that I don't regard you as important. It's that my assistant is inept. Blame my assistant, not me."

The problem with this type of excuse is that we rarely get away with it—and it's hardly an effective leadership strategy.

The more subtle excuses appear when we attribute our failings to some inherited DNA: "I'm impatient" or "I am horrendous at time management. I guess that's just the way I am." The next time you hear yourself saying, "I'm just not good at . . ." ask yourself, "Why not?"

Habit No. 13: Clinging to the Past

People who cling to the past—who want to understand why they are the way they are—can't change the past, rewrite it, or make excuses for it. All they can do is accept it and move on.

But for some reason, many people enjoy living in the past, especially if going back there lets them blame someone else for anything that's gone wrong in their lives. That's when clinging to the past becomes an interpersonal problem. We use the past as a weapon against others. We also use the past as a way of contrasting it with the present—usually to highlight something positive about ourselves at the expense of someone else, for example, "When I was your age . . ."

Habit No. 14: Playing Favorites

If we aren't careful, we can end up treating people at work like dogs—rewarding those who heap thoughtless, unconditional admiration on us.

The net result is obvious: You're encouraging behavior that serves you, but not necessarily in the best interest of the company. If everyone is fawning over the boss, who's getting the work done? Worse, it tilts the field against honest, principled employees who won't play along. This is a double hit of bad news. You're not only playing favorites but favoring the wrong people!

Habit No. 15: Refusing to Express Regret

Whatever the reason, refusing to apologize causes as much ill will in the workplace as any other interpersonal flaw. People who can't apologize might as well wear a T-shirt that says, "I don't care about you." The irony is that all the fears that lead us to resist apologizing are actually erased by an apology. When you tell someone "I'm sorry," you turn people into your allies.

The best thing about apologizing is that it forces everyone to let go of the past. When you employ it on co-workers it can have a great effect on how they feel about you and themselves.

Habit No. 16: Not Listening

People will tolerate all sorts of rudeness, but the inability to pay attention holds a special place in their hearts. When you're not listening you're sending out an armada of negative messages. The reality for leaders of the past and leaders in the future is that *in the past, very bright people would put up with disrespectful behavior, but in the future they will leave!*

Habit No. 17: Failing to Express Gratitude

Often, the two sweetest words in the English language are "Thank you." Although there's no art to saying it, people have a tough time executing this rudimentary maneuver.

If you don't know what to say, your default response to any suggestion should be "Thank you." Almost any response other than this has the potential to stir up trouble. Intentionally or not, you appear as if you are attacking the person talking to you.

Habit No. 18: Punishing the Messenger

Punishing the messenger is not merely the unjust retaliatory action we take against a whistle-blower or the angry tirade we heap on an employee who tells us something we don't enjoy hearing. It's also the small responses we make throughout the day whenever we are inconvenienced or disappointed.

It's the expletive you neglect to delete in a meeting when a subordinate announces a deal fell apart. If you had calmly asked, "What went wrong?" no damage would be done. The subordinate would explain and everyone in the room would be wiser for it.

However, the flash of temper sends a different signal. It says: "If you want to tick off the boss, surprise him or her with bad news." To stop this bad habit, all you need to say is "Thank you."

Habit No. 19: Passing the Buck

This is the behavioral flaw by which we judge leaders. A leader who cannot shoulder the blame is not someone we will follow blindly into battle. Passing the buck is the dark flip side of claiming credit that others deserve. Instead of depriving others of their rightful glory for a success, you wrongfully saddle them with the shame of your failure.

You're not fooling anyone—except perhaps yourself—and no matter how much you think you're saving your hide, you're actually killing it.

Habit No. 20: An Excessive Need to Be "Me"

This is the chronic behavior, both positive and negative, that we think of as our inalterable essence. If we're chronically poor at returning phone calls—whether because we're overcommitted, we're simply rude, or we believe if people really need to talk to us they'll call again until they get through—we mentally give ourselves a pass every time we fail to get back to callers: "Hey, that's me. Deal with it."

It's easy to make a virtue of our flaws—simply because flaws constitute what we think of as "me." This is one of the toughest obstacles to making positive long-term change in our behavior. But it doesn't need to be.

That's because it's not about you. It's about what other people think of you. The less you focus on your need to "be me" and the more you consider what your staff is feeling, the more it will benefit you.

FOUR STEPS TO POSITIVE RECOGNITION

1. Make a list of all the important groups of people in your life.
2. Write down the name of every important person in each group.
3. Twice a week, review the list of names and ask, "Did someone on this page do something that I should recognize?"
4. If the answer is yes, give quick recognition, either by phone, e-mail, voice mail, or a note. If the answer is no, do nothing.

Within a year, your reputation for providing positive recognition can improve from poor to excellent.

THE TWENTY-FIRST HABIT: GOAL OBSESSION

Goal obsession stands apart from the other twenty habits, not because it is a flaw, but because it is often the root cause of an annoying behavior. The habit is the force at play when we get so wrapped up in achieving our goal that we do it at the expense of a larger mission.

Goal obsession comes from misunderstanding what you want in your life. You think you'd be truly happy if you made more money, lost thirty pounds, or got the corner office. So you pursue those goals relentlessly. You don't appreciate until later that in obsessing about making more money, you might be neglecting the loved ones for whom you are presumably securing that money.

It also comes from misunderstanding what others want you to do. A boss tells you that you have to show 10 percent revenue growth for the year, so when it appears you will miss that target, goal obsession forces you to adopt questionable, less-than-honest methods of hitting the target. If you examine it more closely, you're not obsessed with hitting the 10 percent growth; your true goal is pleasing your boss.

PRACTICING "FEEDFORWARD"

Feedforward is feedback going in the opposite direction. If feedback reports on how you functioned In the past, then feedforward comes in the form of ideas that you can put into practice in the future. Feedforward asks you to do four simple things:

1. Pick one behavior you would like to change that would make a significant difference in your life.
2. Describe this objective in a one-on-one dialogue to anyone you know.
3. Ask that person for two suggestions for the future that might help you achieve a positive change in your selected behavior. The only ground rule is there can be no mention of the past. Everything is about the future.
4. Listen attentively to the suggestions. Take notes if you want. The only ground rule is you are not allowed to judge, rate, or critique the suggestions. You can't even say anything positive. The only response you're permitted is "Thank you."

These are the classic conditions of the goal obsessed, which makes it all the more important to reflect:

- Am I achieving a task—and forgetting my organization?
- Am I making money to support my family—and forgetting the family I am trying to support?
- Am I on time to deliver a sermon to my staff—and forgetting to practice what I preach?
- After all this effort I don't want to find myself at a dead end, asking, "What have I done?"

Part III: How We Can Change for the Better

FEEDBACK

Feedback has always been with us. Formal up-the-ladder feedback designed to help managers appeared in the middle of the twentieth century with the first suggestion box. A more recent development is 360-degree feedback, which is solicited from everybody at all levels of the organization. Here are five ways to get feedback by paying closer attention to the world around you:

1. *Make a list of people's casual remarks about you.* Examples: "That was really smart" or "You're late." Then do it the next day and the next. Do it at home too, if you want. Eventually you'll compile enough data about yourself to establish the challenge before you.
2. *Observe how people deal with you.* Do they listen when you have the floor or are they drumming their fingers? A variation on this drill is to make sure you're the first person to arrive at a meeting. Observe how people respond to you as they enter. Do they pull up a chair next to you? Or do they barely acknowledge your presence and sit across the room?
3. *Complete the sentence.* Pick the one thing you want to get better at, then list the positive benefits that will accrue to you and the world if you achieve it. For example, "If I get in shape, one benefit to me is that . . ." and then complete the sentence. As you get deeper into this exercise, your answers will become less corporately correct and more personal. That's when you know you've hit on an interpersonal skill that you really want and need to improve.
4. *Listen to your self-aggrandizing remarks.* None of us is immune to this phenomenon. What do you boast about? It's possible that if you assess this alleged "strength" as closely as your friends do, it's really a weakness. You shouldn't be bragging about it at all.

5. *Look homeward.* Your flaws at work don't vanish when you walk through the door at home.

Feedback tells us what to change, not how to do it. But when you know what to change, you're ready to start changing yourself and how people perceive you. You're ready for the next step: telling everyone you're sorry.

TELLING THE WORLD, OR ADVERTISING

After you apologize, you must advertise. You have to declare in what area you intend to change. You have to be your own press secretary. You can't just apologize and say you're trying to be better just once. You have to drill it into people repeatedly, until they've internalized the concept. Here's how to act like your own press secretary:

• Treat every day as if it were a press conference during which your colleagues are judging you, waiting to see you trip up. That mind-set will boost your self-awareness enough to remind you to stay on high alert.
• Behave as if every day is an opportunity to hit home your message—to remind people you're trying really hard.
• Treat every day as a chance to take on all challengers. There will be people who don't want you to succeed. So be a little paranoid. If you're alert to those who want you to fail, you'll know how to handle them.
• Think of the process as an election campaign. You don't elect yourself to the position of "new improved you." Your colleagues do.
• Think of the process in terms of weeks and months, not just day to day.

LISTENING

Eighty percent of our success in learning from other people is based on how well we listen. Most people think listening is a passive activity. Not true. Good listeners regard what they do as a highly active process—with every muscle engaged, especially the brain. There are three things good listeners do:

1. Think before they speak.
2. Listen with respect.
3. Gauge their response by asking themselves, "Is it worth it?"

The ability to make a person feel that he or she is the most important (and only) person in the room is the skill that separates the great from the near-great. The great ones do it all the time.

EXPRESSING GRATITUDE

Thanking people works because it expresses one of our most basic emotions: gratitude. When someone does something nice for you, they expect gratitude—and think less of you for withholding it.

The best thing about saying "Thank you" is that it creates closure in any potentially explosive discussion. What can you say after someone thanks you? You can't argue with them. You can't try to prove them wrong. You can't trump them, get angry, or ignore them.

FOLLOWING UP

People need to go back to all their co-workers every month or so and ask for comments and suggestions. If you do this every month, your colleagues eventually begin to accept that you're getting better—not because you say so but because it's coming from their lips.

Follow-up is the most protracted part of the process of changing for the better. It goes on for twelve to eighteen months. It's the difference-maker in the process. More than anything, though, follow-up makes you do it, because by engaging in the follow-up process, you are *changing*.

Part IV: Pulling Out the Stops

CHANGING: THE RULES

The following eight rules will help you get a better handle on the process of change. If you obey them, you'll be stacking the deck in your favor.

1. You might not have a disease that behavioral change can cure. Sometimes feedback reveals a symptom, not a disease. For instance, one CEO's feedback was all positive, but he felt completely at sea with changing technology. The solution was not behavioral change, but getting a tech guru to mentor him.
2. Pick the right thing to change. Successful people have a tendency to overcommit. If you list seven flaws, you'll want to tackle all of them. Turn your attention to the one vital flaw that needs fixing.
3. Don't delude yourself about what you *really* must change.
4. Don't hide from the truth you need to hear.
5. There is no ideal behavior. The perfect benchmark human being, like the perfect benchmark organization, does not exist. No matter how many of the successful attributes for the model executive you could list that you *don't* embody, the real question is, how bad is the problem?

6. If you can measure it, you can achieve it. Measuring is the only way you can know for sure how you're doing.
7. Monetize the result, then create a solution. There are all sorts of ways to encourage people to change their behavior—from bonuses to vacations.
8. The best time to change is now. It's time to stop dreaming of a time when you won't be busy, because the time will never come. Ask yourself, "What am I willing to change now?"

YOU ARE HERE NOW

Research was conducted involving more than two hundred high-potential leaders from companies around the world. These are people who could jump at a moment's notice to better-paying positions elsewhere. Each was asked a simple question: "If you stay in this company, why are you going to stay?" The three top answers were:

1. "I am finding meaning and happiness now. The work is exciting and I love what I am doing."
2. "I like the people. They are my friends. This feels like a team, like a family."
3. "I can follow my dreams. This organization is giving me a chance to do what I really want to do in life."

The answers were never about money. They were always about happiness, relationships, following dreams, and meaning. Use that wisdom now. Don't look ahead.

Look behind. Look back from your old age at the life you hope to live. You are here. You can get there! Let the journey begin.

JUDGMENT
by Noel M. Tichy and Warren G. Bennis

Management gurus know how to transmit their leadership wisdom in compelling and thoughtful ways, and both Dr. Noel M. Tichy and Warren G. Bennis more than qualify for the title. After spending decades studying leadership and advising top CEOs, including General Electric's Jack Welch and Starbucks's Howard Schultz, these two authors have discovered how important leadership judgment can be for leaders and their organizations.

When Tichy and Bennis write about decision making in their book *Judgment: How Winning Leaders Make Great Calls,* they combine experiences from two careers spent analyzing those discoveries and helping top leaders make valuable judgment calls. Their personal histories in business and academia span many decades of making important choices and advising others how they can exercise the best judgment at the right time.

The judgments that define effective leadership are those that entail people, strategy, and crisis. In *Judgment,* Tichy and Bennis reflect on the process of making smart decisions by dividing it into three parts: preparation, the judgment call, and the execution of the decision that has been made. By illustrating the process with the experiences of dozens of successful and failed leaders at the tops of a variety of organizations, they help managers and executives discover how they can make better decisions and support better decision making within their organizations.

Tichy and Bennis are experts in judgment because they both have worked with world leaders and CEOs at many Fortune 500 companies, including GE, Best Buy, PepsiCo, Coca-Cola, GM, Nokia, 3M, Daimler-Benz, and Royal Dutch Shell, helping them make better judgment calls on numerous issues. These calls include selecting strategy, choosing team members and CEO succession, creating organizational and self-knowledge, and managing crises.

Tichy had an enormous impact at GE in the mid-1980s as the head of Crotonville, GE's world-renowned leadership center in upstate New York. While serving as the manager of management education for GE, he directed its global development efforts at Crotonville. Before that, he served for nearly a decade as a faculty member at Columbia University Business School. Today, Tichy is a professor at the University of Michigan Business School and advises CEOs around the world.

BusinessWeek and *Business 2.0* have rated Tichy as one of the "Top 10 Management Gurus." His book *The Leadership Engine: How Winning Companies Build Leaders at Every Level*, written with Eli Cohen, was a *BusinessWeek* "Book of the Year." He is also the author of *The Ethical Challenge, Control Your Destiny or Someone Else Will*, and *The Cycle of Leadership*.

Warren Bennis's career as a pioneer of the contemporary field of leadership studies is equally remarkable. Back in 1961, in a *Harvard Business Review* article titled "Revisionist Theory of Leadership," he set a new path for leadership studies by converting his work at MIT into a challenge to the prevailing thinking of the times. In that article, he proclaimed that leaders with more humanistic, democratic styles are better suited to lead in a marketplace that is charged with more complexity and change than those of previous eras.

Bennis is also the author of *On Becoming a Leader, Reinventing Leadership*, and many other best-selling business books. In addition, he is the founding chairman of The Leadership Institute at the University of Southern California. Today, as a USC professor of business administration and a consultant for many Fortune 500 companies, he spends his days helping future and current leaders make better judgments.

In *Judgment*, the authors write that judgment is the essence of leadership. Leading any group of people entails challenges, including ambiguity, conflicting demands, time constraints, and money pressures. These pressures require sound judgments by smart leaders. Tichy and Bennis explain that the main way leaders add value to their organizations is through the decisions they make and the actions they take to enact their choices. Good judgments—including the smart execution of those judgments and their results—define the leaders who make them.

Judgment explores the wide range of decisions that have pulled organizations together and torn them apart. Examining the role of decision making in the business world and beyond, Tichy and Bennis have helped to expand the scope of the judgment discipline into a unique and viable field of study. By recognizing the potential gains in management and leadership understanding that can be made by growing the field of judgment with deeper study and observation, they bring greater insight into the ways managers and leaders make the best choices.

JUDGMENT

How Winning Leaders Make Great Calls

by Noel M. Tichy and Warren G. Bennis

CONTENTS

THE SUMMARY IN BRIEF

Two titans of effective leadership, Noel M. Tichy and Warren G. Bennis, have identified the fundamental essence of leadership as the ability to make consistently good judgment calls, especially when the stakes are high, information is limited, and the right call is far from obvious.

The authors of *Judgment* clarify an important concept that is often misunderstood. Many assume that good judgment is an inborn trait, but Tichy and Bennis show that it's actually a skill that can be developed, refined, and nurtured throughout an organization.

Leaders do, at some moment, make a judgment call, a determination about how things should proceed. Judgment resides at the core of leadership. The authors explain that judgment is a contextually informed decision-making process encompassing three domains: people, strategy, and crisis. And within each domain, leadership judgment follows a three-phase process: preparation, the call, and execution.

Leaders are remembered for their best and worst judgment calls. In the face of ambiguity, uncertainty, and conflicting demands, the quality of a leader's judgment determines the fate of the entire organization.

Tichy and Bennis show how to recognize the critical moment before a judgment call, when swift and decisive action is essential, and also how to execute a decision after the call.

This summary provides ground rules for leaders. Whether they are running a small department or a vast corporation, the authors' insight will help leaders achieve greater success by exercising good judgment.

What You'll Learn in This Summary

- A useful framework that will help leaders make better judgments and help shape the next generation to do the same.
- How to address the most vexing questions leaders confront when making their most important judgments.
- How to improve your own judgment-making faculties.
- How to do a better, more intentional job of developing good judgments in others.
- Why some leaders are better equipped to deal with crises than others.

THE COMPLETE SUMMARY

JUDGMENT AND LEADERSHIP

On November 1, 1997, AT&T was a $130 billion company when Michael Armstrong became CEO. It wasn't the powerhouse it had been for much of its hundred-plus-year history, but it had a stockpile of cash and plenty of opportunity. For the next eight years nothing seemed to work for AT&T, and Armstrong's long string of poor strategic judgments finally caught up with him, bringing his career to an unenviable end. In 2005 a nearly dead-broke AT&T was acquired by its former subsidiary SBC (Southwestern Bell Corp.) for a paltry $16.9 billion. Only its name survived on the combined company.

General Electric Co.'s stock had suffered in the wake of the stock market crash of 2001, but Jeff Immelt was succeeding CEO Jack Welch, dubbed "manager of the century" by *Fortune* magazine and *BusinessWeek*.

Welch had left GE after failing to complete the huge $47 billion acquisition of

Honeywell he had attempted in the final hours of his twenty-year reign. But the company was still a huge dynamo, and Immelt's job was to find a way to keep generating more power. With revenues of $130 billion in 2000, Immelt would have to come up with $3.5 billion in new revenue every quarter to maintain the torrid 10 percent annual growth pace set by Welch. To do that, Immelt took bold steps to reinvent the company. He shifted the company's primary business model to capitalize on emerging technologies and emerging markets. By mid-2007 the stock market was rewarding his efforts. Immelt had succeeded in delivering average growth of some 8 percent per year, no small feat for a $100-billion-plus juggernaut.

Armstrong, former AT&T CEO, could not turn his company around and lost significant shareholder value in a short span of time and ultimately lost his job as well. Immelt and Welch at GE faced no easier challenges, yet they and their organization ride from success to success. When they stumble they are able to recover quickly. Why is that? It's a matter of *judgment*.

Judgment Calls

The cumulative effect of the leaders' judgment calls determines the success or failure of their organizations.

The essence of leadership is judgment. The single most important thing that leaders do is make good judgment calls. In the face of ambiguity, uncertainty, and conflicting demands, often under great time pressure, leaders must make decisions and take effective actions to assure the survival and success of their organizations. This is how leaders add value to their organizations. They lead them to success by exercising good judgment, by making smart calls, and by ensuring that they are well executed. A keen sense of judgment is what makes or breaks a leader.

Getting the Important Ones Right

The thing that really matters is not *how many* calls a leader gets right or even what *percentage* of calls a leader gets right. Rather, it is how many of the *important* ones he or she gets right. Good leaders not only make better calls, but they are able to discern the really important ones and get a higher percentage of them right. They are better at a whole process that runs from seeing the need for a call to framing issues to figuring out what is critical to mobilizing and energizing the troops.

FRAMEWORK FOR LEADERSHIP JUDGMENT

Despite the implications of the word *call*, the judgment calls that leaders make cannot be viewed as single, point-in-time events. Like umpires and referees, leaders do, at some moment, make a call. They make a determination about how things should proceed. But unlike umpires and referees, they cannot—without risking total failure—quickly forget them and move ahead to the next play. Rather, for a leader, the moment of making the call comes in the middle of a process.

That process begins with the leader recognizing the need for a judgment and continues through successful execution. A leader is said to have "good judgment" when he or she repeatedly makes judgment calls that turn out well. These calls frequently turn out well because the leader has mastered a complex, constantly morphing process that unfolds in several dimensions. There are three phases to the process:

1. *Time*. This includes what happens before the leader makes the decision, what the leader does as he or she makes the decision that helps it turn out to be the right one, and what the leader must oversee to make sure the call produces the desired results.
2. *Domain*. The three critical domains in which the majority of the most important calls are required are judgments about *people*, judgments about *strategy*, and judgments in time of *crisis*.
3. *Constituencies*. Leaders make the calls, but they do it in relation to the world around them. A leader's relationships are the sources of the information needed to make a successful call. A leader must interact with different constituencies and manage those relationships to make successful calls. The four types of knowledge needed to do this are self-knowledge, social network knowledge, organizational knowledge, and contextual knowledge.

The Three Judgment Domains

People, strategy, and crisis are the three domains that make the most difference to the survival and well-being of any institution. If they are unattended or if bad calls are made in these domains, it can be fatal to an organization.

1. *People judgment calls*. If leaders don't make smart judgment calls about the people on their teams, or if they manage them poorly, then there is no way leaders can set a sound direction and strategy for the enterprise, nor can they effectively deal with crises.
2. *Strategy judgment calls*. The role of the leader is to lead the organization to success, so when the current strategic road isn't leading toward success, it is his or her job to find a new path. How well a leader makes strategic judgment calls is a function of both (1) his or her own ability to look

over the horizon and frame the right question and (2) the people with whom he or she chooses to interact.

3. *Crisis judgment calls.* Crisis calls require that a leader have clear values and know his or her ultimate goal. Crises not handled well, where good judgment calls were not made, can lead to the demise of an institution.

The Process of Judgment Calls

In all three domains, people, strategy, and crisis, good judgment calls always involve a process that starts with recognizing the need for the call and continues through to successful execution:

- *The preparation phase.* This phase includes sensing and identifying the need for a judgment call, framing and naming the judgment call, and mobilizing and aligning the right people.
- *The call phase: Making the judgment call.* There is a moment when, based on his or her view of the time horizon for the judgment and sufficiency of input and involvement, the leader makes the call.
- *The execution phase: Action—make it happen.* Execution is a critical part of the exercise of good judgment. Once a clear call is made, then resources, people, capital, information, and technology must be mobilized to support it. If they aren't, the decision making simply goes down the tubes. Good judgment calls always produce good results.

Resources and Constituencies

The quality of a person's judgment depends to a large degree on his or her ability to marshal resources and to interact well with the appropriate constituencies. Most of the time the resources and the interested constituencies overlap. A good leader uses four types of knowledge to make judgment calls:

1. *Self-knowledge.* Leaders who exercise good judgment calls are able to listen, reframe their thinking, and give up old paradigms. GE's CEO Jeff Immelt said, "It is an intense journey into yourself."

2. *Social network knowledge.* Leadership is a team sport; there must be alignment of the leader's team, the organization, and critical stakeholders to create the ongoing capacity for good judgment calls. The leader must consciously work to encourage teamwork, draw on the best resources of each individual, and help individuals learn to make better judgments in their own areas of responsibility.

3. *Organizational knowledge.* Good leaders work hard to continuously enhance the team, organizational, and stakeholder capacity at all levels to make good judgment calls.
4. *Stakeholder knowledge.* Good leaders engage customers, suppliers, the community, and boards in generating knowledge to support better judgments.

HAVING A STORYLINE

How a leader works the judgment process depends to a great extent on who the leader is. Winning leaders, the ones who continually make the best judgment calls, have clear mental frameworks to guide their thinking. They have stories running in their heads about how the world works and how they want things to turn out. And they have the all-important qualities of character and courage. They have the internal discipline and the guts to make the right calls and to follow through.

Teachable Points of View

Winning leaders are teachers. They drive their organizations through teaching, and they develop others to be leaders/teachers.

Winning leaders are good at this because they have made the effort and spent the time to develop Teachable Points of View (TPOVs). TPOVs are what enable leaders to take the valuable knowledge and experiences that they have stored up inside their heads and teach them to others. Winning leaders/teachers use their TPOVs to convey ideas and values to energize others and to help them make clear, decisive decisions.

While TPOVs are essential to transformational leadership and to developing others as leaders, TPOVs have an equally crucial role to play in guiding leaders' own decisions and actions.

The TPOV comes alive and is most valuable when a leader weaves it into a storyline for the future success of the organization. As a living story, it both helps the leader make the judgment calls that will make the story become a reality and enlists and energizes others to make it happen.

TPOVs and Storylines

Dr. Martin Luther King Jr.'s "I Have a Dream" speech, delivered at the Lincoln Memorial in 1963, is one of the most famous and compelling examples of a leader transforming a clear, logical TPOV into a vivid and inspirational storyline. The goal of achieving it drove both King's decisions and the success of the civil rights movement.

Winning leaders' storylines specifically address three areas of questions:

1. *Where are we now?*
2. *Where are we going?* The inspirational storyline here adds to the motivation for change, but more important, it lights the beacon. It defines the goal.
3. *How are we going to get there?*

The storyline is never complete and is always being modified by the judgments the leader makes. However, without a solid storyline, the leader's judgments are disconnected acts that may or may not move the organization forward.

Jack Welch and Peter Drucker

In the case of Jack Welch, interactions with management pioneer Peter Drucker had a powerful impact on his strategic thinking. Soon after he became CEO of GE, Welch had a meeting with Drucker. As they discussed GE's various businesses, Drucker, Welch recounts, asked him at one point: "If you weren't already in this business today, would you go into it?" It was a question that crystallized Welch's thinking and ultimately resulted in his famous "#1, #2, fix, close, or sell strategy."

CHARACTER AND COURAGE

What does it mean to have character? It means having values. It means having a moral compass that sets clear parameters for what one will and will not do. Character is all about knowing right from wrong and having worked these issues out long before facing tough judgment calls. It is about knowing what your goals and standards are and sticking with them.

Integrity

We often use the word *integrity* to describe a person of character, a person whose values and principles are above reproach. Psychiatry speaks of such people as *integrated*. Character plays the guiding role in how honest personal feedback and coaching are in the organization, how internal competition and politics are handled, and how suppliers and customers are treated. The CEO's character sets the stage for all the important judgment calls.

Character also means putting the greater good of the organization, or of society, ahead of self-interest. As management legend Peter Drucker put it, it is about worrying about "what is right" rather than "who is right."

Courage

Judgment is about more than decision making. It is about not only coming up with the right solution to the right problem, but it is also producing results. And this is where courage comes in. Having the courage to act on your standards is an integral part of the bundle of what it takes to exercise good judgment. The standards by themselves aren't enough. If you don't act on your "standards," there is some question as to whether they really are your standards.

It's the courage that Procter & Gamble showed in closing down plants in Africa for a year rather than pay bribes. It is the courage to take the hard road, despite all the obstacles, because you should.

Leading with Character

Trust is the emotional glue that holds teams together. Steelcase CEO Jim Hackett said, "You can't lead if you don't have trust, and you can't have trust if you don't have integrity."

Leading with character gives wise leaders clear-cut advantages. They are easier to trust and follow; they honor commitments and promises; their words and behavior match; they are always engaged in and by the world; they are open to "reflective back talk"; they can admit errors and learn from their mistakes. They can speak with conviction because they believe in what they are saying. They feel at ease in the spotlight and they enjoy it there. They tend to be more open to opportunity and risk.

People Judgment Calls

To make good people judgments, a leader has to recognize the need, frame the issue, and mobilize and align the parties who can provide the information and advice needed to make a good call. Then the leader must make the call at the appropriate moment and follow through on the execution to make sure that the result turns out as well as possible.

People judgments are the most complex of the three domains for several reasons. First, a judgment about whether someone will be a good leader is a judgment call about how well the person will do making other judgment calls. Will he or she be able to build a good team? Develop effective strategy? Deal with the inevitable crises?

Complex Dynamics

People calls also have other distinct challenges. Unlike strategies, the "objects" of people judgments are humans who make their own judgment calls and engage their own political circles even as the process unfolds. In a competitive world, no judgment call is ever made in a static situation. But in people calls, the dynamics are more complex, if not more fluid, than in other realms.

No matter how hard-nosed some leaders may appear, they all have emotions that affect their judgments. They have feelings about other people. They become attached to them or maybe detest them. And it's these feelings that can keep them from making good, objective calls.

Wayne Downing

Wayne Downing, the retired four-star general who ran the United States Army Special Forces, said that "most of my bad judgment calls were generally about people. There have been times when I knew I had to take people out of a position. I knew they weren't going to change, and they weren't going to do what had to be done. But it's traumatic when you do that. The higher up you go, the more traumatic it is for the organization to remove people, and you don't like to do that, but in the final analysis you have to."

Aware that the ultimate goal is to produce a successful outcome, leaders who have good judgment track records are always vigilant. They are constantly checking to make sure that conditions are as favorable as they can possibly make them to support the success of the judgment. If they need to take time and expand the decision-making process, they do.

People judgment comes first. If there is not a team of trusted leaders, it is impossible to make good strategy judgments as the people politics will undermine what is good for the enterprise.

PEOPLE JUDGMENT: CEO SUCCESSION

Who heads up an institution is by far the single most important people judgment. CEO succession in any type of organization is the key determinant of organizational performance. This seemingly obvious premise must be examined in light of the empirical reality of success in the last decade. The track record in many companies has been abysmal. Given the importance of this judgment, the grade among blue-chip companies is probably no more than a D, as many blue-chip companies have failed to develop a successor CEO.

Not to have a successor at the top of an institution is the ultimate in bad people judgment. The preparation phase includes a long-term commitment to developing a stream of talent, a leadership pipeline, designed to develop leaders at all levels and ensure a flow of leaders. There are multiple candidates and a succession pipeline that feeds opportunities at lower levels in the organization.

Bad CEO Judgments

Bad CEO judgments happen because of broken leadership pipelines; that is, there are no good candidates and the building of appropriate leadership bench strength has not occurred. There are a variety of underlying causes. In some cases it is family nepotism, such as putting Bill Ford in as CEO at Ford. After only a few years, Ford stepped out of the role and brought in an outsider, Alan Mulally from Boeing, as CEO in mid-2006.

Other causes of broken leadership pipelines include lack of a disciplined succession planning process, board neglect, poor understanding of changing world and talent requirements, and ego issues with the CEO not wanting to let go. Any combination of these problems contributes to bad CEO succession judgment.

Key Elements of Good People Judgments

Here are six lessons for making good people judgments:

1. Anticipate the need for key people changes.
2. Specify the leadership requirements looking into the future, not the rearview mirror.
3. Mobilize and align the social network to support the "right" call.
4. Make the process transparent and judged fair.
5. Make it happen.
6. Provide continuous support to help the leader succeed.

STRATEGY JUDGMENTS

For a leader, developing strategy is a never-ending job of crafting the storyline for success. It is rarely an "aha" clear vision. It is an evolving story that starts off fuzzy. It gets continuously revised and becomes clearer as strategic judgments are made. Each big acquisition or divestiture, or judgment on a big R&D investment, changes the company's position and the possibilities for the future. These judgments are not only manifestations of the storyline, but also shapers of it going forward.

Jeff Immelt's Storyline

Immelt's judgment about the acquisition of Amersham by GE Healthcare for close to $10 billion reflected his storyline of building a medical business around tomorrow's technology for personalized medicine. Thus he manifested his storyline by making an acquisition consistent with where he wanted the business to go. The judgment then sets up a process of reshaping the business in new and unforeseen ways; the Amersham judgment leads to authoring the next chapter of the future. The iterative process of making judgments to further the storyline, which then helps write and revise the future storyline, is how leaders like Immelt drive successful transformations.

Good Strategic Judgment

Good strategic judgment is built on the leader's capacity to intellectually frame the world of opportunity and the organization's potential, as well as the leader's ability to mobilize and align key leaders to help make a smart judgment and get it executed. Like all good judgments, strategic judgments need to be a process: (1) preparation, (2) the call, and (3) execution.

Strategy judgments alter where the organization is heading. They require the leadership to have a clear TPOV and storyline and then have the courage to make the calls and see that they follow through on the execution.

STRATEGY JUDGMENTS AT GE

CEO Jeff Immelt was on the line in 2007 for his GE strategy judgments. He spent five years repositioning GE for future growth; he needed to now demonstrate that his strategic judgments would yield the promised results. His is a work in progress. He has dropped businesses from the portfolio, a never-ending process, and is adding new ones through acquisitions and organic growth to create the GE future engines of growth. Five years into the transformation, his judgments were showing clear evidence of being rewarded in the stock market.

Immelt states: "To be a reliable growth company requires the ability to conceptualize the future. We are investing to capitalize on the major growth trends of this era that will grow at multiples of the global GDP growth rate. We are using our breadth, financial strength, and intellectual capital to create a competitive advantage." Immelt is relentless in sharing his storyline and relentless in driving the strategy execution.

CRISIS JUDGMENTS

Good judgments made during times of crisis follow the same process as judgments made under less stressed circumstances. There is a preparation phase, a call phase, and an execution phase. The preparation phase, however, needs to be done before the crisis occurs.

The most effective leaders prepare for crisis even before knowing what kind of crisis will occur. It is perhaps even more true in crisis situations than with judgments about people and strategy that the likelihood of making successful calls is vastly increased if they are made in the context of a pre-existing

Teachable Point of View (TPOV) and on the platform of the storyline for the future.

Leaders generally make bad crisis judgments either because they lack a clear TPOV and storyline or because they have made bad people judgments. For leaders to handle crises effectively, they must have an aligned team. Otherwise, the crisis situation will splinter the team just when smart, coherent action is needed most. Bad people judgments or bad strategy judgments can precipitate a crisis, but once one happens, teamwork and focus make all the difference between survival and disaster.

Crisis Judgment Compresses Time and Root Causes

The reason crisis is one of the three categories of key leader judgments is that all leaders have to deal with them. The fundamental process of judgment is the same as with people and strategy. Have a solid TPOV, and make sure the judgments you make are consistent with the TPOV or at the very least do not hinder execution of the storyline for where you want to ultimately end up.

CRISIS AS A LEADERSHIP DEVELOPMENT OPPORTUNITY

Why are some leaders better equipped to deal with crises than others? The answer is because they anticipate crises. They aren't psychics. But they clearly understand that some crises *are* going to come down the pike, and they prepare themselves and their organizations to respond effectively and efficiently when they do. These leaders know that in order to survive crises, and perhaps even come out ahead because of them, they must have three things:

1. An aligned and highly trusted team.
2. A TPOV and storyline for the organization's future success.
3. A commitment to developing other leaders throughout the crisis.

Navigating Through Crises

David Novak, CEO of Yum! Brands, and Phil Schoonover, CEO of Circuit City, are two leaders who have successfully navigated their organizations through several crisis situations. Both Novak and Schoonover do three things simultaneously:

1. Effectively, in real time, deal with their crises.
2. Mobilize, align, and engage the right social network of leaders in their organizations by tapping their brains and their emotional energy to handle the crises.

3. Focus explicitly on developing the leaders engaged in the process, taking the time to teach and coach in real time.

Leaders who succeed in crises are able to do so because they work on developing their own capabilities and on building them into the fabric of their organizations. Every crisis that Novak has faced has led to good judgments. They have also given him the platform to keep developing other leaders who will be better and better at handling the inevitable and unforeseen crises. The lesson for others is to clearly have mechanisms in place that provide quick responses to crises and that develop the next generation of leaders.

KNOWLEDGE CREATION

The first imperative to being a good leader who makes good judgments is a commitment to be a learner, to keep building one's knowledge and wisdom. Leaders have two imperatives when it comes to knowledge creation. First and foremost, they must continuously strive to make themselves smarter and better at judgments by the kind of self-journey to improvement that GE's CEO Jeff Immelt and other leaders have taken.

In addition, leaders need to garner the support of their teams; their organizations; and their stakeholders in people, strategy, and crisis judgment making. While striving to make themselves better with the support of others, they must simultaneously invest in the development of leadership judgment in others: namely, their team, their organization, and the organization's key stakeholders. This duality, making oneself better while teaching and developing others' judgment capacity, is the key to good leadership.

Self-Knowledge Creation: A Journey into Yourself

Good leaders are on a transformational journey starting with themselves, which carries over to their teams and organizations. To do this, leaders need the paradoxical combination of self-confidence and humility to learn.

Self-knowledge creation has to be a central agenda item of the leader. It takes commitment to self-learning, significant time, relentless willingness to "look in the mirror," and a paradoxical self-confidence and humility.

"An Intense Journey into Yourself"

Jack Welch chose Jeff Immelt to succeed him as CEO in large part because he recognized that Immelt was a leader with an insatiable thirst for being better, who invested himself in self-knowledge creation. Immelt told an incoming class of MBAs at the University of Michigan: "The first part of leadership is an intense journey into yourself. It's a commitment and an intense journey into your soul . . . more than anything else, the burning desire inside me was to get the best out of what I could be and go on that journey."

The leader's knowledge creation journey is the necessary condition for focusing on knowledge creation at the social network, organizational, and contextual levels where the leader not only mobilizes these domains to support the judgment process, but also builds his or her capacity to develop judgment knowledge capacity.

Social Network/Team Knowledge Creation

It is up to the leader to build knowledge creation processes for his or her team and to ensure that these processes are executed.

Virtually every leader relies on a group of trusted advisers. For most leaders, their team is the group with which they spend the most time. When there are difficult judgments to be made, they convene their team to debate and deliberate. Building a social network that keeps developing knowledge creation capacity is central to the success of a leader.

Organization Knowledge Creation

Building judgment capacity means creating processes that engage leaders in judgment muscle strengthening activities.

All leadership development, from new hires through senior leaders, needs to be geared toward knowledge creation for better leadership judgments, both to support real-time judgments and to develop the next generation's capacity for leadership judgment.

Contextual Knowledge Creation

The final knowledge creation arena is how to work with the stakeholders, the board, the suppliers, the customers, and the communities in which the organization operates. Leaders need to develop customer and supplier interactive processes for developing new knowledge.

JUDGMENT FOR FUTURE GENERATIONS

Mayor Michael Bloomberg and Joel Klein, the chancellor of the New York City school system, want to help shape good judgment in 1.1 million New York City children. To do that, it takes leadership in the New York City schools, where there are eighty thousand teachers and fourteen hundred principals. To deliver on the Bloomberg and Klein strategy judgment, the focus had to be on the principals. This is the leadership role that has the maximum impact on the children; a good principal is the key to good teachers.

The New York City Transformation Journey

When Mayor Bloomberg changed careers, from a very successful entrepreneur to mayor of New York City, he sensed and identified the need for revitalizing the human capital side of New York, namely, its schools and the next generation of young people.

Judgment number one was to frame and name the issue. Bloomberg said, "We have a leadership problem in our school system and schools, and it needs to be fixed to impact outcomes." Bloomberg had witnessed years of emphasis on curriculum and teacher education but very little on who was leading the schools.

Bloomberg's Teachable Point of View included an assumption that organizational performance was dependent on a good leader. The key leader was the one closest to the students, namely, the principal. For these front-line leaders to succeed, the top leaders needed to provide the context and the selection and development pipeline; that was the challenge for Bloomberg, who needed a leader who could execute his judgment to tackle the public education problem in New York City.

That is how Mayor Bloomberg framed it. He made a bold people judgment call and recruited Joel Klein, a non-educator with a successful career in business and law, to be school chancellor. He wanted Klein to be his partner in transforming public education in New York. Klein had a vision of a leadership academy for principals.

Principals and Teachers Shape Our Future

Bloomberg and Klein mobilized a social network of leaders to join in the very difficult execution phase of their yet-to-be completed strategic judgment. Execution required organizational processes, namely, the establishment of the New York Leadership Academy and a mechanism to drive large-scale development and transformation of the schools by focusing on the principals as the key to better schools.

CONCLUSION

The process of judgment begins with the leader recognizing the need for a judgment and continuing through successful execution. Leaders are said to have "good judgment" when they repeatedly make judgment calls that turn out well. And these calls often turn out well because they have mastered a complex process that unfolds in several dimensions: time, domain, and constituencies.

This framework can help you improve your judgment-making faculties, to do a better job of developing good judgment in others and to encourage a more vigorous conversation about judgment. We need more leaders with better judgment.

SMALL GIANTS
By Bo Burlingham

S ome people need to write. Many writers get distracted in careers as editors, managers, or marketers, but a few are tugged back from these jobs to their keyboards by their love for documenting the freshest stories around them. Some writers are compelled by their creative forces to record the new lessons they learn. Bo Burlingham is one of those rare writers.

Burlingham received widespread recognition as a writer for a variety of publications, including *Harper's, Esquire, Boston Magazine,* and *Mother Jones.* After a healthy career as a freelance writer, he was hired by *Ramparts* magazine as a managing editor. He rounded the next bend in his career when he joined Fidelity Investments as a writer for the executives there, including Peter Lynch and Ned Johnson. The next year, 1982, he joined *Inc.* magazine as a senior editor. He was soon promoted to the position of executive editor, a role he would play for the next seven years until he tendered his resignation to become *Inc.*'s editor-at-large. He made this decision because he needs to write.

Soon after he quit his executive editor position, Burlingham wrote two books with Jack Stack, the president and CEO of SRC Holdings Corp. and a pioneer of open-book management. *The Great Game of Business* was the first of those books, and it has become a blueprint for managers who are ready to embrace the idea of open-book management. *A Stake in the Outcome,* Burlingham's second book with Stack, describes how managers and executives can best run an employee-owned company. Both books were successful examples of how forward-thinking management can improve a company as well as the people it employs.

Burlingham continues to embrace his love of business ideas while working with progressive company leaders who expand his horizons. In the 1990s, he served on the board of The Body Shop Inc. Around the same time, he founded the international networking group PAC World with Tom Peters, which gives him the opportunity to meet many forward-thinking businesspeople from around the globe.

In 2003 Burlingham began the research that would eventually lead to his breakthrough book *Small Giants*. While writing articles for *Inc.* about several companies that were able to become successful and maintain that success while staying close to their roots, the central ideas found in *Small Giants* emerged.

While most companies work hard at getting to the "next level" by growing and swelling with staff and real estate, Burlingham observed a new class of companies that were either growing in very unconventional ways, actually choosing not to grow at all, or consciously choosing to scale back their operations. These "small giants" intrigued Burlingham, so he continued to research their leaders and management practices. The result was a book of stories and lessons other leaders can use within their own organizations. With an investigative journalist's eye for the next big story, Burlingham turned the ways small giants pursue goals beyond revenue growth and geographical expansion into a guide other companies can follow when considering their next stage of growth.

Most business writers extol the merits of former GE CEO Jack Welch's idea that a business is not worth owning if it is not first or second in its niche. Burlingham, on the other hand, follows the path less trod and investigates the secrets behind companies that are quite content to be smaller in scale and quietly successful, away from the media glare that comes with giant mergers and acquisitions.

Most companies are small and privately owned. Their financial objectives don't have to be more important than the goal of being great at what they do. In *Small Giants*, Burlingham pays tribute to companies that make being a great place to work a priority. The leaders of these companies contribute to their communities and find satisfying ways to live their lives. This is how their wealth emerges. The stories in *Small Giants* are valuable because they demonstrate a perspective that challenges the ideas found in the majority of reporting in the mainstream business press.

As an insightful writer, Burlingham recognizes the greatness of those who do not follow the business superhighway toward infinite financial goals. In *Small Giants*, he describes how the small roads that have been ignored by the frantic rush of commerce can take businesses to the same, and sometimes better, rewards.

SMALL GIANTS

Companies That Choose to Be Great Instead of Big

by Bo Burlingham

CONTENTS

THE SUMMARY IN BRIEF

It's a widely accepted axiom of business that great companies grow their revenues and profits year after year. Yet quietly, under the radar, some entrepreneurs have rejected the pressure of endless growth to focus on more satisfying business goals. These goals include being great at what they do, creating a great place to work, providing great customer service, making great contributions to their communities, and finding great ways to lead their lives.

In this summary, veteran journalist Bo Burlingham takes readers deep inside fourteen remarkable privately held companies, in widely varying industries across the United States, that have chosen to march to their own drummer. He searches for the magic ingredients that give these companies their unique "mojo" and the lessons other companies can learn from them. These companies include Anchor Brewing, CitiStorage Inc., Clif Bar & Co., ECCO, Hammerhead Productions, Righteous Babe Records, Union Square Hospitality Group, and Zingerman's Community of Businesses.

Size and growth rate aside, these small giants share some very interesting characteristics. They are all utterly determined to be the best at what they do. Most have been recognized for excellence by independent bodies inside and outside their industries. All have had the opportunity to raise much capital, grow very fast, do mergers and acquisitions, expand geographically, and generally follow the well-worn route of other successful companies.

To stay on the road less traveled, these companies have remained privately owned, with the majority of the stock in the hands of one person or a few like-minded individuals. They were founded by and still are run by unique entrepreneurs who recognized the full range of choices they had about the type of company they could create and allowed themselves to question the usual definitions of success.

In addition, this summary will show you:

- How a new class of great companies has been quietly and gradually forming under the radar.
- Why some companies have made conscious decisions to scale back their operations.
- Why successful companies have chosen not to focus on revenue growth or geographical expansion.
- What goals are considered by some companies to be more important than getting as big as possible, as fast as possible.
- How wealth can be the byproduct of success in areas other than growth.

THE COMPLETE SUMMARY

INTRODUCTION

There's a feeling one gets when coming into contact with hot companies just as they are hitting their stride—Apple Computer, Fidelity Investments, People Express Airlines, Ben & Jerry's, Patagonia, and even *Inc.* magazine. They had a buzz. There was excitement, anticipation, a feeling of movement, a sense of purpose and direction, of going somewhere. It happens when people find themselves totally in sync with their market, with the world around them, and with each other. Everything just seems to click. Most companies eventually lose that quality, but some companies manage to retain it.

What Is "Mojo"?

What is "it"? Gary Erickson of Clif Bar came closest to identifying the quality itself. He had begun thinking about it at a critical moment in the company's history, when he was struggling to figure out what kind of company he wanted

Clif Bar to be. At a trade show in the fall of 2000, he met a well-known marketer of consumer products who complimented him on the buzz around Clif Bar's booth, pointing to a competitor's booth that was dead by comparison. "They lost their mojo," the guy said.

Whatever mojo was, some smart people evidently thought that it was important, and that Clif Bar had it. In any case, it was something to which Erickson needed to pay attention. From then on, "mojo" became his watchword. In his book *Raising the Bar*, Erickson said he thought Clif Bar's mojo was "something about the brand, product, and way of being in the world that was different. I realized that mojo was an elusive quality and needed to be tended carefully."

The word is just right for the mysterious quality seen in Clif Bar, CitiStorage, Union Square Hospitality, and many other companies.

How Companies Create Mojo

What do companies do to create mojo? The answer to this question can be found in the common threads among the companies identified as having mojo. These are:

1. Unlike most entrepreneurs, their founders and leaders recognized the full range of choices they had about the type of company they could create.

2. The leaders had overcome the enormous pressures on successful companies to take paths they had not chosen and did not necessarily want to follow.

3. Each company had an extraordinarily intimate relationship with the local city, town, or county in which it did business—a relationship that went well beyond the usual concept of "giving back."

4. They cultivated exceptionally intimate relationships with customers and suppliers, based on personal contact, one-on-one interactions, and mutual commitment to deliver on promises.

5. The companies also had unusually intimate workplaces that strove to address a broad range of their employees' needs as human beings.

6. These companies came up with a variety of corporate structures and modes of governance.

7. The leaders of these companies brought passion to what the company did.

FREE TO CHOOSE

Fritz Maytag may be the grandson of the giant appliance company's founder, but he has an unabashed fondness for small, beautiful things, in business as elsewhere. At sixty-five, he could look back on forty years as the owner and CEO of Anchor Brewing, the premier microbrewery in the United States. In the early 1990s, Maytag was forced to make a choice that all successful entrepreneurs are faced with sooner or later. To his great relief, Maytag had recognized his choice in time and made the one that was right for him.

In the early 1990s, Maytag had owned and run Anchor Brewing for twenty-seven years. While turning the century-old company around and saving its sole product, Anchor Steam Beer, Maytag launched a revolution in beer making with the first nationally recognized microbrews: high-quality, handcrafted beers and ales, made with the finest ingredients using traditional recipes and brewing techniques.

Reaching Capacity

By 1973 his beers had become so popular that demand had maxed out his brewery's capacity. When the MGM Grand Casino in Reno wanted to put Anchor Steam on tap in every bar in the house, rather than sacrifice the authenticity of his product by hiring other microbrewers to do additional brewing, he chose to reject the order.

After moving to a new building with the capacity to handle the growth his company was experiencing, Maytag faced the possibility of going public. With his top three people, he asked several questions: What would the new investors expect? Why are we in business anyway? What do we enjoy doing? What are our goals in life? They considered the various possible outcomes and realized they all had reservations. They weren't sure they wanted the company to get much bigger. They loved it as it was.

"We Made the Decision Not to Grow"

Maytag recalls, "It occurred to me that you could have a small, prestigious, profitable business, and it would be all right. You can stay as you are and have a business that's profitable and rewarding and a source of great pride. So we made the decision not to grow."

If the business survives, you will sooner or later have a choice about how far and how fast to grow. There is a choice, and the payoff for choosing the less traveled path can be huge. It can affect every aspect of your business—from your relationships with your fellow colleagues to the control you have over your time and your destiny, to the impact you have on the world around you, to the satisfaction and fulfillment you get out of your personal life.

Unfortunately, many people have to pass through a major crisis to recognize the choice they have. They have a moment of revelation—often right as they're about to make an irrevocable decision—when they suddenly see they have another option. For Fritz Maytag, that moment came as he was getting ready to take Anchor Brewing public. For Gary Erickson, the moment arrived as he was preparing to sell his $39-million-a-year company, Clif Bar, to a midwestern food conglomerate for $120 million. At the last minute before signing the deal, he backed out. After agreeing to pay his partner $65 million over five years, he took over as CEO and, he says, created "a healthy, sustainable company that grows by natural demand and that is profitable."

With the help of the people in his company, Clif Bar survived and prospered. Over the next five years, the company more than doubled its sales, from $39 million in 1999 to $92 million in 2004, and it did so without taking on any outside investors or even greatly expanding its workforce.

If you want to have the choice, you have to fight for it. All successful businesses face enormous pressures to grow, and they come from everywhere—customers, employees, investors, suppliers, and competitors. Those forces will make the choice for you if you let them, in which case you will lose the opportunity to chart your own course.

WHO'S IN CHARGE HERE?

It is important to take note of the pressures that entrepreneurs have to deal with and that can push any company in a direction its founder never intended to go. You can't build a small giant if you're in an industry where your success depends on how big your company becomes. The pressure to grow fast is irresistible, and sooner or later you'll have to look for outside financing.

Even if you don't go into a scale-based business, you're still likely to face enormous pressure to bring in outside investors, simply because of the economics of growth. You almost always lose a significant portion of your independence when you sell stock to outsiders, even if the business remains privately owned. As a result, it becomes much more difficult to make the kinds of choices that the small giants have made.

Pressures

Even if you manage to keep ownership inside the company, you still have to contend with other forces pushing you in directions you didn't necessarily want to go. In some cases, you may feel pressure from big competitors, or the fear of big competitors. Suppliers, too, will urge you to grow as fast as you can. But the most intense pressure often comes from two sources that both determine and define your success as a business, namely, your employees and your customers.

A great company needs to have great people working for it, but you can't attract or hold on to them unless they have room to grow. That is why many owners wind up putting their companies on a path of aggressive growth, even if they themselves might prefer to rein it in. "I didn't feel I had a choice," says Jim Ansara, the founder and chairman of Shawmut Design and Construction in Boston.

The small giants have all had to keep their best people engaged and challenged or run the risk of losing them. In most cases, the answer has been a kind of controlled growth that has preserved the company's culture while creating new opportunities for employees. Growth is a natural byproduct of the company's success in pursuing its central purpose and reason for being, whatever that may be.

Market Pressure to Grow

It's the market pressure to grow that is the most problematic for any company to deal with. For openers, there's the psychological factor. The pressure is there, after all, because people like your product or service and want a chance either to buy more of it themselves or to make it available to large numbers of customers who don't have access to it now. Either way, the pressure is a powerful indicator of your success. It's the fulfillment of the dreams you had when you started the company.

Many people can't say no, especially male entrepreneurs. Even if he knows that his company and his people aren't ready to handle the growth, even if he realizes that the growth may transform the company in ways he can't foresee and may not like, he has trouble turning business away. By the time you realize that the company is too big, you've made many commitments—to customers, employees, and suppliers—that are hard to break. At that point, you find out just how deeply you care about being the best at what you do.

Ego

There is one other major source of pressure to grow. It comes partly from the social and cultural environments in which we all live and work, and partly from something in the entrepreneurial psyche. Robert Catlin, founder and CEO of Signature Mortgage Corp. in Canton, Ohio, is one person who has struggled with it. He developed a system that allowed his sixteen employees to outperform mortgage companies with three or four times as many people.

The company was wildly successful. Friends, colleagues, customers, and utter strangers said they couldn't understand why he didn't do the same thing in other midsize markets around the country. "People tell me all the time, 'You're crazy, pal. You're missing a golden opportunity,'" he explains. "I say, 'Hey, I'm doing just fine. I have control. I have freedom. I have family time and travel time. What more can I ask for?'"

The notion that bigger—and more—is better has so pervaded our culture that most people assume all entrepreneurs want to capitalize on every business opportunity, grow their companies as fast as they can, and build the next Microsoft or Citicorp. That widespread assumption, in turn, can become another pressure to grow, especially when considerations of status and prestige come into play. "It's really tough—because it can be an ego thing," says Catlin. "I spend a lot of time soul searching. What is most important to me? What's this all about? What do I want to do with my life? The world says, 'Go. Get bigger. Go. Go.' But I don't see why I should."

A Positive Difference

A small giant's mojo comes, in part, from an active appreciation of a business's potential to make a positive difference in the lives of the people with whom it comes into contact. That appreciation makes possible the intimacy the small giants are able to achieve with employees, customers, suppliers, and the community—an intimacy that is both one of the great rewards and one of the crucial generators of the mojo they exude.

THE MONA LISA PRINCIPLE

The Asbury Delaware Methodist Church stands on the main road leading into Buffalo, New York. It's one of the city's many architectural masterpieces that date back to its glory days in the late nineteenth century. Today, it is the home of Righteous Babe, the music company founded by singer-songwriter Ani DiFranco. It's also a symbol of hope for the city of Buffalo.

Ani DiFranco grew up in Buffalo playing her guitar and singing her songs in local clubs, and she has remained fiercely loyal to the city even after she became a star. She has hundreds of thousands of fans around the world and has sold millions of her CDs, plus a smaller number by other artists, under the Righteous Babe Records label.

Creating Local Jobs

DiFranco could have located her business anywhere, but she's chosen Buffalo over New York, Los Angeles, or other cities with modern recording facilities and many musicians. She and her business partner, Scot Fisher, insist on using local suppliers to make the company's T-shirts and other merchandise, to print its album notes and posters, and to manufacture its cassette tapes and CDs. In the process, DiFranco has played a major role in building at least three local businesses in addition to her own and is directly responsible for creating about 125 jobs in a city with one of the highest unemployment rates in the Northeast.

But it is what she's done with the church that has made the biggest impression on the city's psyche. The building was a ruin by the time Righteous Babe got involved. The church would have been demolished in 1995 had not Fisher, an ardent preservationist, helped raise $50,000 to make emergency repairs. In 1999 Fisher and DiFranco decided to buy the church, restore it, and use it to house the company's headquarters, as well as a new concert venue, a jazz bar, an art gallery, and the offices of the city's leading avant garde arts organization.

Intimately Connected

All of the small giants are so intimately connected to the place where they're located that it's hard to imagine them being anywhere else. Anchor Steam is a San Francisco institution. CitiStorage is Brooklyn to the core. The same could be said for Clif Bar and Berkeley. And the influence runs both ways. The companies shape their respective communities, and the communities shape them.

Danny Meyer of Union Square Hospitality Group, for one, views the community as a critical factor in deciding where he will open a restaurant, and what type of restaurant it will be. "I don't want to do a new project unless it's special in some way, and that means the context has to be right," he says. "I don't know what's special about the way the Mona Lisa is framed, hung, and lit, but I do know that the effect would not be the same if it were framed, hung, and lit in a different museum, in a different city, in a different country." That's one reason he and his colleagues at Union Square Hospitality Group turned down developers who wanted them to open a Union Square Café or a Gramercy Tavern in Las Vegas. "Those restaurants are part of their community, and the community is part of what they are. They wouldn't fit in in Las Vegas, given the transience of the people and the nature of the place. It's the wrong context."

Deeply Rooted in the Community

The small giants are all deeply rooted in their communities, and it shows. Each has a distinctive personality that reflects the local environment, often in ways that may seem superficial or quirky on the surface but that actually play an important role in the business's success.

Righteous Babe is a good example. It has the feeling of a small, home-town business, despite its national renown and international customer base. Fisher believes the city has something to do with the company's longevity. "IRS Records wanted to sign Ani, and we went to see them in Los Angeles," he says. "They had this beautiful office. I thought, Who's paying for this? I couldn't see anything they had that we really needed. IRS had a phone; we had a phone. IRS had a fax machine; we had a fax machine. They said they could get Ani's music to a larger audience, but we didn't think she needed them to do that. Now IRS is gone, and we're still here. We must have done something right. And I think that staying in Buffalo all this time, working in a modest office, was a factor. It helped us keep things in perspective."

All the small giants have similarly symbiotic relationships with the communities in which they've grown up, and the vitality of those connections is part of their mojo. The companies' owners and employees have a strong sense of who they are, where they belong, and how they're making a difference to their neighbors, friends, and others they touch. All that contributes to buzz around the business, as well as the passion people feel for what they're doing.

Social Responsibility

When it comes to social responsibility, there's a difference between people spending their own time and money on a cause and a corporation spending somebody else's time and money on it. What the small giants do is consistent with that distinction. Not only do they generally avoid taking initiatives that carry the whiff of ulterior motives but they also follow the rule that—to be a meaningful expression of generosity and support—an act of charity has to be individual, personal, and largely unheralded (though not necessarily secret).

TIES THAT BIND

Extraordinary customer service has always made good business sense, no matter what you have to do to provide it. From eye-popping service come industry legends, rave reviews in the media, and the fabulous word-of-mouth, which is the most effective marketing tool a company can have.

Danny Meyer of the Union Square Hospitality Group calls the service at his restaurants "enlightened hospitality." He doesn't deny the importance of traditional customer service, but he regards it as a set of technical skills. Enlightened hospitality, on the other hand, is an emotional skill involving the ability to make customers feel that you're on their side. Examples include the manager who offers to return by messenger or Federal Express the handbag that the customer left behind, rather than simply holding it for her until she comes to get it. Or the maitre d' who puts a rose on Table 27 for Mr. and Mrs. Knightly, knowing they always sit there on their anniversary because that's where he proposed to her. Beyond that, Meyer can provide staff members with a computer system that will help them remember such details.

Personal Customer Service

"Personal" is the key word. Great customer service involves demonstrating to customers that you value their business and will go the extra mile to keep it. Enlightened hospitality means showing them that you care about them personally. You don't want them just to be satisfied; you want them to be happy. It's a step beyond service, and it requires the company to develop an emotional connection with customers through individual, one-on-one, person-to-person contacts.

You don't have to be in the restaurant business to connect with customers in that way. The other small giants don't call it enlightened hospitality, but they do much the same thing. It is a key element of their mojo, and the one most visible to the outside world.

Intimate customer relationships also figure prominently in the mojo of the small giants in manufacturing, but the challenge they face is different from—and, in some ways, more complex than—the one confronting retail businesses and service companies. It requires organizing the entire company around tailoring products to customers' individual needs.

Supplier Relationships

Customers are not the only outsiders with whom the small giants have intimate relationships. There are also the suppliers that make it possible for them to achieve the level of excellence to which they aspire.

Companies that succeed in developing a sense of community with their customers and suppliers through integrity, professionalism, and the direct, human connection find themselves in possession of one of the most powerful business tools in the world.

It's generally not the people at the top of the mojo companies who create the intimate bonds. It's the managers and employees who do the work of the business, day in and day out. They are the ones who convey the spirit of the company to the outside world.

A CULTURE OF INTIMACY

ECCO is a company located in Boise, Idaho. It is the leading manufacturer of backup alarms and amber warning lights for commercial vehicles. CEO Ed

Zimmer has a lot of contact with his employees. Among other things, he holds a regular monthly lunch with all the people who have a birthday that month, and they talk about themselves, the company, and whatever else they want to discuss. There's also a companywide meeting each month to go over the financials, as well as a steady flow of financial information between meetings.

"Things aren't secret here," says nine-year company veteran Michelle Howard. "Everything is shared, which makes me feel safe. ECCO cares about the people who work here, and we care about each other. I can't imagine going anywhere else. I'll stay here as long as they'll have me. I want to help make this company as successful as it can be."

The small giants have cracked the code to creating a motivated workforce. Indeed, the relationship between the employees and the company is the entire basis for the mojo they exude. Unless a significant majority of a company's people love the place where they work; unless they feel valued, appreciated, supported, and empowered; unless they see a future full of opportunities for them to learn and grow, mojo is simply not in the cards. This is because everything else that makes a company extraordinary—a great brand, terrific products or services, fabulous relationships with customers and suppliers, a vital role in the community—depends on those who do the work of the business, day in and day out.

Creating Intimacy

This is not just about morale. The other factor that promotes a profound sense of belonging, of psychic ownership, is intimacy: a relationship so close employees never doubt that the company, its leaders, and the other people with whom they work care about them personally and will stand by them through thick and thin as long as they hold up their end of the bargain.

Obviously, the ability to create such intimacy has something to do with size. There is generally an inverse correlation between the number of people who work for a company and the strength of their emotional ties to it. There is a limit to the number of employees a company can have and still maintain those intimate, personal connections. The limit varies from company to company.

On one end of the spectrum is Anchor Brewing, whose owner and CEO, Fritz Maytag, has consciously strived to keep the number of his employees as low as possible. For most of the past twenty years, the head count has hovered around fifty full-time people. He has never been tempted to hire more. In an interview with *Harvard Business Review*, he said his idea was "to have a small group of people, where everyone knows they're interrelated and where, as far as possible, everybody is in charge and nobody is looking over anyone's shoulder and there are no time clocks."

Direct Contact

A company's ability to achieve the kind of intimacy the small giants create depends to some extent on the relationship between the person in charge and the employees. If you have no direct contact with a substantial number of the people depending on you for their livelihood, it is extremely unlikely they will feel the intense, emotional attachment to the business seen in close-knit organizations where everybody spends time together, has important experiences together, and knows what's going on in one another's lives.

Such personal connections alone do not produce the kind of commitment seen in the small giants. What exactly can be done to create an environment in which people feel their lives are so intimately tied to the business that, as a matter of personal pride, they do everything they can to help it achieve its aspirations and become the best at what it does? First, get the basics right. Make sure you have the right people on the bus, and keep the bus in good running condition. Also, if you want a company that cares, you need people who care, and they need to be motivated by more than money.

There are three broad imperatives that all small giants pursue in different ways and with different means. These imperatives must be a priority if the company wants to create a culture of intimacy and the mojo that goes with it:

1. *Articulating, demonstrating, and imbuing the company with a higher purpose.* The higher purpose makes the work people do meaningful; it continually reminds them how their contribution matters and why they should care about giving their best effort.

2. *Reminding people in unexpected ways how much the company cares about them.* The crucial word is "unexpected." The small giants go out of their way to make sure the message gets through, either by doing what most companies wouldn't dream of doing or by using one of the standard tools in an unusual way.

3. *Collegiality.* This refers to feelings that employees have toward one another, the mutual trust and respect they feel, the enjoyment they get out of spending time together, their willingness to work through any conflicts that might arise, their collective pride in what they do, and their collective commitment to doing it well.

GALT'S GULCH

Every new business represents an attempt by its founder, or founders, to reorder the world in some way. Most founders do so, however, without giving it much thought; and very few, indeed, think about how far they can go in reordering the world—which is not surprising.

The founders, owners, and CEOs of the small giants stand out in part because of the extent to which they have thought about and worked on the basic questions about the kind of culture and organization they want.

They have various management philosophies, and their companies have quite different cultures and ways of operating. But together they illustrate the range of possibilities that a closely held, private company has in shaping the world inside its walls. In that sense, each company is its own version of Galt's Gulch in *Atlas Shrugged*—a haven for people who have a common vision of the kind of society in which they want to live and work.

One other element needs to be considered in any discussion of how the founders of small giants create organizations that have such a powerful impact on the people with whom they come in contact—especially their employees. A few founders have thought about the way they are perceived, analyzed it, and incorporated it into their management philosophy.

Fritz Maytag of Anchor Brewing says, "I think there's a certain amount of magic to all this, and the more you understand it, or think you do, the more you may lose it. Good management in a small company involves a certain freshness and responsiveness and natural feeling that is by definition partly unspoken, unarticulated, undefined."

HOW HAMMERHEAD ATTRACTS TALENT

The four movie industry veterans who started Hammerhead Productions, the visual effects company in Studio City, California, wanted a business that would allow them to pursue their creative passions. They felt constrained at the large visual effects companies and didn't have the flexibility they needed to do the kind of work they most cared about. They also wanted a culture that was more open and less hierarchical than those of most larger special effects companies, a culture in which people would work autonomously, without supervision. The founders wanted it for themselves and because they believed it would help them attract the kind of animators they were looking for.

You can't have real intimacy without a good deal of freshness, responsiveness, and natural feeling. The bigger the role those spontaneous qualities play in the way the company is managed, the more mojo it is likely to have.

PASS IT ON

A small giant faces no greater challenge than making its mojo last. That's hard enough to do under the best of circumstances, as history attests. It is infinitely more difficult to do so while simultaneously undergoing a transfer of ownership and leadership.

To begin with, it almost always requires the owners to make significant sacrifices. Among other things, they must be willing to accept a lower price for their stock than they could get if they simply sold to the highest bidder.

Even if the owners are willing to sell the company for less than they might otherwise receive, there's still the problem of finding buyers with the vision, the passion, and the talent to guide the business while continuing to nurture the qualities that have given it its mojo in the past. Most likely, those people are already working in the company. They understand better than anyone else what it takes to create mojo in that particular business because they've been part of making it happen.

Given both the complexity and the emotional ramifications of the issues involved, it's no wonder that most owners of private companies put off dealing with succession as long as they can—often until some life-threatening event forces them to face up to their mortality.

Making Mojo Last

Making mojo last does not mean keeping the company the way it is, or was. Mojo does not insulate a business from the marketplace. Small giants must adapt to changes in the competitive environment just like every other business, but they usually have an easier time of it, thanks to the same practices and beliefs that give them their mojo to begin with. They have an easier time in the first generation, while the founders are still around and driving the change, but the founders' very success can often become a significant obstacle to the leaders who follow them, especially when it becomes necessary to make fundamental changes in the way a company does business.

For some small giant founders, succession is not in the cards. Some companies' mojo will last only as long as they themselves are involved because the business can't survive without them. When a company is built around the unique talents of artists—such as Selima Inc., the dress company of Selima

Stavola, and Righteous Babe, the music business of Ani DiFranco—it is almost impossible to imagine the company without its founder.

THE ART OF BUSINESS

What is the essence of the mojo all the small giants have? The answer has more to do with the people than with the businesses. The owners and leaders of these companies stand out for being remarkably in touch with, and focused on, what most would probably agree are the good things in life. They are very clear in their minds about what life has to offer at its best—in terms of exciting challenges, camaraderie, compassion, hope, intimacy, community, a sense of purpose, feelings of accomplishment, and so on—and they have organized their businesses so that they and the people with whom they work can get it. When outsiders come in contact with such a business, they can't help but feel the attraction. The company is cool because what's going on inside it is good, it's fun, it's interesting, and it's something with which you want to be associated. From that perspective, mojo is more or less the business equivalent of charisma. Leaders with charisma have a quality that makes people want to follow them. Companies with mojo have a quality that makes people want to be part of them.

All that starts, however, with the creative impulse to which Bernie Goldhirsh referred when he talked about entrepreneurs as the artists of the business world. If there's one thing that every founder and leader of a small giant has in common with the others, it is a passion for what their companies do. They love it, and they have a burning desire to share it with other people. They thrive on the joy of contributing something great and unique to the world.

Selima Stavola feels that passion for her art of clothing design. "I tell you, I wake up in the morning, and it's the best hour for me—because I'm so excited about going to work," she says. "It all comes down to, are you happy with yourself when you tackle a new day?"

There is a balance between art and business in all the small giants. They demonstrate that it's possible for the business side and the creative side to live in harmony. What makes it possible are the company's priorities. The business is the means people are using to pursue their passion, and not the other way around.

Mojo is not as scarce as some might suppose. Companies that have it are all over. Small giants are the heart and soul of the American economy, and they are setting a new standard for excellence on Main Street.

It's a standard to which thousands of companies can aspire, and many can achieve. What businesses do and how they do it have an impact that extends far beyond the economic sphere. They shape the communities in which we live, the values by which we live, and the quality of the lives we lead. There are no businesses that hold themselves to higher standards than do the small giants.

CHOOSING TO SAY NO

Danny Meyer of the Union Square Hospitality Group says, "I've made much more money by choosing the right things to say no to than by choosing things to say yes to. I measure it by the money I haven't lost and the quality I haven't sacrificed."

DEALING WITH DARWIN
by Geoffrey A. Moore

G eoffrey Moore's books have the broad appeal that makes them bestsellers. They also contain the specific lessons that make them textbooks at
the world's top business schools. *Crossing the Chasm, Inside the Tornado,*
Living on the Fault Line, and *Dealing with Darwin* help to define modern thinking on
strategic management in terms of robust innovation. Leaders worldwide devour
his business survival guides for smart tactics and techniques they can use in their
companies to face an increasingly competitive marketplace.

Dealing with Darwin shows leaders how to face the future by moving forward
with precision, courage, and proper timing. If your company is not focused on innovation, Moore advises, the time to rewrite business plans from the ground up is
now. He writes that "the sooner you start, the sooner you will be able to extract
yourself from those commitments that make you vulnerable and establish those
commitments that will strengthen your new position."

After graduating from Stanford, Moore received a doctorate in English
literature from the University of Washington. His growing reputation as a skilled
communicator of strategy and innovation helped him to become a principal and
partner at Regis McKenna Inc., a high-tech marketing strategy and communications company. Now he is a managing director at TCG Advisors and a popular
speaker.

The in-depth management analysis found in *Dealing with Darwin* comes from
Moore's unprecedented study of Cisco Systems. With unlimited access to the
company granted to him by Cisco's CEO John Chambers, he learned how Cisco's
innovations have helped the company to mature into a global enterprise. *Dealing
with Darwin* shows how SAP, IBM, Cisco, Intel, Avnet, and others have been able to
overcome the inertia that threatens bold innovations.

Moore believes in making innovation a highly centralized activity that surges
forward in many directions at once. A portfolio of options offers companies more
choices. What does he learn from HP's inability to surpass Dell and IBM? Managers must make strong decisions and be decisive about which innovation to pur-

sue, Moore explains, so the entire enterprise can align itself around differentiation and separation from competitors in the marketplace.

Managers must seek the glories of "breakaway status," "breakaway differentiation," and "breaking away from the herd," Moore writes, because these are the lofty goals for which leaders must strive to stay competitive in the twenty-first century and beyond. By asking questions about core versus context, Moore instigates the deeper discussions that get pushed aside by safe budgets that hedge all bets. Revenue collection cannot overshadow the achievement of competitive advantage, Moore professes.

Moore's principles and intriguing models help leaders address the big picture of strategic organizational change. He writes, "[T]he leadership supervising the change is more likely to come from within than without." Being trusted within the company culture helps a leader lead through a transformation, he adds. "When the CEO has less trust, renewal strategies come from acquisition renewal rather than organic renewal. Transformation needs management to risk investing in a fledgling business even when mature businesses are its cash cows."

For example, why did Apple put so much of its advertising budget toward the iPod even when it was less than 10 percent of the company's revenues? Moore writes that "bold gestures" such as this are required to communicate a leader's depth of commitment to a change.

DEALING WITH DARWIN

How Great Companies Innovate at Every Phase of Their Evolution

by Geoffrey A. Moore

CONTENTS

1. Foundational Models

2. Managing Innovation

3. Managing Inertia

THE SUMMARY IN BRIEF

Business is becoming increasingly competitive—globalization, deregulation, and commoditization have taken their toll everywhere you look.

Companies are forced to innovate or fold; it's a constant pressure that goes beyond mere competition—it's about survival. Who will the survivors be? They will be the ones that win the scarce resources of customer purchases; the ones that gain customer preference because of their innovation; the ones creating next-generation offers and raising the bar for the future. It's evolution in every sense of the word. Survival of the fittest. Dealing with Darwin.

In this summary, best-selling author and consultant Geoffrey A. Moore puts into clear relief the fact that innovation is not an optional "nice-to-have" in business—to innovate forever is a design specification. Innovation is no longer a strategy; it's a requirement. Those companies that survive over the long haul must not only innovate, but they must also deal with the cyclical inertia that affects all organizations. How can you extract and repurpose resources to feed and foster new product offers? How do you differentiate your company's products and services from those of your competition, creating sufficient separation to win revenue? According to Darwin, evolution took millions of years—you don't have nearly that long to build a strong competitive position. You must evolve and innovate now or suffer the consequences down the road.

In addition, this summary will describe the following:

- *The economics of innovation.* Innovation can help you neutralize a competitor's advantages in the marketplace, improve your overall productivity, and avoid waste in your business.
- *The maturation of offer categories.* Understanding the category-maturity life cycle will help you determine where your offers are in their development before you set your innovation strategy.
- *Recognizing and managing innovation.* Knowing the types of innovation is the first step toward managing innovation successfully.
- *Extracting resources from context.* You must build resources for core differentiating activities by repurposing those resources from other areas of various mission-criticality.

THE COMPLETE SUMMARY

FOUNDATIONAL MODELS

The economic argument in favor of innovation focuses on pricing power—avoiding commoditization and the resulting vendor price wars brought about by consumers simply searching for the best deal. Over time in these situations, the market stabilizes at prices at or below cost, creating returns for investors below the cost of capital. Investors do not stay in marketplaces like these very long. When innovation is applied, however, offers become more and more differentiated from one another, leading to different ones becoming the preferred choice for different market segments. Vendors in those segments then have pricing power, and the markets stabilize at prices well above cost, creating returns above the cost of capital, attracting more investment.

The Economics of Innovation

When innovation creates differentiation, it creates attractive economic returns. This is not, however, the only possible outcome from innovation. In addition to differentiation, there are three other possible outcomes:

- *Neutralization*. The goal of neutralization is to eliminate differentiation by catching up either to a competitor's superior performance or to a market standard one has fallen short of. Netscape, for example, achieved differentiation with the Internet browser; then Microsoft achieved neutralization with its own browser: Explorer. Neutralizing is an important adaptation to changing competitive dynamics, and it does call for innovation. It does not, however, create as great a positive return as differentiation, in part because its function is to eliminate a negative return.

- *Productivity improvement*. Here the intent is not to affect market outcomes but rather to achieve them at a lower cost. While productivity improvements can create differentiation if they are radical enough, the majority of them are simply designed to cost-reduce a set of existing processes in order to either invest the savings elsewhere or increase profits. Productivity improvement is essential to evolutionary adaptation because it frees resources that other forms of innovation can use. It requires significant innovation focused largely on reengineering existing processes based on either a better understanding of their dynamics or a better set of tools.

- *Waste*. Waste innovation falls into a number of classes. The first simply comprises those attempts at any of the other three goals that don't succeed. This is just part of business.

The other forms of waste are more pernicious. Neutralization efforts that go beyond the good-enough goal have lower returns because you overspent the market requirement. Productivity efforts that go beyond cost-reduction or cycle-time improvement and branch into nice-to-have enhancements also represent waste. The worst kind of waste, however, occurs when an innovation project actually succeeds in meeting its specified targets but fails to achieve competitive separation in the marketplace because it *did not go far enough*.

Underperformance

There are two deep-seated causes for innovation underperformance. These are:

1. *Risk-reduction mentality.* This encourages people to shun bold actions that jeopardize existing assets and relationships. It is based on staying close to norms, thereby leveraging the experience of the herd. As such, it is actually a positive evolutionary response to situations that do not reward differentiation. These situations are called *context*. Risk reduction is the sensible strategy for managing context, but it is a horrible tool to deal with core. *Core* describes innovation that creates differentiation. To succeed with core, you must take your value proposition to such an extreme that competitors either cannot or will not follow. That's what creates the separation you seek. So risk-averse behavior here is a losing strategy.
2. *Lack of corporate alignment.* To achieve breakaway differentiation requires a highly coordinated effort across the entire enterprise. At the end of the day, every function in the corporation has to realign its priorities in order to amplify the innovation to breakaway status. Anything less is simply too easy to neutralize.

In order to break away from the herd, we must overcome risk-reduction mentality and lack of corporate alignment. Neither is a natural act.

Innovation and Category Maturity

To be successful with innovation, you have to understand that different categories reward different types of innovation at different points in time. It is important to locate where your category is in its life cycle before you set your innovation strategy. The framework for this process is the category-maturity life cycle.

The model comprises five phases: (A) New Category Initiation, (B) Growth Market, (C) Mature Market, (D) Declining Market, and (E) End of Life.

The Category-Maturity Life Cycle

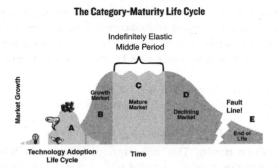

The first phase covers the emergence of a new category. In the development of any specific market, individual choices are masked in the statistics of the group, resulting in five strategies interacting to create a pattern described by the technology-adoption life cycle.

Technology-Adoption Life Cycle

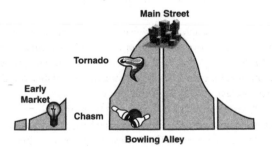

Here are the six stages to consider:

- *Early market.* When a disruptive innovation is first introduced, it initially attracts the attention of technology enthusiasts (who see it as cool) and visionaries (who see it as potentially disruptive). The category is given a name, but it is not yet clear if it will be just a flash in the pan.
- *The chasm.* Having now been in the marketplace for some time, the offer has lost its novelty; visionaries no longer see it as a source of dramatic competitive advantage and pursue disruptive opportunities elsewhere. As a result, the market stalls.

- *Crossing the chasm.* The only reliable way to exit the chasm is to target on the other side a niche market made up of pragmatists united by a common problem for which there is no known solution. These pragmatists are motivated to help the new technology cross the chasm if it is packaged as a complete solution to their problem.
- *Bowling alley.* In this phase, the technology has gained acceptance among pragmatists in multiple-niche markets where it enables genuine solutions to uncommon problems. Within adopting niches, the new paradigm builds a loyal following among those who see a market in the making. Outside the niches, it is becoming more widely accepted by the general public.
- *Tornado.* The technology has proved its usefulness in niche markets and, in the process, a killer app has emerged—something that makes it both broadly applicable and highly attractive to a mass audience. Overnight it becomes perceived as necessary and standard.
- *Main street.* The initial surge of hypergrowth subsides, leaving behind a market-share pecking order that is likely to persist for a long time to come. Customers have selected their vendor of choice and are now focused on deploying the technology more broadly.

After Assimilation

The technology-adoption life cycle comes to an end once the marketplace has completely assimilated the disruption that triggered it. In the case of automobiles, this happened sometime between World War I and World War II. Once assimilation has occurred, a new set of dynamics emerges. These are reflected in the remaining phases of the category-maturity life cycle. They are:

■ **Phase B, Growth Markets.** Even though the technology has been thoroughly assimilated, the offerings it has spawned remain in high demand for a while longer. This is an exceedingly pleasant time to be a manager because you are presiding over what is essentially category growth generating superior economic returns while entailing little company-specific risk.

■ **Phase C, Mature Markets.** Category growth has flattened, and commoditization is under way. In Darwinian terms, the boundaries of the niche have been reached and the category is experiencing the condition of scarcity for the first time. Growth must come from increasing the yield from the current customer base, or growing it at the expense of another competitor. Natural selection ensues with a wave of consolidation thinning out the bottom of the pecking order.

■ **Phase D, Declining Markets.** The category has become completely boxed in, innovation opportunities harder to find, and even those that dominate the market are experiencing difficulty in creating attractive returns. The market is ripe for some form of disruption, through either an obsoleting technology or radically innovative business model.

■ **Phase E, End of Life.** A disruptive technology has emerged and made significant inroads. As a consequence, the incumbent technology has been rendered obsolete. The only customers left are conservatives and laggards. This is a classic time to take a company private to harvest the remaining economic value in the category, brand, distribution channel, and customer relationships.

SLIDING DOWN THE COMMODITIZATION CURVE

Sliding down the commoditization curve has been the fate of the Chevrolet division of General Motors and the personal computing division of HP, not to mention a whole host of airlines and telecommunications service providers. It is not that these companies do not innovate. It is that their offers do not achieve separation—and here is the kicker—*they were never designed to!*

It's probably hard to picture in your mind a Chevrolet sedan from the past ten years, but it's easy to recall a Chrysler PT Cruiser, a Hummer, or a Mini Cooper. Innovation for differentiation must be bold enough that, if it wins, it achieves separation. That's why Chrysler's failures are more memorable than Chevrolet's successes—the Viper and the Prowler, for two.

MANAGING INNOVATION

It is important for you and your colleagues to come to a unanimous consensus around the single most compelling question driving innovation strategy: What type of innovation will we so excel at that we will leave all our competition behind?

Consider each innovation type as an independent vector, an arrow pointed in its own unique direction. Any vector sufficiently amplified will achieve breakaway separation from your competitive set. What would cause you to choose one over the other? Here are three factors to consider:

1. **Core Competence.** Different companies have different assets to exploit—some latent, some realized, in part a function of their business architecture, in part a function of their particular histories.

2. **Competitive Analysis.** Different sets of competitors leave different openings to exploit, either by neglecting them altogether or by strategically targeting them.

3. **Category Maturity.** Different stages of the category-maturity life cycle reward different forms of innovation. As categories mature, certain forms of innovation become outmoded and new ones are called for.

You should commit to an innovation type appropriate to the maturity of your category and forgo types that are not. Consider each innovation type and debate their relative attractions on your way toward choosing one for a strategic focus.

Types of Innovation

To better understand the various types of innovation, it helps to organize those types into clusters. The innovation types fall into these four clusters or innovation zones:

1. Product Leadership Zone.
2. Customer Intimacy Zone.
3. Operational Excellence Zone.
4. Category Renewal Zone.

Product Leadership Zone

A focus on product leadership is intended to contrast with strategies that do not differentiate the offer but rather the customer's experience of it, or *customer intimacy*, or the value chain's effectiveness at delivering it, that is, its *operational excellence*.

There are four primary types of innovation that leverage product leadership as an underlying value creation engine. These are:

• *Disruptive innovation.* This type of innovation creates new market categories based on a discontinuous technology change or a disruptive business model. Examples include the technological discontinuity of digital photo processing introduced by Shutterfly and Ofoto and the business-model disruption of digital media distribution heralded by Napster and made far more palatable by Apple iTunes. Disruptive innovations are incompatible with existing standards and the existing value chain, and they develop fresh markets.

BOSTON SCIENTIFIC: DISRUPTIVE INNOVATION IN A GROWTH MARKET

Stents are plastic tubes that are inserted into blocked arteries to open them and keep them open. The problem is that blockages often reform around the stent, requiring additional intervention. Boston Scientific pioneered the introduction of drug-eluting stents that release plaque-reducing chemicals at the point of use. These stents have revolutionized the treatment of arterial sclerosis, and the company dominates the market.

- *Application innovation.* Also known as solution innovation, this type develops new markets for existing products by finding unexploited uses for them, often by combining them in novel ways. One example is the adaptation of the Macintosh to desktop publishing in advertising and media. Application innovations introduce new standards but leverage existing value chains, albeit by giving them a new focus.
- *Product innovation.* This innovation type focuses on existing markets for existing products, differentiating through features and functions that current offers do not have. This form of innovation depends on fast time to market, although patents sometimes keep competitors at bay.

XEROX AND MEDTRONIC: PRODUCT INNOVATION IN A GROWTH MARKET

Xerox introduced the photocopier in 1960, building the franchise both in a complex-systems direction, with copy-center systems like DocuTech, as well as in the volume-operations direction with desktop copiers. Despite failing to commercialize on many of its other product innovations, including Ethernet, Smalltalk, and graphical user interface computing, this one major success has led to a $15 billion global corporation.

Another similar story belongs to Medtronic, which introduced the pacemaker the same year Xerox introduced the copier. The company remains the worldwide market leader today, earning about half its $9 billion in revenue from cardiac rhythm management products.

- *Platform innovation.* This type of innovation interposes a simplifying layer to mask an underlying legacy of complexity and complication, thereby freeing a next generation of offers to focus on new value propositions. The most successful platform innovations reposition an already ubiquitous product to take on this new role. For example, Oracle repositioned its relational database from a component ingredient of the minicomputer to a universal enterprise application software enabler.

Customer Intimacy Zone

Innovation types in mature markets all have an optimizing flavor. They are either leveraging customer intimacy to make the offer a little bit more attractive to the customer or leveraging operational excellence to make it a little bit more profitable to the vendor. There are four innovation types in this zone, arranged in a sequence migrating from closest to the product to closest to the customer:

- *Line-extension innovation.* This type of innovation makes structural modifications to an established offer to create a distinctive subcategory. The goal is to expand a maturing market by engaging with a new customer base or re-engaging more compellingly with an old one. For example, when the minivan and SUV were introduced in the automotive sector, the underlying infrastructure of the sector remained unchanged, thereby allowing the vendor to leverage amortized investments and keep development risks low.
- *Enhancement innovation.* This type of innovation continues the trajectory begun by line extensions, driving innovation into finer and finer elements of detail, getting closer and closer to the surface of the offer with less and less impact on the underlying infrastructure. The goal is to improve existing offers in existing markets by modifying a single dimension, thereby reawakening customer interest in what was becoming an increasingly commoditized category. One example is cherry flavoring in Coke.
- *Marketing innovation.* This type of innovation focuses on differentiating the interaction with a prospective customer during the purchase process. The goal here is to outsell your competitors rather than "outproduct" them. One example is the use of viral marketing on the Web to create buzz about a new movie.
- *Experiential innovation.* The ultimate refinement in this trajectory of customer intimacy is experiential innovation, where the value is based not on

differentiating the functionality but rather the experience of the offering. This is particularly suited to consumer markets where the product has become a commodity, and the purchase decision has become risk free. Examples include business hotels that remember your newspaper preference, and restaurants that supply patrons with pagers so they can roam while waiting for a table.

Operational Excellence Zone

Complementing the customer intimacy zone's focus on differentiating the offering on the demand side of the market, the operational excellence zone focuses on differentiating on the supply side. Here the primary reward is a lowered cost structure that enables either price reductions, capital reinvestment, or higher profits. Innovation types in the operational excellence zone include the following, organized in a sequence migrating from closest to the product to closest to the processes that enable it:

- *Value-engineering innovation.* This type of innovation extracts cost from the materials and manufacturing of an established offer without changing its external properties. It usually calls for substituting low-cost standard parts and preintegrated subsystems for an earlier design's high-cost manually integrated custom components. Examples include the television, PC, and cell phone, all of which have seen reduced costs from value engineering.
- *Integration innovation.* This type of innovation reduces the customer's cost of maintaining a complex operation by integrating its many disparate elements into a single, centrally managed system. Typically it permits backward compatibility with existing systems.
- *Process innovation.* This type of innovation focuses on improving profit margins by extracting waste not from the offer itself but from the enabling processes that produce it. The goal is to remove nonvalue-adding steps from the work flow. Examples include Dell's direct-retail model and Wal-Mart's vendor-managed inventory process.
- *Value migration innovation.* This type of innovation consists of redirecting the business model away from a commoditizing element in the market's value chain toward one richer in margins. A good example of this is the switch in focus from products to consumables, as with razors to razor blades or printers to ink-jet cartridges.

Category Renewal Zone

Sooner or later all market categories enter into a decline. It is important to remember that when you are faced with a declining market, any market that is still an ongoing concern is in itself a valuable asset. From the vendor's point of view, there are two basic options to explore, usually in tandem: Renew your franchise by refocusing the majority of your resources on a new category while simultaneously optimizing returns for the remainder of the present category's useful life following a harvest-and-exit strategy. The pertinent types of innovation are:

- *Organic innovation.* On this path the company uses its internal resources to reposition itself into a growth category. In industrial markets, this repositioning typically involves reconnecting with its most valued customers and finding new problems to solve for them, following the approach laid out in application innovation. IBM did this when it repositioned itself as an e-commerce-enabling company. This represents a return to product innovation. The vendor stays within the same sector but repositions its product line.
- *Acquisition innovation.* This type of innovation solves the problem of category renewal externally through merger and acquisition. One can play this game as either an acquirer or an acquiree. When BEA bought WebLogic, it repositioned itself from the Unix market to the Internet and dramatically improved its performance. On the other hand, when Lotus could not renew itself organically via its Notes platform, it sold itself to IBM, thereby acquiring the sophisticated distribution and services capabilities that Notes required to be successful.

NOKIA: ORGANIC RENEWAL IN A DECLINING MARKET

For most of the twentieth century, Nokia was known as a diversified corporation in paper and pulp products, rubber manufacturing, and cable. It was through the cable side of the house, first with coaxial cable for computer networks, that it entered the electronics sector. In the 1990s, it entered the mobile-phone business. The company invested heavily in building handset manufacturing capability, drawing on the cash cows of paper, pulp, and rubber products. Once it completed the transition, Nokia divested itself of those other businesses, and today it is the leading mobile-phone supplier in the world.

MANAGING INERTIA

You have just crafted a superb innovation strategy, one that gives every promise of creating the separation you need from your direct competitors, earning the customer preference your profit margins require. Now you must overcome the inertia of your own organization that fosters resistance to making the changes necessary to implement it.

Inertia is not the enemy of innovation, but it does resist it at the point of change. Therefore, at that very point, management must learn to deconstruct inertia in order to reconstitute it elsewhere. You must extract resources from context in order to repurpose them for core. Context includes most of the things you do to meet commitments to key stakeholders and to comply with industry laws and standards. Core is that which differentiates your company to create sustainable competitive advantage.

Extracting resources from context to repurpose for core accomplishes three key objectives:

1. It solves your balance sheet problem, enabling you to fund your future from your current asset base.
2. It solves your income statement problem, enabling you to increase the revenues and margins earned by your current asset base.
3. It solves your inertia problem. By taking mass out of context, you reduce its inertial resistance to core. The more mass you move from context to core, the more powerful this change dynamic will be.

Extracting Resources from Context

We know that we want to prioritize resource allocation for core, but our decision is complicated by the presence of mission-critical risk. As managers we must allocate resources to guard against this downside. Mission-critical context—product shipments, financial transactions, computer security, inventory supply, etc.—is laying claim to the very resources we need to deploy to the next generation of core, but we dare not release them from their current assignments.

To ensure that mission-critical context components do not fail, we assign experienced employees to these tasks and experienced managers to supervise their work. We build systems that track this work and escalate problems should they arise. We tie up many valuable resources to guard against the downside of a mission-critical failure.

What the Future Should Look Like

A desired future state is one in which valuable resources are being extracted and repurposed. Innovation begins where the focus is on core, but the project is contained to minimize risk. This is the domain of non-mission-critical core, an experimental side of the business where risk is encouraged in the quest for differentiation, and the rest of the enterprise is protected by restricting the scope of consequence.

When the innovation is judged ready for wider rollout, it moves into the domain of the mission-critical core. This is the time to release the next generation product line, launch the next new marketing campaign, etc. It is where enterprises expect to make their highest returns because they have distinctive competitive advantage, and they are exploiting it at maximum scale. Innovations stay here for as long as competitive differentiation is sustained, the longer the better.

Eventually, however, Darwinism has its day, and competitors find a way to neutralize the advantages being exploited at their expense. When this happens, the work migrates to the domain of mission-critical context.

Once management realizes that a class of work no longer contributes to competitive advantage, its attitude toward it must change. The work must still be done, but the focus now shifts from differentiation to productivity. Management attention shifts to systems, automation, and any other tool that will free up talented people for other tasks.

To maximize resource extraction, companies must convert mission-critical context into non-mission-critical context, wringing out the risks that lay claim to high-value resources. Organizations will still retain a thin veneer of management to oversee pertinent relationships, but the bulk of once-committed, scarce resources can now be released and used to fund the next cycle of innovation.

Repurposing Resources for Core

In the move toward a global economy, workforces in developed economies have been threatened by offshore outsourcers leveraging low-cost labor. This trend shows no signs of subsiding, and companies that do not avail themselves of this opportunity are severely challenged to price their goods and services competitively.

The problem of creating alignment must be solved by the corporations themselves: management and labor collaborating with each other for the collective good of customers, employees, and investors. Together they must build a solution that actively embraces both outsourcing and offshoring while simultaneously building a stronger in-house domestic workforce compensated commensurately with its local standard of living.

Outsourcing

The essence of the problem with outsourcing is highlighted in the diagram below.

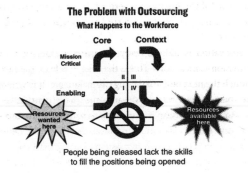

The Problem with Outsourcing
What Happens to the Workforce

People being released lack the skills
to fill the positions being opened

The human resources that are freed up in the context-enabling quadrant IV do not generally have the skill sets required to be repurposed in the core-enabling projects in quadrant I. When layoffs occur, it is Darwinism at its meanest and most parochial, eroding culture and values, devaluing experience, and dismissing loyalty. It sends shock waves through the entire workforce, diminishing productivity everywhere. This is a very bad model indeed.

But what else can be done? Resources need to be properly recycled. What people in quadrant IV bring to jobs in quadrant III is experience and expertise in managing context. By freeing up someone in quadrant IV, a company can reasonably expect that person to have the aptitude for work in quadrant III.

What people in quadrant III bring to tasks in quadrant II is experience and expertise in managing mission criticality. Whether the work is core or context, if it is mission critical, it must be done on time, on spec, and on budget. The class of people who thrive under this kind of pressure are the ones who were getting stuck in quadrant III managing mission-critical context and thus were unavailable in quadrant II to help deploy the next generation of mission-critical core. By recycling people from quadrant IV back into quadrant III to pick up their current workload, these people are freed up to bring about the next generation of innovation in quadrant II.

Finally, what people in quadrant II can bring to tasks in quadrant I is experience and expertise in managing core. Core work is always in some sense unprecedented, or else it would not be differentiating. That typically requires outside-the-box thinking and ongoing iterative experimentation. Quadrant II people don't have to be trained for quadrant I because what they do precedes what trainers would know.

Managing Inertia in Your Enterprise

An aggressive agenda can redirect the inertial momentum of your enterprise from context to core. The seven essential steps of that agenda are as follows:

1. *Conduct a core/context analysis of your current business.* Begin with categorizing your various market segments in terms of the four quadrants. In complex systems enterprises, these will typically consist of multiple grids to represent how core and context play out by product category, customer industry, and geography. In volume-operations businesses, one is likely to develop views by product category, consumer demographics, and sales channel. These placements help guide resource-allocation decisions downstream.

2. *Conduct a resource-allocation analysis to complement your core/context analysis.* Do not get distracted by budgets here. Focus on head count, specifically on identifying and locating your top performers in invention, deployment, and optimization, whose leadership or functional expertise can change the outcome of a project. You want to leverage these people's skills to the maximum.

3. *Set a more ambitious agenda.* Once you have mapped out how things are, turn to determining how you want them to be. How would you improve your enterprise's current performance?

4. *Plan out your moves as a team.* Extracting resources from context to repurpose for core is a collaborative effort. Don't withhold even a single key resource. Get the timing right—it does no good to free up resources if the work they are meant to do is not yet ready to be done.

5. *Focus on time to market.* Create a necessary and proper sense of urgency. Make a direct assault on the scheduling assumptions of your plan of record.

6. *Get the gears moving.* Focus initial efforts on freeing up top-performing deployers from their current mission-critical context assignments. Assign optimizers to attack their workloads with a five-lever approach. Set a date for their last day in their current roles.

7. *Keep the gears moving.* Once resource recycling has begun, do not let it stop. Each new learning curve is paid for by the margins created by the last curve and in turn is expected to generate high-margin returns to fund the next one.

Evolution in Action

Natural selection is a game with no time-outs. It does, however, allow for unlimited substitutions. Resource recycling not only delivers efficiency; it also provides refreshment. There is respite for the weary as long as it is followed by an energized willingness to re-engage. Communities need abiding sources of employment. Customers need stable sources of supply. Governments need a vital tax base. Investors need opportunities to create attractive returns. We are all more or less strategically aligned. We are just being asked to execute at a new level of competitiveness.

That's what evolution is all about—a continual raising of the bar. It's how countries raise their standard of living. It's why new companies get formed every year. It's why each of us must learn new skills throughout our careers. We may get tired, but we are not likely to get bored. Mostly we just have to perform.

THE FIVE LEVERS

The five levers represent a sequence of management actions that systematically reengineers mission-critical workloads to first extract risk so that one can then extract resources.

Here's how the five levers play out:

1. *Centralize.* Bring operations under a single authority to reduce overhead costs and create a single decision-making authority to manage risk.
2. *Standardize.* Reduce the variety and variability of processes delivering similar outputs to further reduce costs and minimize risks.
3. *Modularize.* Deconstruct the system into its component subsystems and standardize interfaces for future cost reduction. This requires specialized support, such as consultants or an in-house Six Sigma team.
4. *Optimize.* Eliminate redundant steps, automate standard sequences, streamline remaining operations, substitute lower-cost resources, and instrument the process for monitoring and control.
5. *Outsource.* Drive processes out of the enterprise entirely to further reduce overhead, variabilize costs, and minimize future investment.

WIKINOMICS
by Don Tapscott and Anthony D. Williams

Modern technology creates amazing advances in more than just the electronic devices and conveniences with which we live, work, and play. Along with the many latest and greatest digital toys and tools, we have also gained new ways to use this gadgetry and the Internet to improve our work as managers. The possibilities created for better management are brimming with hope for better relationships and collaborations thanks to the connections that are now possible with innovations such as Wikipedia, Linux, MySpace, YouTube, the Human Genome Project, and a variety of other new "planetary networks of partners who work as peers."

To define the benefits and possibilities of our increasingly interconnected and global web of access, Don Tapscott and Anthony D. Williams wrote *Wikinomics: How Mass Collaboration Changes Everything*. Through painstaking research and collaboration with others, the authors have written a valuable guide to mass collaboration for people at all levels of business in a variety of fields and disciplines.

Tapscott and Williams point out how our collective capabilities are increasingly vast, yet much of our genius for innovation and growth goes untapped. *Wikinomics* expertly defines the current state of the world's interconnectivity while exploring the ways we can use that knowledge to improve collaboration on a mass scale.

Although Wikipedia, YouTube, MySpace, and Flickr have exhibited the remarkable powers of mass collaboration for several years, Tapscott and Williams are the first writers to create a succinct road map for using these types of open, peering, sharing, and global tools to help companies and organizations create massive online communities. While writing about the changes that are taking place around the globe, the authors also declare that the old-school, inwardly focused, self-contained corporation is exhaling its last breath.

Who would dare to challenge the tried and true corporations that deny their vulnerability to new forms of critical mass until their businesses become obsolete? Don Tapscott, the best-selling author and CEO of the strategy consultancy New Paradigm, and his research director there, Anthony D. Williams, are the brave souls who defy old-fashioned, conventional business wisdom. While showing companies where they currently fall short, they also demonstrate new ways organizations can cope in an increasingly global and interconnected marketplace.

Williams holds a master's of research degree from the London School of Economics, where he also teaches. Tapscott keeps one foot in the academic world as a teacher at the Joseph L. Rotman School of Management at the University of Toronto, and his other foot in the business realm as the leader of his New Paradigm consultancy since the early 1990s. As academics and successful strategy consultants, Tapscott and Williams both stride confidently between higher learning and industry.

Tapscott has been writing about the cutting edge of business strategy for decades. Before *Wikinomics,* he wrote ten books that tackle the conflict between twentieth-century thinking and twenty-first-century marketplace demands, including the best-selling *Paradigm Shift, The Digital Economy, Growing Up Digital, The Naked Corporation,* and *Digital Capital.* After honing his craft and leadership skills with these books, he teamed up with researcher Anthony D. Williams to write *Wikinomics.*

In *Wikinomics,* they describe how a new era is at hand—one in which we will need to create more learning opportunities for ourselves if we want to survive in the new economy where "old business reflexes" are no longer sufficient to compete. *Wikinomics* describes the principles of success in a new marketplace where being open, producing with peers, sharing information, and acting globally offer unparalleled possibilities for growth and innovation. Tapscott and Williams present readers with key insights into the profound changes this new era entails. Through the work of these two top business experts, the fields of management and business leadership have been expanded to include an updated perspective on the phenomenon of global collaboration that is becoming more prevalent every day.

WIKINOMICS

How Mass Collaboration Changes Everything

by Don Tapscott and Anthony D. Williams

CONTENTS

THE SUMMARY IN BRIEF

Based on a $9 million research project led by best-selling author Don Tapscott, *Wikinomics* shows how masses of people can take part in the economy like never before. Billions of connected individuals can now actively participate in innovation, wealth creation, and social development in ways we once only dreamed.

For companies to succeed, leaders must think differently about how to compete and be profitable, and embrace a new art and science of collaboration the authors call "wikinomics." This is more than open source, social networking, smart mobs, crowd wisdom, or any other idea that touches upon the subject. Rather, it's about deep changes in the structure and modus operandi of the corporate entity and our economy, based on new competitive principles such as openness, peering, sharing, and acting globally.

The authors describe the rapid growth of new collaborative enterprises such as MySpace, InnoCentive, Flickr, Second Life, YouTube, and others. They also offer examples of how mature firms such as Boeing, BMW, Procter & Gamble, and others have seized on collaboration and self-organization as ways to cut costs, innovate faster, and co-create with customers and partners.

In this summary, Don Tapscott and Anthony D. Williams challenge our most deeply rooted assumptions about business. They describe what happens when masses of people and firms partner openly to drive innovation and growth, and they offer compelling reasons why anyone in business over the long run should pay close attention to this fundamental evolution.

What You'll Learn in This Summary

- The weapons of mass collaboration and how to use them in your organization.
- How technology, demographics, and global economics are converging for the first Category 6 business revolution.
- The "ideagoras" that are becoming marketplaces for ideas, innovations, and uniquely qualified minds.
- Why consumers are becoming prosumers, and how customers are becoming co-innovators.
- How sharing and peer production will replace traditional ways of conducting business.
- How to live in the new "wiki workplace."

THE COMPLETE SUMMARY

BUILDING THE COMMUNITY OF THE FUTURE

While hierarchies are not vanishing, profound changes in the nature of technology, demographics, and the global economy are giving rise to powerful new models of production based on community, collaboration, and self-organization rather than on hierarchy and control.

Smart companies are encouraging, rather than fighting, the heaving growth of massive online communities. As a growing number of firms see the benefits of mass collaboration, this new way of organizing will displace the traditional corporate structures as the economy's primary engine of wealth creation.

WIKINOMICS

Due to deep changes in technology, demographics, business, the economy, and the world, we are entering a new age in which people take part in the economy like never before. The growing accessibility of information technologies puts the tools required to collaborate, create value, and compete at everybody's fingertips. This new mode of innovation and value creation is called peer production or peering.

New low-cost collaborative infrastructures—from free Internet telephony to open-source software to global outsourcing platforms—allow thousands of individuals and small producers to co-create products, access markets, and delight customers in ways that only large corporations could manage in the past. People can contribute to the "digital commons" at very little cost to themselves, which makes collective action attractive. Indeed, peer production is a very social activity.

These changes are ushering us toward a world where knowledge, power, and productive capability will be more dispersed than during any other time in our history. A power shift is under way and a tough new business rule is emerging: Harness the new collaboration or perish.

The New Promise of Collaboration

A new art and science of collaboration is emerging—called "wikinomics." This isn't just about developing online encyclopedias such as Wikipedia and other documents. A wiki (Hawaiian for "quick") is more than just software for enabling multiple people to edit Web sites. A wiki is a metaphor for a new era of collaboration and participation.

The new promise of collaboration is that with peer production we will harness human skill, ingenuity, and intelligence more efficiently and effectively than anything we have witnessed previously. The ability to integrate the talents of dispersed individuals and organizations is becoming the defining competency for managers and firms.

To innovate and succeed, the new mass collaboration must become part of every leader's playbook and lexicon. Learning how to engage and co-create with a shifting set of self-organized partners is becoming an essential skill, as important as budgeting, R&D, and planning.

The Principles of Wikinomics

Wikinomics is based on four powerful new ideas: openness, peering, sharing, and acting globally.

■ **Being Open.** Today, companies that make their boundaries porous to external ideas and human capital outperform companies that rely solely on their internal resources and capabilities. People and institutions that interact with firms are gaining unprecedented access to important information about corporate behavior, operations, and performance.

■ **Peering.** Peering succeeds because it leverages self-organization—a style of production that works more effectively than hierarchical management for certain tasks. Its greatest impact today is in the production of software, media, entertainment, and culture.

■ **Sharing.** Smart firms are treating intellectual property (IP) like a mutual fund—they manage a balanced portfolio of IP assets, some protected and some shared. Of course companies need to protect critical IP. But companies can't work together effectively if all of their IP is hidden.

■ **Acting Globally.** The new globalization is both causing and caused by changes in collaboration and the way firms orchestrate capability to pioneer and produce things. Winning companies will need to know the world, including its markets, technologies, and people.

THE PERFECT STORM

The new Web is the natural habit for a new cohort of collaborators called the "Net Generation." For them the Web is the new glue that binds their social networks. Phenomena like MySpace, Facebook, Flickr, 43things, Technorati, and del.icio.us aren't just Web sites, they're dynamic online communities where sprawling and vibrant clusters of interaction are forming.

As the new Web and the Net Gen collide with the forces of globalization, we are entering what might be considered a perfect storm, where converging waves of change and innovation are toppling the economic order.

The New Web

Today, the Internet is evolving from a network of Web sites that enable firms to present information into a computing platform in its own right. Whether people are developing, sharing, or socializing, the new Web is principally about joining in rather than about passively receiving information.

Today's most exciting and successful Web companies and communities are stitching together their own services from shared databanks and Lego-style pieces of Web software. They use Web services to design platforms for people to engage and co-create with their peers.

What does the programmable Web mean for users? Increasingly, we are all witting and unwitting co-conspirators in building one massively sophisticated computer. The Web is no longer about idly surfing and passively reading, listening, or watching. It's about peering: sharing, socializing, collaborating, and, most of all, creating within loosely connected communities.

Growing Up Collaborating

A new generation of youngsters has grown up online, and they are bringing a new ethic of openness, participation, and interactivity to workplaces, communities, and markets.

The Net Gen spends time searching, reading, scrutinizing, authenticating, collaborating, and organizing. The Internet makes life an ongoing, massive connection, and this generation loves it.

The Net Gen's modus operandi is networking. It would be easy to dismiss online social networking as another fickle youth fad. But online social networking is uniquely attuned to the Net Gen's cultural habits and will be part of the social fabric going forward.

The opportunity to bring Net-Geners (and other customers) into the enterprise as co-creators of value possibly presents the most exciting long-term engine of change and innovation that the business world has seen.

The Collaboration Economy

Traditional corporations are finding themselves thrust aside by an entirely new kind of business entity. That new entity is the business web, or the b-web. B-webs are clusters of businesses that come together over the Internet. While each company retains its identity, the companies function together, generating more wealth than they could ever hope to generate individually.

The future lives in collaboration across borders, cultures, companies, and disciplines. Effectively, it's globalize or die.

In the collaboration economy, the real advantage of global sourcing is not cost savings, but the endless possibilities for growth, innovation, and diversity. The greatest growth engines of the twenty-first century will be business webs that fuse the resources and competencies of the developed and developing worlds into unbeatable combinations.

THE PEER PIONEERS

Peer production is emerging as an alternative model of production that can harness human skill, ingenuity, and intelligence more efficiently and effectively than traditional firms. The way companies address peer production will shape the future of industry and affect their very chances for survival. In its purest form, peer production is a way of producing goods and services that relies entirely on self-organizing, egalitarian communities of individuals who come together voluntarily to produce a shared outcome.

Communities of producers typically use "general public licenses" to guarantee users the right to share and modify creative works, provided that any modifications are shared. By opening up the right to modify and distribute, these open-source licenses allow larger numbers of contributors to interact freely with larger amounts of information in search of new projects and possibilities for collaboration.

Peering works best when at least three conditions are present: (1) The object of production is information or culture, which keeps the cost of participation low for contributors; (2) Tasks can be chunked out into bite-size pieces that individuals can contribute in small increments and independently of other producers; and (3) The costs of integrating those pieces into an end product, including the leadership and quality-control mechanisms, must be low.

The Future of Open Source

Open source, it seems, may at last be coming of age. Embracing open source means embracing new mental models and new ways of conceptualizing value creation. Profiting from peer production groups like Linux is a new skill that requires companies to recognize and seize chances to build new products and services on top of vibrant open ecosystems.

Peer Production Is Here to Stay

Peer production will continue to grow in importance because key enabling conditions are present and growing. These include access to computing power and applications, transparency, globalization, the democratization of knowledge and skills, and the increasing complexity of systems. Firms must invest in the technology and business architecture to become truly networked and open enterprises, and engage in collaborative networks that help build the culture and strategic capabilities to leverage peer production.

IDEAGORAS

Ninety thousand scientists from 175 countries have registered with Inno-Centive to provide solutions to companies such as Boeing, Dow, DuPont, Novartis, and Procter & Gamble. Launched by U.S. pharmaceutical giant Eli Lilly as an e-business venture in 2001, InnoCentive now enables some thirty-five Fortune 500 companies to extend their problem-solving capacity. This visionary matchmaking system links experts to unsolved R&D problems, allowing these companies to tap the talents of a global, scientific community without having to employ everybody full time.

The authors call these marketplaces ideagoras, much like the bustling agoras that sprang up in the heart of ancient Athens to facilitate politics and commerce among the burgeoning Athenian citizenry. Modern-day ideagoras such as InnoCentive make ideas, inventions, and scientific expertise around the planet accessible to innovation-hungry companies. As more companies embrace the principles of wikinomics—openness, peering, sharing, and acting globally—these ideagoras will come to fruition, fueling an increasingly active trade in technology, intellectual capital, and other key innovation ingredients.

Questions and Solutions

Ideagoras come in two principal flavors: solutions in search of questions and questions in need of solutions. Solutions in search of questions are those 70 percent to 90 percent of ideas and inventions that go unutilized. Questions in need of solutions are just that: unanswered problems, queries, or uncertainties that have not been addressed internally.

In the late 1990s, Procter & Gamble launched an internal survey and discovered it was spending $1.5 billion on R&D, generating lots of patents, but using less than 10 percent of them in its own products. CEO A.G. Lafley saw it as a wake-up call and led the charge to open up the patent portfolio. P&G now makes every patent in its portfolio available for license to any outsider, as long as it has existed for at least five years or has been in use in a P&G product for at least three years.

THE KEY BENEFITS OF PEER PRODUCTION FOR BUSINESSES

Harnessing External Talent. Smart firms can harness innovation by using peer production to involve more people and partners in developing customer solutions than they could ever hope to marshal internally.

Keeping Up with Users. If you do not stay current with users, they invent around you, creating opportunities for competitors.

Boosting Demand for Complementary Offerings. Participating in peer-production communities can boost demand for complementary offerings and provide new opportunities to create added value.

Reducing Costs. By collaborating with open-source communities, companies can reduce costs dramatically.

Shifting the Locus of Competition. Publishing intellectual property in non-core areas that are core to a competitor can undermine your rival's ability to monopolize a resource that you depend on.

Taking the Friction out of Collaboration. Avoiding the problems related to ownership and exploitation of intellectual property is one reason why a growing number of firms are embracing open models of collaborative innovation.

Developing Social Capital. When firms join a peer-production community, sharing is the continued price of admission to the community from which the firm derives various benefits.

P&G is not alone in its affinity for IP licensing. In fact, virtually all companies with sizable patent holdings are now busy mining their portfolios, looking for licensing-out opportunities and taking technologies off the shelf that can bring in revenue. Using online marketplaces such as yet2.com allows them to cast wider nets across multiple, and often unrelated, industries.

Other mature, innovation-based companies face the same dilemma. The potential for growth is out there, but it's distributed across thousands, perhaps millions, of individuals, organizations, and firms. That's where ideagoras come in—they help link all of these individuals, companies, and organizations together by establishing connections and facilitating transactions between buyers and sellers of ideas and technology.

Not only can ideagoras enable companies like P&G to innovate well beyond what they could muster internally, they help them hone their true value-adding capabilities and avoid reinventing the wheel.

Harnessing Ideagoras

With the emergence of global ideagoras, companies can pursue a wider set of strategic possibilities. Learning how to create, find, and reapply great ideas in a global ideagora means turning the R&D organization on its head. Some of the big changes include refining its approach to intellectual property, sharpening its external radar, and creating an R&D culture that supports the acquisition of external ideas and technologies. Smart firms will harness a portfolio of approaches ranging from corporate ventures to customer co-creation to peer-producing value in open communities.

Ideagoras lower the costs of communicating, collaborating, and transacting and could very well revolutionize the way firms conduct R&D. Companies that learn how to harness ideagoras will divest themselves of non-core activities and conserve their resources for cutting-edge challenges and opportunities.

Internal R&D will still be important in the new world of ideagoras. But in-house innovation alone will not be enough to survive in a quickly changing and intensely competitive economy. Increasingly, the corporate R&D process must look two ways: toward its internal projects and competencies, and toward the external marketplace to leverage new IP and capabilities. Ideagoras are the place where companies can tap a wealth of new ideas, innovations, and uniquely qualified minds.

THE PROSUMERS

Two forces are converging to position the customer as a co-innovator. One is that customers use the Web as a stage to generate prosumer communities, so what was once fringe activity is increasingly out in the open. Second, companies are discovering that "lead users"—people who stretch the limits of existing technology and often design their own product prototypes in the process—often develop modifications and extensions to products that will eventually appeal to mainstream markets. Companies that learn how to tap the insights of lead users can gain competitive advantage.

Customer innovation is going self-serve with the rise of prosumer communities. One of the earliest, and still most vibrant, prosumer communities has formed around Lego products. Lego's fusion of mass customization and peer production remains rare enough in today's consumer products market to make the idea particularly outstanding. Customers can make whatever they want, and Lego transforms its legion of youthful customers into a decentralized virtual design team that invents and swaps new Lego models.

Control Versus Customer Hacking

Here's the prosumption dilemma: A company that gives its customers free rein to hack risks cannibalizing its business model and losing control of its platform. A company that fights its users soils its reputation and shuts out a potentially valuable source of innovation.

Customer hacking will live on. Smart companies will bring customers into their business webs and give them lead roles in developing next-generation products and services. This may mean adjusting business models and revamping internal processes to enable better collaboration with users.

That is a small price to pay to keep customers loyal to your business. In fact, the opportunity to generate vibrant customer ecosystems where users help advance, implement, and even market new product features represents a largely untapped frontier for farsighted companies to exploit.

Nothing illustrates the opportunities and trade-offs of prosumption better than the growing propensity of young people to weave fluid and participatory tapestries of music content into their own unique and inviting creations. Call it "the remix culture."

The most popular form of Do-It-Yourself (DIY) creativity is what participants call "mashups," "bootlegging," "bastard pop," and a variety of other labels. The common theme is that aspiring artists fuse songs digitally from completely different genres to produce hybrid singles and, increasingly, full-length mashup albums. Unorthodox? Yes. Illegal piracy? Perhaps. Innovative and enjoyable? Most definitely.

Democratization is a scary word for those accustomed to ironclad control over the creation and distribution of music. But the music industry—and all industries for that matter—must resist the temptation to impose their will on consumers as a matter of convenience or, worse, as a result of a lack of ingenuity and agility. Rather, music labels should develop Internet business models and offerings with the right combination of "free" goods, consumer control, versioning, and ancillary products and services. This includes new platforms for fan remixes and other forms of customer participation in music creation and distribution.

Harnessing Prosumer Communities

Prosumption is becoming one of the most powerful engines of change and innovation that the business world has ever seen. Co-creating with customers is like tapping the most uniquely qualified pool of intellectual capital ever assembled. But it comes with new rules of engagement and tough challenges to existing business models.

The old customer co-creation idea was simple: Collaborate with your customers to create or customize goods, services, and experiences, all while generating a built-in market for your wares. This is the company-centric view of co-creation.

In the new prosumer-centric paradigm, customers want a genuine role in designing the products of the future. Products that don't enable and invite customer participation will be anathema.

If you expect to be around in the next decade, your organization will find ways to join and lead prosumer communities.

THE NEW ALEXANDRIANS

The Alexandrian Greeks were inspired by a simple but powerful idea. Take the sum of mankind's knowledge, store it in one building, and share it for the betterment of science, the arts, wealth, and the economy. At its crowning glory, estimates suggest that they had accumulated more than half a million volumes in their library.

We are fortunate to be living through the fastest and broadest accumulation of human knowledge and culture ever. Thanks to a new generation of Alexandrians, this fountain of knowledge, past and present, will soon be accessible in ways our ancestors could only dream of. Digital libraries are important, but the Alexandrian revolution extends far beyond the way we archive knowledge, to the way we develop and harness knowledge to drive economic and technological progress.

Collaboration, publication, peer review, and exchange of precompetitive information are now becoming keys to success in the knowledge-based economy. In fact, we have entered the age of collaborative science.

Just as collaborative tools and applications are reshaping enterprises, the new Web will forever change the way scientists publish, manage data, and collaborate across institutional boundaries. All the world's scientific data and research will at last be available to every single researcher—gratis—without prejudice or burden.

The New Alexandrians understand that creating a shared foundation of knowledge on which large and diverse groups of collaborators can build is a great way to enhance innovation and corporate success.

HOW TO HARNESS PROSUMERS

More Than Customization. Customization occurs when a customer gets a product adjusted to his or her specification. The problem is that mass customization entails mixing and matching prespecified components, significantly limiting flexibility and innovation for users. True prosumption entails deeper and earlier engagement in design processes and products that facilitate customer hacking and remixing.

Losing Control. Customers will treat your product as a platform for their own innovations, whether you grant them permission or not. If you do not stay current with customers, they invent around you, creating opportunities for competitors. It is preferable to sacrifice some control than it is to cede the game completely.

Customer Tool Kits and Context Orchestration. Make your products modular, reconfigurable, and editable. Set the context for customer innovation and collaboration. Make it easy to remix and share.

Becoming a Peer. Your real business is not creating finished products but innovation ecosystems.

Sharing the Fruits. Customers will expect to share in the ownership and fruits of their creations. If you make it profitable for customers to get involved, you will always be able to count on a dynamic and fertile ecosystem for growth and innovation.

Some companies use cross-licensing and patent pools to lower transaction costs and remove friction in their business relationships. Some industries embrace open standards to enhance interoperability and encourage collaboration. Others invest in a precompetitive knowledge commons to boost the productivity of downstream product development. Regardless of which method—or combination of methods—firms choose, the result is usually the same: a more dynamic and prosperous ecosystem.

PLATFORMS FOR PARTICIPATION

Today, with open platforms for innovation inviting unprecedented participation in value creation, cumulative innovation is going into overdrive. The companies that figure out how to harness the power of open platforms while providing adequate incentives to all stakeholders are poised to reap great rewards. Retail sites such as Amazon, eBay, and Apple demonstrate how platforms for participation can give rise to vibrant ecosystems around a simple activity like shopping.

Platform Incentive Systems

Should open-platform orchestrators compensate the people and organizations that add value to their platforms? And would monetary incentive systems spur more value creation, or possibly taint the dynamics that have made online communities successful?

Platforms for participation represent an exciting new kind of business that thrives on mass collaboration and embodies all of the wikinomics principles. Though the early examples are most evident on the Web, nearly all businesses can become open platforms, with enough imagination and ingenuity.

THE GLOBAL PLANT FLOOR

Peer production of physical things is coming of age, and smart companies are getting with the program. The old monolithic, multinational corporation that produces value in a closed hierarchical fashion is dead. Even the stodgy, capital-intensive manufacturing industries are no exception to this rule. Indeed, there is no part of the economy where this opening and blurring of corporate boundaries has more revolutionary potential.

The new reality in manufacturing, as in other spheres, is that boundaries are constantly blurring. In an age of modularity, open architectures, instant communication, and globally dispersed capabilities, the answers to who will do what and where the value will be developed are constantly changing.

Harnessing the Global Plant Floor

The rise of peer and collaborative processes for designing and building things is not unique. These processes are emerging in industries where intellectual property is widely dispersed and production capacity is fragmented among hundreds of specialized firms.

By organizing into loosely coupled networks of firms that jointly design and develop products for customers, both the suppliers and global integrators win. But harnessing the global plant floor means learning from the examples being set. Companies must focus on the critical value drivers; add value through orchestration; instill rapid, iterative design processes; harness modular architectures; create a transparent and egalitarian ecosystem; share the costs and risks; and, finally, keep a keen futures watch.

THE WIKI WORKPLACE

The workplace is becoming a self-organizing entity where centralized and tightly controlled processes are increasingly giving way to more spontaneous and decentralized forms of mass collaboration. This impacts five typical workplace functions: teaming, time-allocation, decision-making, resource-allocation, and communication.

Waking Up to the Wiki Workplace

Where might this new wiki workplace take us in the future?

- Workplaces will become smaller and teams will be more distributed, with participants drawn from all over.
- Employment relationships will necessarily become more fluid, definitely less long term, and undoubtedly more horizontal.
- The creation of ad hoc self-organized teams that come together to accomplish specialized tasks will become the norm.
- Expect new guildlike formations with codes of conduct that set the formal and informal norms and rules that govern how a growing number of people carry out their trade.
- Look for new peer-to-peer reputation-rating services to play a greater role in identifying high-quality, reliable collaborators.
- Talent agencies, auctions, and markets will play a larger role in managing the interface between employers and employees.

Don't expect overnight change. But a truly self-organized and distributed way of working is not far off on the distant horizon. Mass collaboration is already transforming the way goods and services are developed throughout the economy, and it is now becoming a growing force in today's marketplace.

COLLABORATIVE MINDS

Each model we have discussed represents a new and unique way to compete, but they all share one thing: These new forms of peer production enable firms to harvest external knowledge, resources, and talent on a scale that was previously impossible. Companies that adopt these models can drive important changes in their industries and rewrite the rules of competition.

There has probably never been a more exciting time to be in business, nor a more dangerous one. We are in the midst of a paradigm shift. New paradigms cause disruption and uncertainty and are nearly always received with coolness, hostility, or worse. Vested interests fight against the change, and leaders of the old are often the last to embrace the new. Consequently, a paradigm shift typically causes a crisis of leadership.

The lesson of history is that profound changes favor the newcomer and, in rare cases, the incumbent firms that learn to think differently. The choice facing firms is not whether to engage and work with peer-production communities, but determining when and how. The chance for customers and competitors to get the jump on new innovations in your area of business increases daily.

Thinking Differently

Smart firms will be able to harness external resources and talent to achieve unparalleled growth and success. The hard part will be rewiring your brain and turning off those old business reflexes so that you can capitalize on what the new world of wikinomics can offer.

■ **Being Open.** A growing number of smart companies are learning that openness is a force for growth and competitiveness. Amazon, eBay, Google, and Flickr open up their applications and business infrastructures to increase the speed, scope, and success of innovation.

■ **Peering.** IBM joins the Linux peer producers and gives away hundreds of millions of dollars of software and resources to support them. Has IBM lost its head? No, it's stumbled onto a new mode of production called peering.

■ **Sharing.** Smart firms today understand that sharing is more than playground etiquette. Organizations like the Bill and Melinda Gates Foundation and the Tropical Disease Initiative are leveraging open-source drug discovery to launch an unprecedented attack on neglected diseases such as cholera and African sleeping sickness.

■ **Acting Globally.** Like others in the aerospace and defense industries, Boeing has found that the costs, risks, and expertise required to engage in large-scale development projects such as designing and building new aircraft are simply too large for it to do alone. So Boeing reached beyond its walls to co-create its new 787 passenger jet with a network of partners that stretches over six countries.

Wikinomics Design Principles

So how should leaders go about applying the principles of wikinomics in their businesses?

Your planning must allow for a high degree of learning on your part and the flexibility to respond to new opportunities that arise out of the interplay among participants in your business web. Peering is a design and production innovation, and the firm must learn how to operate in this new environment. You must:

• Take cues from your lead users.
• Build critical mass.
• Supply an infrastructure for collaboration.
• Take your time to get the structures and governance right.
• Abide by community norms.
• Let the process evolve.
• Hone your collaborative mind.

For the business manager, the number-one lesson is that the self-contained inwardly focused corporation is dead. Regardless of the industry or whether your firm is large or small, internal capabilities and a handful of b-web partnerships are not sufficient to meet the market's expectations for growth and innovation.

Managers should treat wikinomics as their playbook and harness its core principles to achieve success. Leaders must prepare their collaborative minds.

Is your mind wired for wikinomics?

MANAGING CRISES BEFORE THEY HAPPEN

by Ian I. Mitroff with Gus Anagnos

very crisis has the potential to disrupt an organization and shake it to its foundation, but preparing for a crisis before the event can mean the difference between a disaster and an opportunity to shine. Telling the truth is at the core of the message Ian Mitroff delivers: a simple answer to many of the problems that arise from an unexpected accident.

The powerful concepts that crisis management expert Mitroff explores go beyond the usual immediate response mode that follows an unforeseen event. Instead, he aims for early detection by showing leaders how they can carefully scan the horizon for the warning signs that always precede a crisis. He also demonstrates the systems that can be actively in place before a crisis to improve response and help a company emerge prepared from the rubble of a catastrophe. In his many crisis management books, Mitroff offers practical ideas such as anticipating risk factors, constructing "worst case" scenarios, and looking outside your industry for solutions.

The succinct brevity of *Managing Crises Before They Happen* is testament to Mitroff's clear sense of purpose, developed over years spent studying leadership and writing definitive books on many business and social issues. These include *Crisis Leadership, Break-Away Thinking, Corporate Tragedies, A Spiritual Audit of Corporate America, The Essential Guide to Managing Corporate Crises, Why Some Companies Emerge Stronger and Better from a Crisis,* and *The Unbounded Mind.*

Published in 2001, *Managing Crises Before They Happen* arrived before the bankruptcy of Enron, the dissolution of Andersen, and Bernie Ebbers's shenanigans at WorldCom became infamous case studies of billion-dollar crises. Mitroff's prophetic words still ring true as much now as they did before the full extent of possible corporate crises was realized. Although September 11 was still months away when *Managing Crises Before They Happen* first appeared, the book aims to fix the kinds of institutional flaws that led to the disaster.

A pioneer in the field of crisis management, Mitroff has gained valuable insight into crises as a researcher, author, professor, and consultant. His lifelong study of disasters has made him an international crisis management guru. As a world-traveling professor of business policy from the Marshall School of Business at the University of Southern California, he keeps students and corporate leaders up-to-date on the latest crisis management techniques.

Mitroff offers a more thoughtful approach to crisis management than simple predictions. He refuses to give an exact definition of a crisis because he's done enough research on plane crashes, political mistakes, and oil spills to recognize that the definition of a crisis changes for each stakeholder in the outcome. His advice calls for a stretching of the imagination to foresee improbable events, envisioning possible outcomes, and becoming "prepared to adapt." He places crisis management within the realm of reengineering.

Through regular surveys of Fortune 500 executives, Mitroff keeps his fingers on the pulse of the most recent trends in crisis management. His studies show that preparing for crises wards off crises, so the best way to prevent and properly deal with crises is to make crisis management part of everyone's job. The next step is creating a job for somebody who understands crisis management. Corporate vulnerabilities can be found when emergencies are anticipated with hard work. That's why some companies look for weaknesses in their security systems by hiring hackers.

The technological world in which we now live is without secrets, so Mitroff's message of telling the truth is even more important today than ever before. Thanks to the omnipresence of pesky camcorders and cell-phone cameras that have access to the world through the Internet, ordinary people are now the investigators who have brought much of what was once private into the public view. The interconnected effects of faraway events make it folly to expect lies to remain hidden.

Where does self-revelation end and the unnecessary revealing of secrets begin? Mitroff advises those in a crisis to tell as much of the truth about themselves as they are able and willing to tell. Then go a step further and tell a bit more. Give the media something to report, but not enough to gloat. Mitroff's sage advice comes from a leader who has studied enough victims and villains to learn how organizations can work to keep both labels away from their public perception.

Mitroff writes that crisis management "is not only the right thing to do, but it is good business." *Managing Crises Before They Happen* provides the cost-effective tools and approaches that can help any company raise profits by experiencing fewer crises.

MANAGING CRISES BEFORE THEY HAPPEN

What Every Executive Needs to Know About Crisis Management

by Ian I. Mitroff with Gus Anagnos

CONTENTS

THE SUMMARY IN BRIEF

While emergency and risk management deal with natural disasters, crisis management is concerned with human-caused disasters—a permanent and prominent feature of today's societies. A sample includes the random poisonings of Tylenol capsules, the devastating *Exxon Valdez* oil spill, the Columbine High School shootings, and the crash of a ValuJet flight into the Florida swamps.

Unlike natural disasters, however, human-caused disasters are not inevitable. They do not need to happen. As a result, the general public is extremely critical of organizations that are held responsible for the crises.

Of course, it's impossible to eliminate crises completely. But with the right crisis management (CM) tools—and attitudes—in place, a company can ensure that it can either anticipate crises or effectively manage them once they occur. This summary presents the following fundamentals about crisis management:

• *The five components of a crisis management framework.* Mitroff and Anagnos present a crisis management framework that includes five components: types or risk categories of crises; mechanisms; systems; stakeholders; and scenarios.

- *How telling the truth is vital to crisis management.* The question is not whether the truth will be revealed, but rather when that truth will become public and under what circumstances. Crises only become worse when a cover-up is attempted.
- *Assume responsibility or pay the price.* If you don't assume responsibility immediately, a chain reaction of crises is guaranteed.
- *Crisis management is an exercise in creative thinking.* Don't go for the obvious response.

THE COMPLETE SUMMARY

THE FIVE COMPONENTS OF A CRISIS MANAGEMENT FRAMEWORK

Completely preventing human-caused crises is impossible. However, with the appropriate planning and preparation, any company can limit both the duration and the damage caused by major crises. Effective crisis management also ensures that a crisis or a series of crises does not derail your major business objectives.

Authors Ian Mitroff and Gus Anagnos have developed a best-practice model that identifies the five factors companies must manage before, during, and after a major crisis. These five factors are: (1) the types and risk categories of crises, (2) mechanisms, (3) systems, (4) stakeholders, and (5) scenarios.

In the first section of this summary, we will look at each of these components in depth.

TYPES AND RISK CATEGORIES OF CRISES

Major crises can be divided into a number of general categories. These categories include:

- *Economic crises,* such as labor strikes, labor shortage, market crash, a major decline in stock price, and fluctuations or a decline in major earnings.
- *Informational crises,* such as a loss of proprietary and confidential information, tampering with computer records, or a loss of key computer information with regard to customers and suppliers.
- *Physical crises,* such as a loss of key equipment, plants, and material suppliers; breakdowns of key equipment and plants; loss of key facilities, and major plant disruptions.

- Human resource crises, such as a loss of key executives, loss of key personnel, rise in absenteeism, a rise in vandalism, and accidents and workplace violence.
- Reputation crises, such as slander, gossip, rumors, damage to corporate reputation, and tampering with corporate logos.
- Crises resulting from psychopathic acts, such as product tampering, kidnapping, hostage taking, terrorism, and workplace violence.
- Natural disasters, such as earthquakes, fires, floods, explosions, typhoons, and hurricanes.

As we've already noted, natural disasters do not necessarily have the same effect on an organization, since the general public will rarely see a company struck by a natural disaster as a villain. Of course, if clear mistakes were made—for example, building flimsy factories in earthquake-prone regions—the company's reputation will suffer.

Prepare for One Crisis in Each Category

Within the general categories or types of major crises, the crises share many similarities. Between the categories, there are sharp differences. The best crisis management approach is to try to prepare for at least one crisis in each of the categories.

Most companies, however, do much less. They will consider, at most, one or two categories.

For example, most companies prepare for natural disasters. Organizations that do broaden their preparations for crises other than natural disasters often do it only for "core or normal" disasters that are specific to their particular industry. The chemical industry, for example, prepares for explosions and fires, since these crises are part of the industry's day-to-day operating experience. The same holds true for fast-food companies that prepare for food contamination and poisoning.

While companies have a legitimate reason to be concerned about crises that they know will occur in their particular industry, they must not assume that the crisis they anticipate will be the crisis they will face. The fast-food industry can be hit with a crisis that has nothing to do with food contamination.

In other words, every organization can be hit with a crisis of any of the types listed above. Take product tampering, which was listed under the "psychopathic acts" category. One naturally thinks of the food or the pharmaceutical industries as being particularly vulnerable. But what about publishing?

This is exactly what happened in France to the publishers of the Larousse encyclopedias. The French being avid collectors and eaters of wild mushrooms, Larousse has a page filled with illustrations of mushrooms that are edible and, on the facing page, illustrations of unsafe mushrooms. One year, the labels on the two pages were reversed, causing the unsafe mushrooms to be labeled safe, and vice-versa. This was a case of a product-tampering crisis in an industry probably unprepared for such a crisis.

In sum, as we said earlier, every organization must prepare for at least one crisis in each of the various categories or types.

WHAT IS A MAJOR CRISIS?

It's not possible to give a precise and general definition of a crisis, just as it's not possible to predict with exact certainty when a crisis will occur, how it will occur, and why.

We can, however, propose a guiding definition of a major crisis. First, a major crisis affects, or has the potential to affect the whole of an organization. If it is an event that will affect only a small, isolated part of the organization, it may not be a major crisis.

A major crisis will also exact a major toll on human lives, property, financial earnings, and the reputation and/or general health and well-being of the organization. Often these effects occur simultaneously. As a result, a major crisis cannot be completely contained within the organization's boundaries.

And some major crises, such as the one suffered by Barron's Bank several years ago, will actually destroy the organization.

Prepare for Simultaneous Crises

Fortunately, you don't have to prepare for every specific type of crisis within each of the categories. As we noted earlier, each of the specific types within a particular category or type share strong similarities. Of course, the broader the range of crises for which you are prepared, the stronger your crisis management capabilities. But in the beginning, it is sufficient to prepare for one particular crisis in each category.

One final and important note: In today's world, any crisis is capable of setting off any other crisis. As a result, companies should prepare not only for each individual crisis they've selected as part of the crisis portfolio, but also for the simultaneous occurrence of multiple crises. In other words, crisis management is strongly systemic. Like total quality management or environmentalism, if it is not done systemically, then it is not being done well.

THE SYSTEMIC NATURE OF CRISIS MANAGEMENT

A complex system involves a number of intertwined parts working together. The separate parts of the system cannot exist nor function in isolation from one another. For instance, you can't remove the heart or lungs from a human body and have the human body survive. Also, because systems are so tightly interconnected, one event in one part of the system can have system-wide effects.

These characteristics of complex systems are reflected in modern society. We are much more interconnected than before. The impact of one event in our society will have much wider implications than in the past.

For example, sixty years ago, the impact of human-caused crises, such as a mine disaster or an explosion, would have been limited to one particular community or region. Today, crises can impact vast areas of the globe in little time. A rogue trader in the Far East, as was recently shown, can bring down one of the oldest blue-chip banks in the world. Or a nuclear disaster such as Chernobyl can threaten the health of people on two continents.

As a result, crisis management must always include the big picture. For example, ask yourself: "How can I temper how a crisis in one area of the company will impact the entire company?" "How can I prevent one crisis from causing another crisis or a chain of crises?"

The systemic nature of crisis management also means that it must be integrated with other important organizational programs in your company, such as quality assurance, strategic planning, environmentalism, or issues management. Crisis management should never be viewed as another separate, stand-alone program.

MECHANISMS TO PREPARE FOR AND RESPOND TO CRISES

We now move onto the second of the five elements of our crisis management model: mechanisms.

The best form of crisis management is preparation before the crisis occurs. For this, the company must put in place a small number of mechanisms that will help your company anticipate, sense, react to, contain, learn from, and redesign effective organizational procedures for handling major crises.

The first of the mechanisms concerns signal detection.

Signal Detection Mechanisms

All crises send out early warning signals. In many cases, of course, these signals may be weak and camouflaged by noise. But if your company has the mechanisms in place to enable signals to be picked up, amplified, and acted upon, then it stands a greater chance of preventing crises before they happen.

For example, make sure that a process exists for front-line employees to be able to communicate with management about their concerns. After the tragic explosion of the space shuttle *Challenger* cost seven lives, it was discovered that a string of memos expressing concern about the design of the shuttle was ignored by management.

The Signal Detection Chain

Dr. Judy Clair of Boston College did extensive research on signal detection in a large insurance company. This company handled billions of dollars in government Medicaid payments. The threat of fraud was extremely high.

Based on her research, Dr. Clair developed the important links in the "signal detection chain."

The first link: the signal detector.

Hearing the Signal

If a company wants to detect signals, it must have signal detectors. Although this may sound obvious, most companies do not have signal detectors in place. In other words, signals of an impending crisis may be clearly visible, but no one is paying attention.

The intensity threshold must also play a role. A signal detector must be able to read a signal and determine whether it has reached a level of intensity that indicates danger or potential danger for the company.

Because different types of crises send out very different types of signals, each company must ask itself: "What would count as a signal of the impending or near occurrence of a particular type of crisis?"

One example might be a pattern of slow, but noticeable increases in the accident rate at a particular oil refinery; this pattern may signal an impending serious accident, such as an oil spill, fire, or explosion.

Of course, if there is no one or no mechanism recording the accidents, then the pattern remains invisible. The signal goes undetected.

There must also be someone at the refinery or at headquarters to read the accident reports and note the pattern. If signals go off but there is no one to recognize, record, and attend to them, the signals are not heard.

Signal Transmission

Once the signal is heard, the next step is to transmit the signal to the right people (and in the right form). If someone picks up a signal in your company but doesn't know to whom to send it, or sends it to people who don't know what to do with it, then, once again, the signal will fail.

In sum, it is important, when putting in place signal mechanisms, to:

- Have signal detectors in place that can pick up the signals.
- Have intensity thresholds established so that people know when a signal indicates a dangerous situation for the company.
- Clearly communicate what people should do with a signal when it is detected.

One final note on signal mechanisms: It is not enough to pick up individual signals from different locations. It is possible that only when two signals are combined does the danger to the company become evident. Companies must be prepared to have a gathering point for signals, in other words, a central location where the signals can be pieced together into a larger whole.

RISK ANALYSIS VS. CRISIS MANAGEMENT

Author Ian Mitroff strongly counsels against traditional risk analysis for companies. The reason: Risk analysis mainly selects crises with which the company or the company's industry is familiar. One of the fundamental steps for traditional risk analysis is to construct models of the probability of occurrence of past crises. These models will give a higher ranking to certain types of crises based on how likely they are to occur. Conversely, the models give low rankings to crises that are least likely to occur.

However, it is precisely those crises that have never occurred before that must be anticipated. Yet, using traditional risk analyses, companies will not prepare for a crisis until it happens—at which point, of course, the unprepared company can be significantly damaged.

Other Mechanisms

Without proper signal detection mechanisms in place, an organization not only makes a major crisis more likely, but also reduces its chances of bringing it under control when it does occur.

Even with the best signal mechanisms in place, however, crises will occur. Thus, your company will also need damage containment mechanisms to keep the unwanted effects of the crisis from spreading. Of course, a damage containment mechanism that is appropriate for one type of crisis will not necessarily be appropriate in containing others. A systemic and systematic CM program will feature a number of damage containment mechanisms.

Finally, your company must also have postmortem mechanisms in place that will allow it to learn from the crisis and redesign the systems and mechanism to improve crisis management in the future. Few organizations conduct postmortems of crises and near-misses—and those that do either do not perform them correctly or don't implement their findings.

When doing a postmortem, the goal is not to assign blame. It is to examine the key lessons that need to be learned. The exception, of course, is in crises that involve criminal malfeasance or negligence.

FOUR TYPES OF SIGNALS

Signals can be differentiated along two dimensions. The first dimension relates to the source of the signal. In this dimension, signals can originate from either inside or outside the organization.

The second relates to the kind of signal. Signals can be either technical (recorded by remote sensing devices), or noticed by people.

If you put these two dimensions together, you have four types of signals that apply to every company:

1. Internal technical signals, such as monitoring devices for hazardous operations.
2. Internal people signals, for example, people working in a plant.
3. External technical signals, such as monitoring of plant emissions carried out by environmental activist groups.
4. External people signals, including members of surrounding communities who may literally "smell" that something is wrong.

ORGANIZATIONAL SYSTEMS

The third component of the crisis management framework involves organizational systems.

A company and its various systems can be illustrated as the layers of an onion. The outermost layer is technology. Then come organizational structure, human factors, organizational culture, and finally, at the core of the organization, top management psychology. These are the systems that govern most complex organizations.

A company's systems are intertwined, interacting with one another in many ways. Complex technologies, for example, are run by humans and thus are susceptible to human errors. Technologies are also embedded in complex organizational structures. These complex structures can also lead to errors as messages and communications must travel across different and multiple layers.

Organizational Culture

Organizational culture is a critical component of the systems involved in crisis management. For example, an organizational culture that establishes reward systems that reward certain kinds of behavior can hinder communication to the right people—and, thus, lead to wrong decisions.

One example of the impact of organizational culture on crisis management involves a power utility that served extreme northern settlements. If the power failed, the inhabitants of these communities would literally freeze to death within thirty-six hours.

The most likely employees of this power utility to find flaws in the electrical generators that served these communities were maintenance workers. Maintenance workers were the signal detectors; they filled out logs at the end of each shift on the state of the generators. However, the culture of this power utility placed maintenance workers at the lowest rung of the company. Therefore, their logs were ignored and their warnings were not taken seriously.

The most prestigious jobs in the company belonged to the linemen, those who climbed the poles to repair the lines. The linemen were macho risk takers—in fact, they made a point never to wear safety equipment.

Obviously, the macho culture of this organization made it susceptible to a variety of crises.

A Defensive Corporate Culture

The impact of a company's organizational culture on crisis management is also apparent when we look at one of the key components of a culture: defense mechanisms. As with humans, organizations have defense mechanisms that rear up to deny vulnerabilities to major crises. These defense mechanisms can take many forms, including denial ("Crises only happen to others"), disavowal ("Crises happen, but their impact on our organization is small"), grandiosity ("We are so big and powerful that we will be protected from crises"), or compartmentalization ("Crises cannot affect the whole of our organization since the parts are independent of one another").

DON'T FORGET YOUR STAKEHOLDERS

The fourth element of your organization that must be involved in crisis management is the company's stakeholders.

Stakeholders include all of the internal and external parties who cooperate, share crisis plans, and participate in the training and development of your company's crisis management capabilities. Stakeholders can range from your employees to such external agencies as police departments, fire departments, and even the Red Cross. Another important external stakeholder is the media, which will not hesitate to judge harshly an inadequate response to a crisis.

Crisis management must include developing the right relationships with stakeholders in advance to ensure the smooth functioning of the organization in the heat of a major crisis.

Make-A-Wish Foundation and Its Stakeholders

The importance of understanding stakeholders in crisis management is illustrated by a story involving the Make-A-Wish Foundation. This well-respected organization grants wishes to terminally ill children. One child, a teenager suffering from a brain tumor, wished to hunt a Zodiac bear in Alaska. When the foundation enabled the teenager to achieve his wish, it suddenly found itself under fire from numerous animal-rights organizations and portions of the general public. The foundation's mistake involved several assumptions about the organization's stakeholders. The first assumption was that the primary stakeholder was the teenager, and that other stakeholders (including the general public which supports the group through donations) would not object to the wishes of the teenager, despite any ethical or moral qualms they might have. The foundation believed those stakeholders would share the foundation's view of the situation: Make-A-Wish had to find a way to grant the wish of a dying child as effectively as possible no matter how offensive it may be to others.

Several crisis management lessons can be drawn from this example. First, never assume the outside world sees a situation exactly as you do. Second, it's a good idea to list as many assumptions as possible about as many stakeholders as you can think of. Be careful not to overlook any stakeholders, or to accept any unwarranted assumptions about stakeholders.

This story also highlights another important point about crisis management situations: Don't solve the wrong problem precisely. The foundation focused on finding a way to fulfill the teenager's wish. Solving that problem led to the crisis.

YOU ARE NOW READY TO DEVELOP CRISIS MANAGEMENT SCENARIOS

Taking into account all of the four elements of the crisis management framework we've discussed above—types of crises, mechanisms, systems, and stakeholders—your company can develop the fifth and final component of the framework: scenarios.

What will happen if a certain crisis occurs? How will your organization and its employees and customers react? What steps will have to be taken? These are the kinds of questions that must be answered in a scenario.

The best approach is to create a "best-case, worst-case" scenario. In the best-case scenario, of course, everything goes as planned in response to the crisis—a crisis that was anticipated. A worst-case crisis scenario, on the other hand, involves a type of crisis that the organization has not considered—and for which it is not prepared. Also, the crisis occurs at the worst possible time—over a holiday weekend, for example. And the most taken-for-granted, well-designed, and well-performing systems break down.

To summarize the framework presented by Ian Mitroff and Gus Anagnos, effective crisis management means:

- Understanding and preparing for the different types of crises.
- Implementing the important mechanisms that will help you prepare for those crises.
- Understanding the impact of your company's systems—from organizational structure and culture to human factors and the psychology of your top management—on crisis management.
- Developing the right relationships with stakeholders in advance of a crisis.
- Establishing best-case, worst-case scenarios.

These five components should be used as a framework for an audit of your company's crisis management program. A crisis audit will reveal any weaknesses in one or more of these areas that might hinder your crisis management capabilities.

HOW TELLING THE TRUTH IS VITAL TO CRISIS MANAGEMENT

The general framework presented here is a key tool in crisis management. But by itself, no framework, while necessary, is sufficient. In addition, crisis management must confront the question of both individual and organizational character. Specifically, crisis management must address two questions:

1. Do we (the individual, the organization) always tell the truth?
2. Do we (the individual, the organization) always assume responsibility?

This article deals with the first issue: telling the truth.

Should the Public Know?

The question is not whether you or your company should lie or tell the truth. The question is: When a crisis occurs, how much of the truth must be made public? Should a company try to fix the crisis in-house, sheltered from prying eyes? For example, if a CEO is caught in a compromising position, should that CEO be fired without any explanation? Or should every detail be made public?

There are no easy answers. But here's an important consideration: In today's society, there are no secrets anymore. None. Technology in general, and television in particular, has invaded every "back stage" that might have once existed in the lives of people and institutions. For example, overzealous police officers might have once been able to step over the limit in their behavior without being caught. Today, police brutality is likely to be captured on videotape by passersby or hovering television cameras. Human rights organizations are even distributing free video cameras to citizens in countries with poor human rights reputations so that they can film incriminating acts by their governments.

The question, therefore, is not whether the truth about an organization or individual will be revealed, but rather when that truth will become public and under what circumstances.

In light of this situation, the best approach is to take the initiative to tell the truth about a crisis. By taking the initiative, you (or your organization) controls who reveals the truth, in what circumstances, and when. Ian Mitroff describes the advice he offers his clients on telling the truth:

"No matter what the crisis situation, I always advise my clients to tell as much of the truth about themselves as they are able and willing to tell. I next ask them to take the additional step and tell a bit more, and a bit more, etc. Only after both of us are satisfied that they have indeed told 'enough' of the truth to ensure that the crisis will not be perpetuated any further can they finally stop. In short, how much 'truth' do I tell my clients to reveal about themselves? More than they can stand to bear, but, unfortunately, not what the world wants to hear and to gloat over!"

ASSUME RESPONSIBILITY OR PAY THE PRICE

The next issue concerning character and crisis management is whether or not to assume responsibility. In this case, the answer is clear and unequivocable: Yes. You or your organization should always assume full responsibility.

In a crisis situation, a company will fall into the role of villain—someone who knowingly causes harm or allows harm to happen.

Villains, however, fall into different categories. "Repentant" villains accept full responsibility for the crisis, promise to correct the situation and to prevent the situation from ever recurring, then take action to back up their promises. One example is Lee Iacocca's response to the substantiated charges that Chrysler was falsely resetting odometers on its cars: "It happened; it shouldn't have happened; it won't happen again."

Unlike repentant villains, "damn" villains are those who knowingly cause harm and then deny that they did it. In other words, they refuse to assume responsibility for their actions. Those who continually engage in stonewalling and denial are what Mitroff calls "damningly, damnable villains." They not only created a crisis in the first place, but their stonewalling sets off a chain reaction that causes additional crises. Or to put it more bluntly, if you don't assume responsibility from the very beginning, a chain reaction is virtually guaranteed. The classic case, of course, is Watergate, in which one isolated incident snowballed until it brought down a sitting U.S. president.

CRISIS MANAGEMENT: AN EXERCISE IN CREATIVE THINKING

Crisis management requires individuals and companies to think about the unthinkable. It is, in other words, an exercise in creative thinking. Creative thinking is especially important in preventing a crisis from escalating into a worse situation.

In this article, we present two case studies showing the power of creative thinking in responding to crises.

Why Benetton Erased Its Colors

In 1999 an international incident arose between the Turkish and Italian governments over the fate of Kurdish rebel Abdullah Ocalan, who had fled to Italy. When the Italian government refused to extradite Ocalan to Turkey, Italian businesses and products in Turkey, including Benetton, Ferrari, and Perelli, were the targets of widespread and violent protests. Many Italian businesses took out newspaper ads pointing to the difference between an Italian parent company and the Turks who operated them. Benetton-Turkey took a different tack. To show its solidarity with the Turkish people, Benetton-Turkey's "corporate response team"—consisting of the president, head of public affairs, and head of corporate finance—developed a crisis plan that was as creative as it was effective. The plan involved going to the heart of Benetton's corporate identity—the logo, "The United Colors of Benetton"—and making a statement by removing those famous colors. In addition to removing the colors from its logo, black wreaths were placed on the storefronts of all Benetton stores throughout

Turkey until the situation was resolved. Also, all of the mannequins in the store windows were dressed in black indicating that the company was in a state of mourning.

Benetton-Turkey's response was exemplary in many ways. Not only was it swift and dramatic, but it recognized that an emotional response, not the logical and rational response of the other businesses, was key in diffusing the crisis. Responding emotionally, and doing the unthinkable, prevented Benetton-Turkey from becoming a hated villain.

Talking Down the Greens

Another example of thinking creatively involves the Swiss chemical conglomerate CIBA. Two German Green Party activists climbed a six-hundred-foot smokestack and unfurled a huge banner declaring that CIBA was harmful to the environment. Rather than following the typical heavy-handed response of having the protesters forceably removed (which would only bring more publicity to their cause and create more enemies), Walter von Wartburg, head of Issues Management for CIBA, sent an emissary up the smokestack to ask them to come down and talk about their issues with him. They were told they could leave their banner up. The two Greens eventually came to talk with von Wartburg over tea.

The lesson of the story: Before adopting any solution to a problem, always ask, "Is the proposed solution likely to create even worse problems?"

NEEDED: ONE CHAMPION

For an organization to successfully instill a crisis management program, it must find an organizational champion to lead the way. This champion should be a leader who has championed other system-wide programs. He or she must be able to see the big picture and make the connections between the various parts of the organization. The champion also needs to understand and be able to explain to top executives how a major crisis will derail the major business objectives of the company.

THE LEADER OF THE FUTURE

by Frances Hesselbein, Marshall Goldsmith, and Richard Beckhard

L egendary management guru Peter Drucker wrote that leadership must—and can—be learned. He saw the million active nonprofit organizations in the United States as excellent opportunities for learning about leadership.

To bring Drucker's ideas to life and "lead social sector organizations toward excellence in performance," the Peter F. Drucker Foundation for Nonprofit Management was founded in 1990. Through the Peter F. Drucker Award for Nonprofit Innovation, the Frances Hesselbein Fellows Program, conferences, partnerships, and publications, the organization—now called the Leader to Leader Institute—works to unite the world's top leaders with the people and information they need to improve voluntary social organizations. *The Leader of the Future* is one of those publications.

Published in 1995 as part of the Drucker Foundation's Future Series, the book was seen as the definitive text on the future of organizations and the role of leaders in the global society of organizations. Drucker wrote that he wanted *The Leader of the Future* to motivate leaders to ask what they can do in their organizations to set an example and make a difference.

Each of the three top management leaders who edited the book has a career that reflects Leader to Leader's social values.

Editor Frances Hesselbein is the founding president of the Drucker Foundation; chairman of Leader to Leader; a former CEO of the Girl Scouts of the U.S.A.; and a recipient of the Presidential Medal of Freedom, the United States's highest civilian honor. In her essay, "The 'How to Be' Leader," Hesselbein writes, "The leader for today and the future will be focused on *how to be*—how to develop quality, character, mind-set, values, principles, and courage."

Leadership development expert Marshall Goldsmith conceived the idea of *The Leader of the Future* and served as the lead editor on the book. Goldsmith is the co-founder of the Learning Network, an association of the world's top consultants, and the founding director of Keilty, Goldsmith and Co., one of the country's key providers of customized leadership development. Hesselbein and organization development consultant Richard Beckhard, the author of six books and a former professor at the Sloan School of Management at the Massachusetts Institute of Technology, provided the editorial support to help Goldsmith make the book a best-selling classic in its field.

In *The Leader of the Future*, the editors collect experienced lessons on leadership from the world's top management thinkers. Essays from Charles Handy, Sally Helgesen, Peter M. Senge, Edgar H. Schein, Rosabeth Moss Kanter, Stephen R. Covey, and many others, offer vital links to the future by examining the success of inspirational role models from the past. These authors show other leaders how they can be successful by applying their own unique vision, hope, and purpose to the people who make an organization work.

The Leader of the Future shows leaders how to predict and anticipate changes and challenges in a new era of business and organizations. Strengthened by their combination, the brightest minds in management offer leaders from all sectors the new approaches, stories, motivations, and principles of leadership that the future will require.

THE LEADER OF THE FUTURE

New Visions, Strategies, and Practices for the Next Era

Edited by Frances Hesselbein, Marshall Goldsmith, and Richard Beckhard

CONTENTS

1. Peter F. Drucker: "Not Enough Generals Were Killed"

2. Gifford Pinchot: "Creating Organizations With Many Leaders"

3. James M. Kouzes and Barry Z. Posner: "Seven Lessons for Leading"

4. Charles Handy: "Earn Authority"

5. Stephen R. Covey: "Three Roles of the Leader"

6. Douglas K. Smith: "The Following Part of Leading"

7. Warren Wilhelm: "Learn from Past Leaders"

8. C. William Pollard: "The Leader Who Serves"

9. **William C. Steere, Jr.: "Foster Creative Tension"**

10. **Alfred C. DeCrane, Jr.: "A Constitutional Model of Leadership"**

11. **Marshall Goldsmith: "Get Input & Follow Up!"**

THE SUMMARY IN BRIEF

This summary is about the future—of our lives, our organizations, and our society. And it's about your role in that future.

Frances Hesselbein, Marshall Goldsmith, and Richard Beckhard are all connected with the Peter F. Drucker Institute for Nonprofit Management. They put out a call to their friends, the leading business writers of our day, for their thoughts on the leadership skills necessary to take advantage of the new century's challenges.

Hesselbein, president of the Drucker Foundation and former head of the Girl Scouts of the U.S.A., sets the tone for this summary by offering a glimpse of the skills needed in coming years. The leader of the future—the "how to be" leader—contrasts with the "how to do it" leader of the past whose knowledge is of little use in the face of the changes ahead.

- The "how to be" leader knows that people are the organization's greatest asset and in word, behavior, and relationships demonstrates this belief. This leader banishes hierarchy and builds a more circular, flexible, and fluid system designed to liberate the human spirit.
- The "how to be" leader builds dispersed and diverse leadership.
- The "how to be" leader mobilizes people around the mission of the organization, making it a powerful force in uncertain times. This leader gives those in the enterprise a clear sense of direction and the opportunity to find meaning in their work.
- The "how to be" leader knows that listening to customers and learning what they value is essential to success.
- The "how to be" leader recognizes the value of a healthy community to the success of an organization.

The Leader of the Future spotlights the ideas of a remarkable set of visionary thinkers like Hesselbein. Its ideas can boost your career—as well as broaden your sense of what is possible in the years to come.

THE COMPLETE SUMMARY

PETER F. DRUCKER: "NOT ENOUGH GENERALS WERE KILLED"
LEADERSHIP CAN AND MUST BE LEARNED

Over the past fifty years, Peter F. Drucker has discussed with hundreds of leaders their roles, goals, and performance. He's come to some strong conclusions. First, while there may be born leaders, there are far too few of them to depend on. Leadership, therefore, can and must be learned.

No Leadership "Personality"

Second, there is no "leadership personality." And "leadership traits" do not exist. Says Drucker, "Among the most effective leaders I have encountered and worked with in a half century, some locked themselves into their offices, and others were ultragregarious. Some (though not many) were 'nice guys' and others were stern disciplinarians."

Some were quick and impulsive, while others studied the situation and took forever to come to a decision. Some were warm, others aloof; some were vain, others self-effacing. Some, finally, were good listeners, while others were loners who listened to nothing but their own inner counsel.

The leaders did have something in common. Not one had much—or any—"charisma."

The most effective leaders know four simple things:

- The only definition of a leader is someone who has followers.
- An effective leader is not someone who is loved or admired. Popularity isn't leadership; results are.
- Leaders are highly visible. They set examples.
- Leadership is not rank, privileges, or money. It is responsibility.

Doers, Not Preachers

When Peter Drucker was in high school in the mid-1920s, his history teacher assigned a number of books on World War I campaigns. When discussing the books, one student said, "Every one of these books says that the Great War was a war of total military incompetence. *Why was it?*"

The teacher, who had been badly wounded in the war, shot back without hesitation: "Because not enough generals were killed; they stayed way behind the lines and let others do the fighting and dying."

LEADERSHIP BEHAVIOR

Effective leaders . . .

- Do not start out with the question, "What do I want?" They start out asking, "What needs to be done?"
- Then they ask, "What can and should I do to make a difference?"
- They constantly ask, "What are the organization's mission and goals? What constitutes performance and results?"
- They tolerate diversity in people; they don't look for clones of themselves. It rarely occurs to them to ask, "Do I like or dislike this person?"

  But they are intolerant when it comes to a person's performance, standards, and values.
- They are not afraid of strength in their associates. They glory in it.
- In one way or another, they submit themselves to the "mirror test": They make sure the person they see in the morning is the kind of person they want to be, respect, and believe in.

  This keeps them from doing things that are popular rather than right, and it keeps them from doing mean, petty, or sleazy things.

Effective leaders are doers, not preachers. While they may delegate many things, they don't delegate the one thing only they can do with excellence, the one thing that makes a difference, the one thing that will set the standards, or the one thing they want to be remembered for. They do it.

GIFFORD PINCHOT: "CREATING ORGANIZATIONS WITH MANY LEADERS"
LEARN TO USE THE "INVISIBLE HAND"

Consultant and speaker Gifford Pinchot believes that as the percentage of knowledge workers in an organization increases, more leaders are needed. Important work that needs to be done includes innovating, seeing things in new ways, and responding to customers by changing the way things are done.

By replacing hierarchy with more indirect methods of leadership, you can allow greater freedom, better allocation of resources, and a strong force for focusing on the common good. Offering workers more room to lead creates an organization ready to meet tomorrow's challenges.

Open Your Markets

Begin by unleashing the spirit of enterprise in your organization. As recent political changes show, the free market seems to be an indispensable institution for improving productivity and prosperity.

That's because the free market, as Adam Smith wrote, acts with an "invisible hand" to guide entrepreneurs pursuing their own selfish ends into serving the needs of their customers and thus the common good.

By introducing a free market system in your organization, you can indirectly motivate and inspire followers to find the most efficient, effective ways to serve the group.

Free Intraprise

Free intraprise—short for intracorporate enterprise—is easy to understand: Don't force employees to use monopolistic staff services. Let them choose among service providers. (And let them become providers if they want to.)

That's what the U.S. Forest Service did, with great results. The Forest Service had two technical service centers, each with a monopoly in its region. Customers—127 national forests—complained often about service. Senior leaders could have defined acceptable standards or changed management at the centers, but they did something better: They let customers choose between them.

This soon transformed the centers into cost-effective, customer-focused organizations.

Organizations of the future will be communities of intrapreneurs selling services to the core businesses. Like the much discussed virtual organization, there'll be a small hierarchy responsible to top leaders for accomplishing the mission.

Virtual organizations, however, buy the components and services that create value for customers from outside suppliers. In a free intraprise system, buyers can choose from groups outside the firm or suppliers part of a free internal market.

The advantages of intraprise? Imagine if the formerly Communist countries had decided to undertake a piecemeal reform. They'd have gotten nowhere by telling local party leaders to take more risks or by asking managers in the central ministries to empower their employees.

To crack the bureaucracy, leaders had to allow entrepreneurs to compete with state-owned monopolies.

So it is with bureaucratic private organizations. Training managers in empowerment isn't enough; you have to let intrapreneurial teams offer services that compete with functional and staff monopolies.

Creating intraprise leaders spreads learning and capabilities across organizational borders. And it creates a feedback system that sorts out the most effective internal services.

Free intraprise takes getting used to, but it can result in better productivity, innovation, and service.

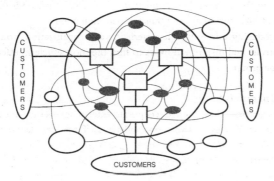

The Intelligent Network Organization. The rectangular line organizations buy from intraprises inside the firm (dark ovals), and from outside suppliers (white ovals).

JAMES M. KOUZES AND BARRY Z. POSNER: "SEVEN LESSONS FOR LEADING"
HELP LEAD THE VOYAGE TO THE FUTURE

The cynics are winning, say James M. Kouzes of TPG/Learning Systems and Barry Posner of Santa Clara University. People are fed up, angry, disgusted, and pessimistic about the future. Alienation is high, and loyalty—to people and institutions both—is falling.

In this climate, how can a leader mobilize a group of people toward some unknown and uncertain future?

Portrait of a New Leader

It can be done, as the story of Charlie Mae Knight shows. Knight, newly appointed superintendent for the Ravenswood School District in East Palo Alto, California, faced a nightmare. The district had the lowest revenue rate in the state, and 98 percent of the children performed in the lowest percentile of achievement.

Buckets to catch rainwater lined school hallways, rats and gophers had taken over in some, and pilfering ran rampant.

GROUP SPREADS TALENTS AROUND DUPONT

When AIDS first started to appear, the New York Blood Bank asked DuPont's Medical Products division to help it create a database to track the history of each pint of blood it distributed. Fearing for innocent lives, the Blood Bank wanted this done in ninety days.

The Medical Products division couldn't do it in ninety days. But an account executive had heard of a DuPont group called Information Engineering Associates (IEA), part of the Fibers division, that had created a database designed to trace the history and quality of Kevlar fiber as it moved through a Virginia plant. One division's staff support group wasn't supposed to help another, but this was an emergency, so IEA got the job. It completed it under the deadline.

IEA's reputation spread, and soon other divisions wanted to use its expertise. DuPont managers allowed this to happen, and soon businesses all over DuPont began getting better information service.

Thanks to "intraprise," DuPont became more productive.

Immediately upon taking office, Knight asked for support from Bay Area companies and community foundations to refurbish a school. Engineers from Raychem Corporation fixed the wiring and phone systems. Volunteers got rid of the rats and painted the school. Hardware stores donated supplies.

The effort rubbed off on nearby homeowners, who planted trees in front of their houses and began to demand more of a say in what went on at the school.

After two years, students passed the goal of scoring in the fifty-first percentile on academic achievement, and the state lauded the district for its innovative programs.

Seven Lessons of Leadership

Kouzes and Posner learned much about leadership from Charlie Mae Knight and thousands of others:

■ **Lesson 1: Leaders Don't Wait.** Knight, for instance, knew she had to produce early victories to get people excited about a new vision. Leaders don't wait for permission to start new endeavors; they act with a sense of urgency.

■ **Lesson 2: Character Counts.** People admire—and willingly follow—those who are honest, forward looking, inspiring, and competent. More than anything, people want leaders who are credible and can be trusted.

People, further, expect leaders to stand for something and have the courage of their convictions. They don't trust those who change positions with every fad or opinion poll.

■ **Lesson 3: Leaders Have Their Head in the Clouds and Their Feet on the Ground.** You must have a sense of direction and a vision for the future. The best leaders have a capacity to paint an uplifting and ennobling vision of the future.

■ **Lesson 4: Shared Values Make a Difference.** Your vision and values must be consistent with the aspirations of your people. Followers have needs, interests, and dreams of their own. If your values are out of step with theirs, you can expect trouble. You must be able to build a community of shared values.

■ **Lesson 5: You Can't Do It Alone.** Leadership isn't a solo act. Extraordinary achievement doesn't occur without the active involvement and support of many people.

■ **Lesson 6: The Legacy You Leave Is the Life You Lead.** In other words, "walk the talk." That's what the new president of Youngstown State University in Ohio did. Youngstown near the campus had become rough, and Les Cochran wanted to begin reclaiming the area from gangs and drug-related crime—and combat the fear, hopelessness, and mistrust that paralyzed the community.

"Together we can make a difference," he declared, and the first thing he did after arriving was fix up an abandoned building on the edge of campus for his residence. No one doubted his sincerity or character.

Credible leaders, in the eyes of followers, "do what they say they will do." That's the golden rule of leadership.

■ **Lesson 7: Leadership Is Everyone's Business.** Leadership is not a title. It's a set of skills and abilities that can be learned. And they are just as valuable whether you're in the executive suite or on the front lines.

CHARLES HANDY: "EARN AUTHORITY"

Renowned management theorist Charles Handy points out that under traditional management structures, power stemmed from your position.

In today's more fluid organizations, however, titles carry little weight. Leaders must prove their competence; authority has to be earned before it can be exercised.

How do top leaders earn authority? How do they lead an organization in which authority must be earned? It requires a combination of attributes:

- *A belief in yourself.* This is the only thing that gives you the self-confidence to step into the unknown and persuade others to go with you. Yet you must combine this with *a decent doubt*, the humility to accept that you can be wrong, and that listening is as important as talking.

- *A passion for the job*. This provides the energy and focus that drive the organization and sets an example. Yet you must also maintain *an awareness of other worlds*—finding time to read, meet people beyond your circle, go to the theater, etc.
- *A love of people*. Those who find people a pain or a nuisance will not be willingly followed. This trait, however, must be balanced by a *capacity for aloneness*. Great leaders must walk alone from time to time.

CHALLENGE ASSUMPTIONS

Leaders challenge the assumptions behind established ways of thinking. For instance, new leaders in law are challenging the assumption that disputes must end in confrontational, win-lose litigation. "Win-win or no deal" options, they know, can create better solutions for all.

In business, new leaders will challenge the assumption that "total customer satisfaction" represents the ultimate service ethic. They'll be more concerned with satisfying all stakeholders by making decisions that benefit all.

STEPHEN R. COVEY: "THREE ROLES OF THE LEADER"
LEAD BASED ON TIMELESS PRINCIPLES

According to Stephen R. Covey, author of *The Seven Habits of Highly Effective People*, leaders of the future will be the people who create cultures or value systems based on principles.

Creating such cultures will be tremendously exciting for future leaders—but only if they have the vision, courage, and humility to learn and grow.

Those with a passion for learning—through listening, seeing emerging trends, evaluating successes and mistakes, and absorbing the lessons that conscience and principles teach—will have enduring influence. These leaders won't resist change. They'll embrace it.

A Changed World

The consumer revolution has accelerated, quality standards are much higher, and many new competitive forces are operating.

The marketplace is demanding that organizations change. We all must be able to produce high-quality goods and services and deliver them in a fast, friendly, and flexible way.

Doing so requires an empowered workforce that gives its creative all. Yet, while thousands of organizations are trying to transform themselves to produce better results, few are succeeding. The main reason is a lack of trust among people.

Put Principles to Work

The competitive global economy is compelling us to see that principles like empowerment, trust, and trustworthiness ultimately control the good results we all seek.

The most effective leaders are thus models of principle-centered leadership. They know we're subject to natural laws, or governing principles, that operate regardless of whether we're aware of them or not. Being effective thus depends on living in harmony with principles such as fairness, service, equity, justice, integrity, honesty, and trust.

These principles are self-evident. You can prove that by trying to imagine if any effective society, organization, or family could be based on the opposite of any of them.

Correct principles point the way. They don't change or shift. They always provide direction.

Having a principle-centered core is thus key to having the confidence, security, power, guidance, and wisdom to address today's needs and opportunities.

Three Roles for a Leader

You can break principle-centered leadership into three basic activities:

1. *Pathfinding*. The essence of pathfinding is in having a compelling vision and mission. Pathfinding gets the organization excited about a transcendent purpose on behalf of customers and other stakeholders.

   Pathfinding then ties your value system and vision to the needs of customers and stakeholders through a strategic plan.

2. *Aligning*. This consists of making sure that your structure, systems, and processes contribute to achieving your mission and vision. That means they don't interfere with them, they don't compete with them, and they don't dominate them.

   The greatest leverage occurs when people are aligned with your mission, vision, and strategy. You have alignment when they share a powerful commitment to accomplishing the vision, and when you invite them to improve structures and systems.

3. *Empowering*. People have enormous talent, ingenuity, intelligence, and creativity—which often lie dormant. But when everyone is aligned with a common mission and vision, you begin to "co-mission" with them.

The purpose and mission of each person are commingled with those of the organization.

That ignites a fire that unleashes their talent and ingenuity; they do whatever is necessary to serve customers and other stakeholders.

LEADERSHIP IN THE COMMUNITY

It's increasingly clear that drugs, gangs, illiteracy, poverty, crime, and the breakdown of the family put every aspect of society at risk.

Leaders of the future realize, further, that government and social groups aren't up to the task of solving these problems. It's not their fault; they need a broader network of helping hands. Everyone thus needs a sense of responsibility and stewardship for the community.

We also need to help develop a similar sense of responsibility in young people. Begin by becoming a role model for your family. Are you serving the community in some way? Are you working to understand community problems to see how you can help solve them? Are you organizing service opportunities for the entire family?

Create a vision of a better society and help bring it to life.

DOUGLAS K. SMITH: "THE FOLLOWING PART OF LEADING"
LEAD FROM BEHIND

The word from consultant and author Douglas K. Smith: Thanks to changes in technology, demographics, and economics, the omniscient leader is obsolete.

Leaders will continue to set direction, make tough decisions, and inspire commitment. But getting good performance now requires relying on the capacities and insights of others.

Leaders thus need to understand when the best choice is to follow.

New Indicators

Organizational performance used to be a well-ordered affair. Ten or twenty years ago, you judged success by a number of financial and market indicators, along with functional and individual contributions. All measures were quantitative.

In that command-and-control world, leaders and followers were strictly divided. The best organizations were well-oiled machines.

Today, it's hard to tell how an organization is doing. "Who knows?" underlies any response. The elegant blueprint of financial, market, functional, and individual indicators is no longer enough. For one thing, organizations must now balance performance with every constituency in mind. Shareholders aren't king, but neither are customers.

Balanced performance now also includes ensuring functional and cross-functional ("process") excellence; reaching goals that are continuous as well as periodic; and watching qualitative measures along with quantitative ones. Further, cycle time and zero defects have joined money and volume as key measures.

To ensure success, workers must now both think and do, manage others as well as themselves, and make decisions and do real work.

Why Follow?

Few who only follow can contribute. Nor can many who only lead. We all must learn to lead and follow.

For instance, those who do a job know best how to make it more responsive to customers. That person's boss must know when to follow. And team leaders now know that performance depends on the team being in control, not one person. The leader must know when to follow.

Finally, those at the top who set rich, promising visions must know when to follow other interpretations of that vision if the organization is to benefit from the creativity of others.

Leaders must learn to follow in three common situations:

■ **Individual Performance.** You must follow a person, regardless of hierarchy, if that person knows best; if that person's growth demands it; and if only that person has the capacity to get the job done.

■ **Team Performance.** As a leader, you must follow the team if the team's purpose and goals demand it; if the team, not you, must develop skills and self-confidence; and if the team's agreed-upon approach requires you to do real work.

■ **Organizational Performance.** As a leader, you must follow others, regardless of hierarchy, if the organization's purpose and performance goals demand it; if the need to expand the leadership capacity of others in the organization requires it; or if living the vision demands it.

It's time to build organizations that celebrate leading *and* following.

WARREN WILHELM: "LEARN FROM PAST LEADERS"

Warren Wilhelm, AlliedSignal's vice president of corporate education, believes that the characteristics of effective leaders of the future will be the same as those of the past:

- Intelligence: the ability to see more faster and to reason effectively.
- Clear and strong values.
- High energy levels.
- A thirst for knowledge.
- Vision. Effective leaders have the ability to collect the same data as everyone else but find new things in them.
- Curiosity.
- A good memory: to remember people as well as things.
- The ability to help followers feel good about themselves.

Effective leaders also have "enabling behaviors":

- Empathy. The best leaders have always been able to put themselves in the minds and situations of others.
- Predictability. It's easier for people to follow predictable leaders.
- Persuasive ability.
- Leadership by example. Effective leaders operate by higher standards of personal conduct.
- Communication skills. This is the core of effective leadership. Good leaders master written, oral, electronic, behavioral, artistic, and emotional communication. Such mastery may require a lifetime to achieve—but it's worth the effort.

WAYS TO FOLLOW

Here's how a leader can follow:

- Ask questions instead of giving answers: "What do you think we should do?"
- Provide opportunities for others to lead you. Go beyond merely looking for growth opportunities for others.
- Do real work in support of others.
- Become a matchmaker instead of a "central switch." Don't consider yourself the central switch through whom all decisions must flow. Help others find their best collaborators: "Have you asked Tim what he thinks?"
- Seek common understanding instead of consensus. Build deep, common understanding around the purpose, approach, and goals of a project. Mutual understanding is more powerful than any one decision to choose A over B.

C. WILLIAM POLLARD: "THE LEADER WHO SERVES"
PROVIDE DIRECTION AND PURPOSE

Samuel Beckett, who won the Nobel Prize for literature in 1969, wrote short stories, plays, novels, and TV and radio scripts that highlight the absurdity and despair in life. His characters usually engage in meaningless tasks to kill time. With no purpose or mission, they accomplish nothing.

In writing about empty lives with no purpose, Beckett may well have been describing people today living in our world of accelerated change and choice without leadership.

But this isn't how things need to be, maintains C. William Pollard, chairman of ServiceMaster. A leader who is willing to serve can provide hope instead of despair. This person, the leader of the future, can be an example for those who want direction and purpose, and who want to accomplish and contribute.

Witness ServiceMaster

ServiceMaster, with divisions in cleaning, maintenance, pest control, and more, has revenues in excess of $4 billion. It has doubled in size every three and a half years for two decades.

Much of its business is routine if not mundane: Many employees are unskilled, uneducated—and often unnoticed. They clean floors and toilets, maintain boilers, kill bugs, or repair home appliances.

The management and leadership challenge, of course, is to train, motivate, and develop these people to be effective and productive on the job—and to be better people.

ServiceMaster's objectives are simply stated: to honor God in all it does, to help people develop, to pursue excellence, and to grow profitably. These objectives provide a reference point for determining what's right and wrong. They define the mission for its servant leaders.

Servant Leaders . . .

What are servant leaders?

- Servant leaders seek to recognize the dignity and worth of all people. They're interested in more than what people do on the job; they're also interested in their growth.
- Servant leaders are committed. Their responsibility is for the long term and not for their short-term benefit. Further, the promises servant leaders make provide the framework for relationships to grow. Servant leaders keep promises to the people they lead. It is their obligation.

- Servant leaders go out and talk with the people they lead. As they listen, they learn.
- Servant leaders make things happen. They initiate and at times create disequilibrium to maintain the vitality of the organization. They delegate authority and responsibility.
- Servant leaders promote diversity, knowing that people's differences can strengthen the group.
- Servant leaders are value-driven and performance-oriented. They lead people to do the right thing the right way. And they provide an example by their actions. As the founder of ServiceMaster said, "If you don't live it, you don't believe it."

A servant leader's results are measured beyond the workplace, and the story is told in the changed lives of others.

SERVANT LEADERS CHANGE LIVES

On a trip to Leningrad, C. William Pollard met a custodian named Olga. Nobody cared about Olga. She'd been given a T-frame for a mop, a filthy rag, and a bucket of dirty water. She wasn't cleaning the floor—she just moved dirt from one section to another.

Olga wasn't proud of what she was doing, and she found no dignity in her work. Though she had great untapped potential—which would help make her a better human being—she was caught in a system that did not care.

Pollard, in London a few days later, met a ServiceMaster custodian who greeted him with a hug and thanked him for all the training and tools the company provided. She then showed Pollard what she'd accomplished that day. It was easy to see how proud she was of her work.

Because a servant leader had showed her what to do and rewarded her efforts, she bought into the result. She was thankful—and looking forward to her next accomplishment.

WILLIAM C. STEERE, JR.: "FOSTER CREATIVE TENSION"

William C. Steere, Jr., chairman and CEO of pharmaceutical firm Pfizer Inc., pinpoints what he calls an "ongoing challenge for the leader of a large company": to build and sustain an appropriate level of positive *creative tension*. This is constructive debate about where and how the firm needs to change, how to respond to customer feedback, and so on.

Building consensus is a necessary leadership skill, because leadership through influence is more effective in building commitment and good results than leadership through position or intimidation.

But consensus without creative tension is dangerous, because:

- Dissent occurs outside meetings rather than in them.
- The gap between true consensus and perceived consensus (the *belief* that people are in agreement) widens.
- Thanks to passive resistance, difficulties increase when decisions are implemented.
- Managers begin to believe direct conflict is dysfunctional, so the ability to read nuances becomes key to survival and advancement.

ALFRED C. DECRANE, JR.: "A CONSTITUTIONAL MODEL OF LEADERSHIP"
TIMELESS CORE LEADERSHIP COMPETENCIES

James Madison and the framers of the U.S. Constitution created a document that contained core principles to guide the lives of citizens and establish a framework for governance.

It's clear they understood that the Constitution had to be worded broadly and flexibly enough to remain a relevant guide for endlessly changing issues, conditions, and challenges. They succeeded grandly.

Similarly, writes Alfred C. DeCrane, Jr., CEO and chairman of Texaco Inc., there's a set of solid, broad, and relevant core leadership competencies that will guide you now or in the future—no matter how conditions change or what challenges arise.

Character

Real leaders, in the words of Thucydides, have "knowledge of their duty, and a sense of honor in action." They are fair, honest, open, and trustworthy. You can achieve short-term wins without these qualities, but lasting leadership and success is impossible without them.

Effective leaders are also infused with humor and humility, and they treat all in the organization equally.

They are inquisitive and approachable, and followers feel safe offering feedback and ideas. Finally, they are action-oriented, moving relentlessly toward clear goals.

Vision

We follow those who can spark the imagination with a compelling vision of a worthwhile end—and who can translate that end into clear objectives.

Successful leaders develop goals to achieve their vision. Their commitment to the goals is, by their actions, obvious to followers.

Behaviors

Once you have clear objectives in mind, the issue becomes how you behave while working with—and through—people to achieve goals. Good leaders:

- Act. Moreover, they are unwilling to rationalize inaction.
- Create and shape change rather than accepting it passively. They challenge the status quo.
- Seize present opportunities while remembering to invest in the future.
- Evaluate and place people based solely on strength, performance, and potential.
- Think positively and never give up. They seek the opportunity that lies in every challenge.
- Communicate constantly by influencing, encouraging, listening.

In addition, leaders convey with the utmost clarity:

- Expectations of high performance for each member of the organization. Everyone, including the leader, is evaluated against those expectations.
- Confidence and trust in employees. That includes a desire to give opportunities to anyone eager to accept the accountability that goes with responsibility.

Confidence

Self-confidence is critical for success. It's essential if leaders are to undertake the difficult ventures necessary to meet goals.

Self-confidence, further, makes it possible for leaders to take prudent risks and encourage others to do the same. Self-confidence is also important to have faith in followers and support their advancement.

Self-confident leaders aren't threatened by the success of others, and they pay no attention to petty politics. They are consumed, rather, with achieving the vision.

MARSHALL GOLDSMITH: "GET INPUT & FOLLOW UP!"

Consultant Marshall Goldsmith believes that the leader of the future will consistently *ask, learn, follow up, and grow.*

A study done by Goldsmith's firm shows the benefits of getting feedback on your leadership capabilities and doing something with it.

NOT ENOUGH MISTAKES

Businesses often stumble because timid leaders send signals that discourage risk taking.

Thomas Watson, Jr., of IBM had the right approach to risk. He once said, while discussing IBM's competitive challenges, "We don't have enough people out there making mistakes."

In the study, eight thousand managers in a Fortune 100 firm asked for feedback on their leadership abilities from direct reports.

After receiving a confidential report on the feedback, each manager was asked to pick three areas for improvement and develop an action plan for change; respond to co-workers by thanking them for the feedback and discussing the plan with them; and follow up with co-workers to check on their progress.

Managers Who Responded and Did Consistent (Periodic) Follow-Up

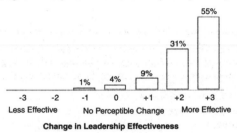

Change in Leadership Effectiveness

After eighteen months, people were asked again to provide feedback. Two questions were added: Had the managers become better leaders? Had they followed up?

The study's findings are dramatic: Managers rated as doing consistent or periodic follow up showed a big gain in effectiveness.

The lesson: Get feedback, respond positively, and follow up!

THE NEXT GLOBAL STAGE
by Kenichi Ohmae

The extended business metaphor that corporate strategist Dr. Kenichi Ohmae uses to describe the increasingly borderless world of the future is a global stage on which all businesses perform. Stage directors and managers work to make the most of the platforms on which the detailed drama of business unfolds. In *The Next Global Stage,* Ohmae offers directions to the players on this international stage, including individuals, companies, national leaders, and regional leaders.

Throughout this engaging book of tactics and tips for applying the new rules of a new marketplace, Ohmae explains how national borders have given way to a global economy in which old theories must be reassessed in terms of the changes that are transforming the ways companies and individuals grow.

As one of the world's top corporate strategists, Ohmae has developed his groundbreaking ideas over a career he spends helping the best and brightest corporate stars shine more brightly. The eloquent words and metaphors found in his lectures and one hundred books describe the complex challenges and opportunities future changes will bring.

In *The Next Global Stage*, Ohmae continues to explain what he hears when he listens closely to the heart of the corporation as he seeks to understand what makes it pump. Published in 2005, Ohmae wrote this book to explain how technology keeps that heart ticking. Stories from GE, Dell, Cisco, and many other technology companies describe in global terms the proper path to a healthy corporate strategy.

Ohmae's accomplishments as a master of management theory and practice are legendary. Born in Japan, he earned a B.S. at Waseda University, one of Japan's top schools. Next, he earned an M.S. at the Tokyo Institute of Technology. After receiving his doctorate in nuclear engineering from the Massachusetts Institute of Technology, he spent twenty-three years as a partner at McKinsey & Co. Today, he is chairman of the strategic consulting firm Ohmae & Associates. His numerous books include the best-selling *Triad Power, The Mind of the Strategist, The Evolving Global Economy, The End of the Nation State, The Invisible Continent, The Borderless World,* and *The Next Global Stage.*

Voted one of the world's top five management gurus by *The Economist,* Ohmae understands the art of strategic thinking so deeply that he imparts great advice in simple reflections. When Ohmae examines the long-term business horizon, he explains that he is excited by the possibilities found in the many developing areas of the world. He says, "I would call this particular time of history an era of global opportunities." As he watches for the signs of economic progress, and the visionary leadership necessary to manage people and organizations in the new borderless world, he says his search for cross-border opportunities shows him real growth opportunities everywhere in the world today.

The story Ohmae presents in *The Next Global Stage* has world-changing implications. It has the power to teach corporate leaders about the importance of education for capturing cross-border growth opportunities, and the need for vision and sustained leadership. By following Ohmae's cues, leaders in all sectors can rise above complacency and improve their chances of succeeding with the restless audience of the twenty-first-century marketplace.

THE NEXT GLOBAL STAGE

Challenges and Opportunities in Our Borderless World

by Kenichi Ohmae

CONTENTS

THE SUMMARY IN BRIEF

A radically new world is taking shape from the ashes of yesterday's nation-based economic world. To succeed, you must act on the global stage, leveraging radically new drivers of economic power and growth. In this summary, legendary business strategist Kenichi Ohmae synthesizes today's emerging trends into the first coherent view of tomorrow's global economy—and its implications for politics, business, and personal success.

Ohmae shows why yesterday's economic theories are collapsing, and explores the dynamics of the new region-state: tomorrow's most potent economic institution. He also shows how China is rapidly becoming the exemplar of this new economic paradigm.

This summary offers a practical blueprint for businesses, governments, and individuals who seek ways to thrive in this new environment. It concludes with a detailed look at strategy in an era when it is tougher than ever to define competitors, customers, and even companies themselves.

What You'll Learn in This Summary

- *What is the "cybercontinent"?* It is everywhere and nowhere. It is populated by the 800 million individuals who live almost everywhere in the physical world and are electronically interconnected.
- *How has the global economy changed the rules of competition?* Prosperity no longer depends exclusively on material wealth. And size is no longer important—companies no longer need a large domestic market in order to be successful.
- *Why are "platforms" so important?* They enable the exceedingly rapid exchange of goods and information, e.g., such phenomena as diverse as ATM cards, global positioning satellites, and the English language.
- *What are the new roles of government in the global economy?* Central governments must make it easier for businesses and investments to come to their countries. The best way: Don't impede entrepreneurial region-states.

THE COMPLETE SUMMARY

Part I: The Stage

WHAT IS THE GLOBAL ECONOMY?

For many, Ireland summons up visions of green, mist-covered fields and valleys. But outside the tourism industry, pleasant scenery does not produce wealth.

When Ireland became independent as a nation in 1922, it was overwhelmingly rural. From the 1960s onward, attempts were made to attract manufacturing industry from abroad. The Industrial Development Authority, a government agency, constructed industrial infrastructure and facilities, while the government offered generous tax breaks for foreign direct investments. These moves were only partly successful.

Location, Location, Location

In the 1970s and early 1980s, physical geography still played a big role in the international economy, and Ireland's location on the far western periphery of Europe meant that it was just too far away from potential markets.

In the late 1980s, emigration from Ireland increased, but those highly educated emigrants often returned after gaining experience and contacts outside the country. A new self-confidence began to take hold. The fact that the country had missed out on industrialization was increasingly seen as a blessing. It meant that the country's economy could take advantage of new trends beyond its borders in the global economy. Ireland could begin from scratch. In the late 1980s, developments in cybertechnology made it clear that jobs and prosperity could come at the end of a telephone line.

In 1992 the vision of Ireland as the "e-hub of Europe" emerged. Ireland is lucky: It is a nation-state that is the same size as a *region-state*. It is therefore capable of tapping into the dynamism of such a region-state. One of the keys to the success of a region-state is being able to brand itself successfully (such as an "e-hub") and to offer something different that sets it apart from the competition.

Innate Characteristics of the Global Economy

The global economy has four innate characteristics:

1. *Borderless*. National borders are far less constrictive than they once were. In terms of the four key factors of business life—communications, capital, corporations, and consumers—the world has attained the position of being effectively without borders.

2. *Invisible.* The potency and prevalence of the global economy is not totally visible to the naked eye. The actions that it performs often take place not on the streets or in the debating chambers of national parliaments, but on computer terminals. Plus, cash transfers occur with a credit card.

3. *Cyber-connected.* The global economy would not be possible without cybertechnology allowing large amounts of data to be transferred incredibly quickly. The Internet is only the most public part of this. Everything and everyone connects.

4. *Measured in multiples.* Money is no longer seen only as a unit of value in the short term. Multiples are signs given to management by shareholders to shoot at the business opportunities on the horizon. Multiples are fictitious, in that they often do not reflect corporate value, but they express an expectation.

OPENING NIGHT

The pivotal year in the evolution of the global economy was 1985: Mikhail Gorbachev became general secretary of the Communist Party, and the finance ministers of the major economic powers created the Plaza Accord, which would allow the dollar to fall in value and thus reduce the overall U.S. debt. Also, Congress passed the Gramm-Rudman Act and made the U.S. budget deficit less of a bogeyman (even though it didn't go away, as the Act intended).

Also in 1985, Microsoft launched its new operating system: Windows. A user-friendly operating system was a very significant innovation. It allowed different types of applications to be run on the same machine, and it enabled many nontechnical people to use computers.

Changes in China

Meanwhile, China was seeking to compress two hundred years of post–Industrial Revolution development into a couple of decades. At the root of the changes was a series of reforms that created stand-alone companies out of state-owned enterprises. The changes were monumental. Capitalism has come to China—but in the most brutal, inhumane, and unsentimental form imaginable. Workers are exploited beyond anything imaginable in the West, and capitalists do anything they want.

The technological background for all of this is the cybercontinent—greater than any country on Earth. For the first time in human history, the world changes its habits in a matter of days rather than years. By the end of 2003, 800 million people were connected to the Internet. They're ready to read, listen to, or watch anything available in cyberspace.

THE END OF ECONOMICS

Traditionally, economics was concerned with relationships between demand and supply—and supply and employment.

But the world has changed dramatically. An "economy" is not confined by national boundaries, nor is the world an assembly of autonomous nation-states, as economists assume. The significant players are independent units, both nations and regions. Some regions have a population of millions; others, such as the European Union (EU), have hundreds of millions.

The global economy powerfully affects national economies: In a borderless world, excess money supply from the central bank can slip out of the country if there are no attractive opportunities within. Thus, governments are constantly disciplined by their own citizens and by the investors in the rest of the world.

There is no model that describes the way the cyber-economy grows as goods, services, and financial instruments are exchanged across borders in ways that are not understood by economists, let alone governments.

The whole system is suffused with funny money: bonds, Treasury bills, and other instruments that don't represent cash or assets—but liabilities. The effectiveness of any government's fiscal policy is thus at the mercy of not only domestic businesses and consumers, but also of governments, companies, and consumers in the rest of the world. In the last few years, derivatives and multiples (assessed values) have added to the amount and kinds of funny money in circulation.

Derivatives and multiples defy traditional business thinking and seem to rely on nonstatistical elements, which are often nonrational or even irrational, such as euphoria. Yet economic education still revolves around the old paradigms.

A New Economic Paradigm

The characteristics of the New Economic Paradigm are:

- *Prosperity doesn't depend exclusively on material wealth, such as natural resources.* You don't have to be rich to get richer. Countries such as Ireland and Finland can be poor in traditional resources, yet still prosper.
- *The world has an excess of capital.* Many areas are cash-rich and are searching constantly for investment opportunities. But regions must show themselves to be worthy of consideration. Money isn't necessary for prosperity—but investment is.
- *Size no longer matters.* Companies are no longer required to develop a substantial domestic market. Nokia is highly successful but has only a tiny domestic market in Finland. In fact, a large domestic market is no longer a competitive advantage.

Part II: Stage Directions

PLAYMAKERS

The geographical and economic unit of the global economy is the region. In a world of near-instant communications and a completely interconnected economy, the nation-state is increasingly irrelevant.

Some regions are parts of the old nation-states; others spill over existing borders. A region-state is not a political unit, but an economic one. Some, such as Singapore, are also political units. Or they can be smaller—the greater Tokyo area has a GNP that is in the world's top three.

A region-state is a unit for creating a positive wealth-cycle. The more new immigrants—and the more varied their backgrounds and skills—the more varied the region becomes over time. Manufacturing is followed by services, financial institutions, and other businesses.

Finding Your Bearings on the Global Stage

A positive cycle thus occurs, and the region becomes a totality with a deeper, wider economic and business base. Industries and service providers—from car dealerships to hospitals—are quickly attracted to a prosperous region, and move there to support some of the industries already spearheading industrial acceleration.

Region-states have been most successfully established in China, where in the 1980s, the government opened up a number of special economic zones to attract foreign direct investment. In GDP per capita, some of these region-states are among the top fifteen economic units in the world.

Within the region-states, there can be smaller industrial clusters, as in northern Italy, where the town of Modena has a cluster of producers of fast sports cars, Parma has famous cheese producers, and nearby Carpi has knitwear manufacturers. Table 1 (see p. 261) provides examples of globally active and prosperous region-states.

Flexibility

The aspiring region or microregion must be flexible—willing not to be imprisoned by the paradigms of the past and, if necessary, to reinvent itself to meet the requirements of the global economy. Thus, Italy is a tapestry of small townships, each of which has been able to thrive by producing pricey items for which there is an inelastic demand.

Also, if regions are to attain their potential, they must devolve decision-making, especially in economic and trade policy. National leaders are not intellectually equipped or politically motivated to embrace the global economy.

There is bound to be tension when an area becomes successful while remaining part of a nation-state built on the nineteenth-century model, just as the traditional, physical stock exchange is becoming less relevant in today's borderless world. Thus, emerging regions must often renegotiate their relationship with the center of power.

Even well-advantaged regions are not guaranteed success. Interference by the central government can undermine a region's prospects. A region can undermine its own success by not being flexible—or by trying to do too many things but specializing in nothing.

Good Marketing

Regions also need good marketing. They must learn from other successful regions but never slavishly copy them. They must be aware of local differences and of what makes their region uniquely attractive.

Most important is the will to succeed. Unless this becomes part of the fabric of the region's identity, participation in the global economy will remain mere rhetoric.

Globally Active and Prosperous
Megaregions, Region-States, and Microregions

Breadth of Industrial Spectrum		Functional Specialist	Multiple but Sporadic	Full Range or Controlling
	Broad	Shandong	Pearl River Delta Greater Shanghai	Tokyo Metropolitan Area
	Sector Specific	Irish CRM Dutch BPO	Singapore Indian BPO (Bangalore/ Hyderabad)	Silicon Valley Greater Boston Medicon Valley
	Niche	Italian Towns	Chinese CRM (Dalian)	Austin

Table 1   Business System Leading to End Users/Customers

The world must start thinking not only smaller (in terms of regions)—but also bigger in terms of the global totality and amalgams of effective and progressive regions. Large economic groupings such as the EU and the countries of ASEAN can play a vital role on the new global stage.

Some complain that globalization is an attempt to impose a particular form of commercial activity on the whole world at the expense of the varied tapestry of cultural differences. Others say that it is equivalent to Americanization.

Both groups are wrong. Globalization realizes and affirms our interdependence as human beings and societies. It exposes the fallacy of self-sufficiency, whether economic or cultural. It is a process of global optimization and the best mechanism to help less-developed nations to grow without artificial subsidies from the rich—but with the legitimate filter of markets.

Globalization is nothing but the liberalization of the individual, consumers, corporations, and regions from the legacy of the nation-state in which they belong.

PLATFORMS FOR PROGRESS

Though we like to think of human development as gradual, made up of small and manageable incremental improvements, the reality is that sudden bursts of energy, often unleashed by or in tandem with technological breakthroughs, have moved us forward. They are groundbreaking when they happen, but then they are added to the aggregate of human progress and become part of our everyday life.

"Platforms" are ways to enable organizations or individuals to communicate with each other to get things done more quickly or more efficiently. Platforms are: (a) open and communal—the technology that powers them is accessible to a wide range of users, and anyone with the appropriate license can participate; (b) two-way and interactive; and (c) adaptable and easy to use.

Information technology has been the platform for the global economy in two ways: first, its impact on the world's money markets; second, the extent to which, through the Internet, it redefines the very concept of the market and the types of relationships that businesses must be prepared to develop.

Recent Breakthroughs

The recent breakthroughs in data-transfer—in the materials through which data must pass, and in the formats in which large amounts of data can be efficiently stored—have totally transformed our world. They have made many products cheaper and given millions of people access to information that was once beyond their reach.

A language can also be a platform, just as English has become the language of the global economy and the standard in cyberspace for the storage of information and two-way communication. The prominence of English in Ireland and India is a major factor in the success of these two countries as electronic hubs for the rest of the world.

Nevertheless, native English speakers should realize that if they do not learn a second language, they might be disadvantaged in their long-term ability to participate in the global marketplace.

Here are other crucial platforms on the global stage:

- *The U.S. dollar*. It is the natural medium of payment for the substantial part of world trade that centers on the United States, as well as a considerable number of other trading partners.
- *Brands*. A borderless world has opened up vast new possibilities for branding. The same brands are almost everywhere. They gain loyalty with the promise of consistently offering certain features. Most major brands are American.
- *A global business culture and language*. Business executives throughout the world communicate in English. They use the same terminology and have the same motivations and professional interests. They read the same magazines and very likely attended the same business schools—or ones that offer a very similar range of teaching materials, lecturing styles, and placement opportunities. The new jargon of business—CRM, EBITA, BPO—is understood internationally.
- *The ATM*. The dispensation of money is now almost completely detached from the physical bank.
- *Credit cards and smart cards*. Programmable cards can now be used for a wide range of purposes—acquiring services, accumulating shopping points, and much more.
- *The global positioning satellite*. This technology now has a rapidly expanding array of uses, such as providing information to travelers on foot, tracking stolen cars, and analyzing traffic patterns from the sky.

BREAKING THE CHAINS

We live in a small and intimate global community where all sorts of information, even rumors, can disseminate in a matter of seconds. It is a global village with a population of 800 million people who could be treated as a single race or tribe. They include the enlightened and curious in the developing and underdeveloped countries. These "cyberites" follow three rules of behavior:

- *Cyberites who have used the Internet for five years or more tend to think and act similarly.* The longer their online experience, the more they take advantage of the Internet's various resources, engage in international trade, become more global in outlook, and gain the confidence that they can live well under the liberated regime of a truly global environment.

- *The number of years it takes to become a true cyberite is (age minus ten) divided by ten.* It takes longer to unlearn twentieth-century assumptions, depending on how long you were exposed to them.
- *Cyberites are proactive consumers.* That is why TV and print advertising is so ineffective. Eight hundred million people now actively seek what they want through their favorite search engines. Marketers must make sure that their advertising is search-engine-triggered, so that it tracks with the growing Internet sophistication of their customers.

The Logistics Revolution

The final part of the revolution is taking place in logistics.

Even though there is still a physical supply chain—and warehouses and inventory are still important—distribution centers are decisive. Once again, technology has triggered the revolution. The relationship between the product provider (who might also be the producer) and the end consumer has been simplified, even collapsed, by e-commerce.

Dell and Gateway exemplify an entirely new business entity—the virtual company—that assembles products not in a single factory, but in a large number of places, and ships them from distribution centers, warehouses, and FedEx facilities.

And companies such as FedEx are getting into the strategic logistics business and using their databases to become a vital link in other companies' supply chains.

A micro tag (only 0.5 mm square) can be buried in books, clothes, and anything that is not going to be eaten. Soon, most items will have these tags built into them, representing the products' ID card, with a radio frequency capability that can be detected remotely.

The result will be a revolution in physical distribution and merchandising. We will no longer have to check out each individual item, so shopping will become quicker and less stressful. Inventory control will also benefit: Companies will know exactly how much of each product they are selling, as soon as it is sold. And because the micro tag contains details about the person to whom the item is being sold, it could have a major impact on theft and shoplifting.

Homogenous Chains

On the global stage, much of the logistics process has been containerized and standardized into homogenous chains, as foods of all types are transmitted worldwide through special equipment (to maintain a consistent environment) and seamless, electronically guided logistics platforms. The result has been a fundamental change to lifestyles.

In time, postal services, which, until recently, haven't given much thought to logistics, will realize that they are fundamentally in the logistics business, and, despite the challenge from e-mail, need to avail themselves of the latest developments.

OUT AND ABOUT

Cross-border business process outsourcing (BPO) is another platform that helps people and businesses communicate, and it is shaping the global stage in a major way. It's about optimization. Activities once done in a high-cost environment are moved to where the labor costs are lower, with no loss in quality. It has been going on for decades, and it is controversial because of the loss of jobs at home. Almost every area of the world has some type of BPO activity.

There is nothing inevitable about BPO. It suits some sectors better than others. For some, it can be very successful; for those poorly prepared, it can spell disaster.

BPO would be unthinkable without present-day telecommunications technology. The two countries that have been most successful in the outsourcing of electronic services—India and Ireland—have made radical improvements in their telecommunications infrastructures.

BPO is happening in other areas, such as clinical drug trials (patents come from various countries at lower costs) and compiling research materials.

HOME OFFICES

Many BPO providers work from their own homes or in a small office environment. This is the most important difference between the Manufacturing Age and the Cyber Age. The reality of BPO is that it is not about sweatshops and exploited labor. BPO brings prosperity and hope to countless millions of people.

Patriotic sentiment and a desire to protect domestic jobs doesn't do much for a company's bottom line. Outsourcing decisions are never based only on lower labor costs—in Ireland, labor costs don't even enter the discussion. Processes are outsourced to environments that can provide the same level of service and expertise—but at a lower price. BPO makes economic sense, despite what its critics say. Also, technology has ensured that it is irreversible.

BPO is a way for companies to seek more competitive ways to grow on the global stage.

The question is: Are we brave enough to apply the new technology? Strenuous opposition to worldwide, supranational markets comes from many places, including local farmers. Perhaps over time, people will adopt the attitude that a particular product need not come from a particular nation (as, for example, with the Japanese attitude about rice) because there are such enormous economic benefits to be realized from the logistics revolution.

Part III: The Script

REINVENTING GOVERNMENT

Governments don't create wealth, except through taxation. Thus, a key priority for politicians is to look into the economic development of their countries and regions. Is bureaucracy preventing local governments and regions from taking initiatives? Is the central government hindering them? Is there a clear chain of command and consistent messages? Are special interest groups or political lobbies blocking the regions' initiatives?

Too many governments still see themselves as distributors of wealth. They see their role as protecting domestic companies, their own population, and certain regions considered vulnerable or disadvantaged. Local industries, protected by taxpayers' money, don't think globally. And governments have not been successful in tempting cyberites, who have the power to send their money anywhere.

Governments of the future, if they want to remain vibrant and relevant, must figure out how to facilitate economic development, introduce more discipline in their public services, and simplify their tax code to increase compliance.

The best government is small government. And the best it can do for its people is to invite capital by welcoming corporations, which will bring in jobs and take over weak companies, so that the government won't have to use taxpayers' money to subsidize them. The smaller the government is, and the more open it is to wealth and investment from outside, the greater the payback will be for the region-state.

Today, the most important success factor is not a well-established domestic industry or home markets, but an educated and motivated workforce—on the factory floor, in the computer room, and in the agencies that provide national services. Also, a region must have good infrastructure, in both technology and logistics.

Challenges and Vision

As governments change their focus, they face several challenges: In a borderless world, they must not overemphasize the national interest. They must also realize that wealth creation is increasingly leveraged. Governments must come up with and deliver an economic vision that attracts many global investors, resulting in high multiples.

A viable vision must adhere to the already-known fundamentals of the global stage. The vision must:

- *Empower individuals.* The wealth of a nation, region, or company is more dependent than ever on the number of talented individuals it can produce.
- *Invite capital from the rest of the world, and minimize obstacles to investment.*
- *Maintain an even keel.* Government must ensure that individuals can grow and prosper, and that regions can interact with the rest of the world.
- *Welcome new technology,* as Ireland did in the early 1990s by providing all primary schools with personal computers.
- *Diminish hindrances to the inflow and outflow of capital.*
- *Eliminate obstacles to companies that want to attract the best people to work for them, at any level and from any geographical area.*
- *Specialize.* The government must decide what industry or range of industries it wants to attract.

THE FUTURES MARKET

On the global stage, change is necessary and inevitable at three fundamental levels: technological, personal, and organizational.

- **Technological.** Technological progress can speedily reshape, even destroy, entire industries. Technology means that industrial death is increasingly a fact of business life.

  It has never been uncommon to see whole sections of industry wiped out by technological progress. We need only think of the impact that the automobile had not only on the carriage industry, but also on saddle makers and the providers of feed and stables for horses. Each new technological wave usually has its victims: those who were unable to change in time.

  Time has now been compressed. In the past, there was usually some time lag between the discovery of a new process or processes, and their complete victory over their predecessors. In the world of the interconnected global economy, such time lags are very rare.

Capitalizing on New Opportunities

- **Personal.** No matter where they are, individuals will have to adapt to the new reality in which one seldom has a job for life and cannot look forward to the certainty of an incrementally improving lifestyle and a postretirement soft landing, in which all or most of his or her needs are provided for.

Instead, people will have to take more responsibility for themselves and take advantage of the vast quantity of new information that is now available—and the opportunities for personal development.

Success in the global economy will also depend on good leadership—of a region-state, a microstate, or a company. The best leaders in the new economy, such as Singapore's Lee Kuan-Yew, have the courage to look into the future and to act according to time intervals longer than the present accounting period or the next elections.

• **Organizational.** The answer to uncertainty is more information. Leaders in the global economy must be well informed about the world around them. They must fully understand and have an instinctive sympathy for and familiarity with the global economy.

The changing structure of organizations requires leaders to be flexible and intuitive, without preconceived attitudes about their role.

E-Everything at GE

An old-line company really can morph itself into a global competitor. General Electric has done an amazing job. It has never become complacent. It has been a leader in outsourcing its support base.

GE was fortunate to have Jack Welch, a true visionary, who once told the company to put the letter "e" in front of all internally used verbs, such as "e-design," "e-sell," and "e-distribute." The idea was to get the entire company to think electronically. And it worked.

Players in the new economy must learn to doubt and even discard the business models of the past. That is why business schools should question the case-study method: Companies rise and fall more quickly than ever before, and students need to learn the dynamics of steering a company—as opposed to balancing static power.

The successful company must be something quite new, owing little to the precedents of the past. Whatever business structure you adopt, customers must know that they are in control. As far as possible, their involvement must be sought and their whims catered to. And instead of the usual sources of information, such as market surveys and statistics, leaders need to develop a feel for what is happening with the 800 million cyberites who are the key drivers of the global economy.

Companies must also divorce themselves from a physical focus on the home office or the country. They must totally embrace the borderlessness of the new economy.

And companies should abandon the old divisions of the business world into industrial sectors, because the global economy can bring a company into areas where it does not expect to be.

Four Areas for Innovation

Companies must also commit themselves to innovation as never before in these four areas:

- Business systems. Companies must ally themselves with the best and cheapest providers of products and services across the entire spectrum of corporate functions. Companies must also learn to make their organizations scalable, so that there's less stress in growing fast.
- Products and services. The need for innovation is obvious, but the challenge is formidable: What we once thought were technological islands, such as mobile phones and PCs, are all converging to form huge "continents." The marketing and technological "territory" in which a company operates is constantly changing.
- Customer interface. Innovation in customer interface is a prerequisite for most companies, because the traditional advertising media are not only cost-ineffective but also inadequate for keeping customers interested.
- Employees, managers, and staff. Power is shifting from those who make rules to those who break or rewrite them. Thus, corporations need to find ways to recruit dropouts, retirees, very young people, and even petty criminals (as in the case of hackers who have been turned into computer security experts). Companies must also find untraditional ways to reward innovation.

Also, companies must learn not to take their traditional identity too seriously. The fact that something has never been tried should not be an obstacle to its future adoption.

Finally, the traditional hierarchy—the pyramid structure of almost all organizations—has to be discarded. The traditional top-down method of leadership is wasteful and ineffective because a company's need to innovate continues to conflict with shared assumptions about loyalty and unquestioning obedience. This situation must change.

THE NEXT STAGE

Some economic units have the potential to adapt successfully to the new realities. Here are the regions that currently have some of the ingredients to attain the level of a prosperous region-state:

■ **Hainan Island, China.** The People's Republic of China has shown the world how region-states can prosper. The province of Hainan Island, with eight million people, is far away from the capital's interference and has an outward-looking government. It has established air routes to Southeast Asia and to Europe. Still, it has not taken off as quickly as other burgeoning Chinese regions.

■ **Petropavlosk-Kamchatsily, Russia.** The climate of this remote region is really no more severe than that of Kalamazoo, Michigan. It would be a wonderful location for e-professionals of all kinds who don't mind the isolation, given that technology enables many more people to work from anywhere in the world.

■ **Vancouver and British Columbia.** British Columbia is geographically the closest Canadian province to Asia, so the Vancouver area is increasingly attractive to Asian tourism and business. It is also a geographical and commercial extension of Northwest Washington State. On its doorstep are the homes of Microsoft, Starbucks, and Amazon. Despite high taxes and onerous regulations, there is a new desire on the part of the provincial government to open up to the rest of the world.

Regions with Potential

Other regions with similar potential include Estonia; the Baltic Corner; Ho Chi Minh City, Vietnam; Khabarovsk, Maritime (Primorye) Province and Sakhalin Island, Russia; São Paulo, Brazil; and Kyushu, Japan. From the investor's point of view, the list of attractive regions is getting longer.

You now have some feel for the new global economy, the coming shape of the geopolitical maps of the future, the key levers corporations can pull, and the dynamic business domains we can tap. Now it is your turn to climb up onto the global stage and perform.

INDEX